Animal Bodies, Renaissance Culture

HANEY FOUNDATION SERIES

A volume in the Haney Foundation Series,
established in 1961 with the generous support
of Dr. John Louis Haney

Animal Bodies, Renaissance Culture

KAREN RABER

PENN

UNIVERSITY OF PENNSYLVANIA PRESS

PHILADELPHIA

Published by
University of Pennsylvania Press
Philadelphia, Pennsylvania 19104-4112
www.upenn.edu/pennpress

Printed in the United States of America on acid-free paper
10   9   8   7   6   5   4   3   2   1

Library of Congress Cataloging-in-Publication Data
Raber, Karen, 1961–
    Animal bodies, Renaissance culture / Karen Raber. —
1st ed.
        p. cm. — (Haney Foundation series)
    Includes bibliographical references and index.
    ISBN 978-0-8122-4536-3 (hardcover : alk. paper)
    1. Animals (Philosophy)—Europe—History—16th
century. 2. Animals (Philosophy)—Europe—History—
17th century. 3. Animal intelligence—Philosophy—
History—16th century. 4. Animal intelligence—
Philosophy—History—17th century. 5. Human-animal
relationships—Europe—History—16th century.
6. Human-animal relationships—Europe—History—
17th century. 7. Human beings—Animal nature—
History—16th century. 8. Human beings—Animal
nature—History—17th century. I. Title. II. Series: Haney
Foundation series.
B105.A55R33 2013
113'.8—dc23

                                        2013004238

Contents

Animal Bodies, Renaissance Culture

Absent Bodies

Giovanni Battista Gelli's *Circe* of 1549 recounts Ulysses' efforts to convince a variety of beasts, transformed from men by Circe, that they should return to their human form and leave her island with him. Ulysses begins with the humblest of creatures, the oyster and the mole (also the simplest and humblest of humans, a fisherman and a ploughman respectively), but upon being soundly rejected, decides to move on to other creatures more likely to understand his appeal to reason: "Thou shalt find some [men] of such knowledge and wit," he remarks to Circe, "that they are almost lyke unto the goddes, and some others of so grosse wytte, and small knowledge, that they seme almost bestes." Assuming he has met only men who were dull witted in their human forms, or "whiles they were men, never knew themselves, nor never knewe their own nature, but they attended onely to the bodye,"[1] Ulysses keeps trying new tacks with new interlocutors. Moving through his own version of a great chain of being to a snake, a hare, a lion, a horse, a goat, a hind, a dog, a calf, and an elephant, Ulysses proposes different arguments in support of human superiority. But in each debate, the famous orator's persuasion returns again and again to the idea that reason is the basis of human excellence; so he tells the lion that animals cannot claim true virtues because "amongst beastes there is no fortitude at all, but onle amonge menne," since fortitude "is a meane, determined with reasonne, betwene boldenes and feare . . . because you have not the discourse of reason, whereby you might eyther knowe the good or the honest, and by occasion thereof, only you put your selves in daungers; but you do it eyther for profyte or for pleasure, or to revenge some injurie. And this is not fortitude" (sig. l4r). Again, he tells the horse, "temperance is an elective habit, made with a right discourse of reason; howe can you then have this virtue in you?" (sig. n4r). However, each and every animal rejects Ulysses' proposed gift of humanity, arguing that its beastly condition is superior. Not until he debates with the elephant, once a human philosopher, does he find someone who shares his philosophical language, and whom he is able to convince that humans are the most noble, the most virtuous creatures because they are rational, and are not limited by the sensory memory, experience, and instinct that is all animals possess. Transformed, the elephant, now restored to human identity as Aglafemos, cries out, "Oh what a marveylous thing it is to be a man!" (sig. t2r).

Of course, having found his convert, Ulysses must then warn him that there are some things that even human beings cannot know, such as the first cause of life, because they are hampered by their bodies and the shortness of their lives. Although he has categorically rejected the claims of all his targets to a better life in animal form by privileging reason and discounting the body, it turns out that the body is a limiting factor even for humans. Indeed, this conclusion of the *Circe* sends us back to reevaluate the positions of even the very simplest of the animals, each of whom makes a strong case that human bodies are, in fact, far inferior to beastly ones. The oyster, for instance, argues that unlike humans animals do not have to labor to create their food and clothing, and goes on: "I have reason, consideringe besides this that nature hath set so litle store by you, for besides the bringing forth of you naked, she also hath not made you any hose or habitation of your own, wher[e] you mought defend you from th'injuries of the wether, as she has made to us, which is a plaine toke that you are as rebelles and banished of this world, having no place here of your owne" (sig. B4r). Likewise, the mole answers the charge that his condition is defined by lack, particularly of sight, by pointing out that humans come into the world weeping because they are embarking on a life of misery and suffering. "And why for syns it [seeing] is not necessarye to my nature, it is sufficient to me, to be perfit in myne owne kynde," concludes the mole, and reiterates, "for that I am perfecte in thys my kynd" (sig. c3r). Even the oyster and the mole, the lowest of low creatures, see themselves as physically and therefore morally perfect in contrast to humans, and assert that it would defy reason—their "perfect" reason, which accepts their god-given condition in life—for them to return to their human forms.

Gelli's dialogue derives its premise from Plutarch's "Whether the Beasts Have the Use of Reason," also titled *Gryllus*, in the *Moralia*. Where Plutarch offers only one recalcitrant pig, however, Gelli explores additional dimensions of animal and human reason and embodiment, as well as issues of class and economic privilege, through his additional animal characters. Gelli's text was popular, enjoying numerous reprints by the end of the century. Its first English translator, Henry Iden, justifies his efforts by recommending the dialogue for those "who know no other language than their owne, to see herein how lyke the brute beast, and farre from his perfection man is, without the understanding and folowinge of dyvyne thynges" (sig. a2r). And indeed, Ulysses' ostensibly rational positions are again and again ignored, inverted, or countered with narrow examples of animal contentment. However, the conversion of Aglafemos hardly counterbalances the influence of the other animals' often compelling positions, nor does it fully vindicate the self-blind and blithely self-congratulatory Ulysses. Where the text underscores human frailty, the tone shifts to pathos, suggesting (perhaps despite its apparent goals) that human reason is small compensation for the evils of existence in a weaker human body, subject to social, political, and economic forces that make life harder, not more rewarding. In this, Gelli expands on elements of Plutarch's original dialogue, in which Gryllus does a pretty good job of defending animal intelligence and impugning human "virtues."

As I've noted, Gelli's Ulysses insists on the perfection of the human based on the exclusive property humans presumably have in reason. Yet the text's debates offer a more complex set of propositions about types of reason, focusing especially on the razor-thin line between sensory knowledge combined with experience and what he calls "understanding," or cognition, the ability to think beyond the body's inputs, to construct scenarios and options that might not exist in reality unconstrained by "quantity, or place, time, or variety, and such like appertaining to ye matter" (sig. r8v). But despite every angle Ulysses covers, arguments about reason and soul, it turns out, cannot be extricated from the condition of the body. The oyster and the mole, being the simplest of creatures, have the simplest connection to their embodiment, and so might be expected to have the most limited perspective on themselves—something Ulysses keeps asserting in defense of his failure to convert them to humanity. Yet the rest of the animals also argue with increasing complexity their superiority to human beings based on the virtues, knowledge, and "perfections" that derive from their particular *physical* relationships to the world and its challenges. The snake, for instance, who was once a physician, details the miseries of human suffering, while celebrating the fact that animals never fall prey to excessive appetites or other vices; the hind was once a woman, and so cannot be persuaded to return to her life of servitude and submission; the dog points out that humans have to borrow animals' natural skills or imitate animal appendages to make many of their inventions work.[2] Gelli's creatures are all convinced that they are happier, are more secure, and have more pleasurable lives than do any and all humans precisely because they *don't* have the type of reason Ulysses keeps trying to establish as exclusively human, since it is attended by imbalanced appetites, dissatisfaction, oppression by their fellows, and so on.

Gelli's creatures assert that they do have "reason," and that deriving that faculty from their sensory, experiential interpretation of themselves in the world they inhabit is preferable to whatever "understanding" is. Although Ulysses keeps reaching for examples of how human reason differs, he is in the end unable to call up any of the imaginative cognition that he celebrates as peculiarly human to defend against the charge that "understanding" is essentially error-driven misinterpretation of sensory phenomena, except to assert that the "understanding" resolves the problem of deception by the senses. In fact, the most imaginative argument Ulysses does offer is a kind of precursor to Schroedinger's thought experiment with his cat: that the mere observation of a thing (in Ulysses' case, claiming any natural object must be variable, in motion, as it were, so never the same at any moment) necessarily changes the condition of the object observed—and so, he asserts, there is no such thing as certainty. Yet this is the one proposition that Ulysses cannot apply to himself: whatever the content or direction of debate, he remains utterly, absolutely persuaded that he alone has the truth about human nobility. Further, Ulysses concludes that humans are exceptional in that they can, through will, come to knowledge of the divine. Of course, the will exerted to remain in their "brute" forms of the creatures he has accosted does not occur to him as a corollary. Nor does he see a contradiction in the fact that he describes human will arising directly from the body's ability to discern: "for that the will is so marvelously united and knyt *unto the senses*" (sig. tlr, my italics).

Anatomical and physiological sameness is at the root of many modern assaults on the supposedly firm boundary between human and animal, and has historically troubled contrasting efforts to establish human exceptionalism. If, after all, we sleep, eat, breathe, procreate, communicate with others of all species, avoid dangers, and pursue pleasures through the same instrument, the body, how is it that these activities come to mean different things if they are performed by a "human," rather than an "animal"? As Ulysses eventually has to concede, we are like animals in that we perceive the world through sensory data and construct knowledge out of it; how then do we establish that the *way* we understand the world is appreciably better than the way animals do, especially when our senses are so often clearly inferior? If we share with animals so many crucial aspects of our physiology, how can we be sure that we are in some invisible, undetectable fashion more perfect than animals?

Modern and postmodern upholders of animal rights and those in the various subfields of animal studies have long argued that humans and animals are not categorically different even in the things that we assume comprise "reason," like logic, extrapolation, language use, and so on. Philosophers and critical theorists challenging the ideological uses of humanism have demonstrated its implication in systems ranging from sexism to colonialism; decentering the category of "the human" has made possible a reevaluation of "the animal" as a necessary or viable category in creating distinctions that can be so exploited. After a long period of resistance to anthropomorphizing animals, various fields of science have begun to make similar moves—brain studies and tests of intelligence being performed right now grant many animals far, far greater capacity for what humans call "reason," or "thoughtfulness," than was once evident. The source for this shift is, I would suggest, grounded in the increasing tendency for moderns and postmoderns to locate what once seemed abstract functions, unrelated to the body, in biology, especially in the structures of the brain and nervous system (so the reason that is a kind of soul in Ulysses' usage becomes, for us, a byproduct of the physical processes and changes in the brain). Because the inception of humanism in the Renaissance requires interrogation of the category of "the animal," early modern writers and thinkers encountered similarly important obstacles to establishing human difference in the sheer fact, as well as the various nuances, of shared embodiment despite their very different religious, cultural, and scientific frameworks for interpreting these terms. In a sense, then, we have come full circle with a difference.

This book begins to chart the questions and issues raised by early modern animal embodiment for both early modern and modern theories of the human. How did early moderns perceive the consequences of shared embodiment? How do animals contribute to human culture? Indeed, how human *is* culture, and how and why have we come to discount animals' roles in constructing it? Given our greater distance in many instances from real animals, our alienation from parts of our environment that once were familiar territory (wild animals, of course, fit this description, but so do many domestic animals), what kinds of interpenetration of the human and the animal do we tend to overlook? Can early modern representations of animal bodies alert us to ways in which we might move forward out of the depressingly deterministic side of biological explanations for emotions, thoughts, attitudes? Despite having begun with a text that thinks it is all about reason, I am particularly concerned to provide an account of animal and human embodiment that does *not* automatically privilege that faculty as if it were somehow free-floating and independent of the bodies that produce it. I hope, that is, to be less a Ulysses, and more an oyster, a mole, a horse, or a hind during this journey through Renaissance culture.

Gelli's dialogue summarizes a larger debate in the Renaissance over the relative felicity, morality, and physical superiority of animals versus humans. From Plutarch's *Gryllus* Gelli would have had available the argument that animals were potentially *more* rational and *more* virtuous than humans, an argument that stemmed from the materiality of the soul in some ancient thought. Erica Fudge explores the lineage of this idea: it derives from Plato rather than Aristotle, the Renaissance's go-to ancient source, but was nonetheless widely influential in Renaissance literature. Reason, Plato believed, inhered in a bodily organ, "the divinest part," the brain; thus, where Aristotle saw a tripartite form of soul—the nutritive, sensitive, and rational, only the last of which belonged to humans—Plato offered a schema in which animals and humans might share not only the fact of having a brain, but the rational capacity the brain generated.[3] In turn, Plutarch suggests that unlike animals, who act merely to satisfy needs and uncomplicated desires, humans are bound by irrational customs, habits, and social imperatives. In many cases these influences determine whether or not they may achieve happiness.

Where Fudge elaborates this conflict in early modern thought between theriophiles and those who would diminish animals based on their unequal access to self-awareness and reason, I want to reframe it through a lesson that Gelli's *Circe* could teach us if we resist obsessing over the validity of human reason—that is, the lesson that only animals' and humans' *shared embodiment* makes the dispute possible at all. For Ulysses to assert a rational soul that is distinct from the sensitive, he must himself understand the sensitive soul—and he must be able to answer the creatures' descriptions of their felicity. Indeed, when Ulysses tries to blame animals for overindulging their bodies, his arguments fail most miserably; it is humans who are most likely to fall into that trap, not animals.

Even the work's English translator falls into logical paradoxes in dealing with the question of reason versus bodies. When Iden justifies his translation by claiming he wants to promote a better appreciation of divine things among humans who wish to avoid resembling beasts, he is being unintentionally ironic on several levels: first, the idea that language is a barrier needing someone to translate (as Iden does) grants Circe, not Ulysses, supreme authority since it is she who enables the beasts to talk. Next, Iden seems to miss the point that if humans can so easily devolve into beasts, they share something rather compelling with animals. And finally, Iden apparently doesn't recognize that Ulysses' own command of language—his ability to translate his ideas so that they raise the animals' attention to divine things—fails utterly. His oratory clearly has no impact on the first ten animals, while the elephant, who presumably commands a level of discourse that the other lower animals don't, ends up actually speaking and arguing the least of all of them. As dialogists, then, the more embodied, less (by Ulysses' definition) rational animals have the most to say.

Renaissance works of medicine and natural philosophy often attempt to provide answers to questions about human superiority, specifically those raised by the relative sameness combined with the observable differences in human and animal bodies—and as often fail to do so satisfactorily. Perhaps the most comprehensive and elegant summary of the position that humans are easily and absolutely distinguishable physiologically from animals appears in Helkiah Crooke's *Microcosmographia*. Crooke is aware of the views expressed in works like Gelli's, that humans are somehow deficient:

> Their unbrideled insolencie is also to bee restrained, that call Nature
> a cruell Stepmother, because shee casts foorth Man into the world
> altogether naked and unarmed . . . and therefore holde him to bee
> of all Creatures the most imperfect. . . . Other Creatures (say they)
> do perceyve and understand their owne Nature; some betake them-
> selves to the swiftnesse of their feete, some trust to the loftinesse of
> their flight. . . . Man knoweth nothing, neyther how to speak, nor
> how to goe, nor how to feede: and in a word, that Creature which
> is borne to rule and governe all the rest, is enclined by Nature to
> nothing else but mourning and lamentation.[4]

Gelli's mole couldn't have put it better. Crooke also notes the physical attributes of animals missing in humans: "Nature hath given other creature divers coverings, shelles, rindes, haire, bristles, feathers . . . whereby they are able both to defend themselves, and offend others; onely Man she hath prostituted in his very nativitie, altogether unarmed, naked, and unable to helpe him-selfe" (9). But Crooke answers these doubters and naysayers with a description of human "excellencie," which he argues far outstrips the supposed beauties or advantages of animals: "The frame and composition which is upright and mounting toward heaven, the moderate temper, the equal and just proportion of the parts . . . Man onely is of an upright frame and proportion" because only man is infused with soul directly from heaven; human bipedal stature allows mankind to exercise the faculties of speech and reason, lets him gaze upward to heaven, and frees his hands to work his will on the world (4–5).

But when Crooke begins to catalogue the differences between animal and human bodies, his ability to draw a bright line of division wavers. For each case it turns out there is an exception: human eyes are multicolored of various hues, while animals' eyes ("the horse excepted") are all in their kind always alike (so all oxen have brown eyes, all sheep "watry" eyes, et cetera). Humans have eyelashes on top and bottom lids, while animals do not—except the ostrich, which does. Human ears are fixed and immovable, while those of animals are not—except in the apes, which most resemble humans (11). "Furthermore, of all creatures (excepting birds) that live upon the land, Man alone is two-footed" (12). In one thing humans and animals are indeed absolutely different, namely the human need to sit, which Crooke tries to turn from a weakness into a sign of human contemplation and a necessity if the hands are to be freed for practicing the arts (12). Gelli's text may or may not be meant as a laughable rehearsal of human superiority discounted by animal narcissism and obtuseness, but Crooke's very serious celebration of human excellency dangerously tends to refute rather than validate the idea that all humans are bodily different from and superior to all animals.

Thomas Browne's *Religio Medici* of 1643 runs into a related problem when he too addresses human physical defenselessness: "Thus have we no just quarrel with Nature for leaving us naked; or to envy the Horns, Hoofs, Skins and Furs of other Creatures, being provided with Reason that can supply them all."[5] Like Crooke, Browne takes stock of human deficiencies, but he is not dismayed by them, because, as Crooke puts it, "Reason doth more availe man, then any naturall gift doth the dumbe creature" (10). With reason, human beings can create substitutes for everything that they lack, and so extend their domination over creation (an argument Ulysses uses in Gelli's *Circe*). Indeed, having particular strengths might encroach on this supremacy of reason by limiting the need for ingenuity. Yet Browne's establishment of reason's compensatory and consolatory role is complicated by the mind's dependence on the information nature provides it. And it turns out, much of what the mind should learn comes from animals: "Indeed," writes Browne, "what Reason may not go to school to the wisdom of Bees, Ants and Spiders?"

(336). Browne confesses admiration for Pythagoras, who believed in metempsychosis (the transfer of souls from one animal to another and from animal to human or vice versa). In such a schema, the body that houses the soul does not define or delimit it; instead, all kinds of bodies are capable of housing all kinds of souls. This rejection of distinction inflects Browne's positioning of human intellect as the student of animal behavior (what we humans can learn from animals applies to us, so we are not substantially different), even if Browne concludes that humans have a greater potential to comprehend at once and in conjunction the many specific examples of animal "wisdom." Browne, like Crooke, wants to establish human exceptionalism but finds that shared embodiment complicates his agenda.

This book investigates a select few examples of Renaissance culture grappling with the many kinds of problems posed by shared embodiment. It joins a growing "body" of critical and historical work on animals, and "the animal" in the period. In the decades since Keith Thomas made an early foray into the field with his chapter on animals in *Man and the Natural World* (1983)—still an important reference for anyone thinking about Renaissance animals—scholars like Erica Fudge, Bruce Boehrer, Laurie Shannon, Simon Estok, Virginia DeJohn Anderson, and Juliana Schiesari (to name just a few) have transformed the study of animals in the Renaissance from hobby history to serious academic subject.[6] At the same time, theories that inform critical animal studies have made consideration of "the animal" an integral part of current debate about "the human." Cary Wolfe's influential *Animal Rites* begins with the proposition that speciesism is prior to and a necessary basis for all forms of discrimination and oppression: "It is this pervasiveness of the discourse of species that has made the *institution* of speciesism fundamental . . . to the formation of Western subjectivity and sociality as such, an institution that relies on the tacit agreement that the full transcendence of the 'human' requires the sacrifice of the 'anima' and the animalistic, which in turn makes possible a symbolic economy in which we can engage in what Derrida will call a 'noncriminal putting to death' of other *humans* as well by marking *them* as animal."[7] Wolfe's tour de force among the theory giants of the last century makes it clear that the category of "the animal" is a lynchpin in Western philosophical and political thought.

In fact, I think it's fair to say that nearly every academic currently working on the subject of animals is in some way influenced by a version of Wolfe's argument that speciesism is the first principle from which all other forms of oppression and exploitation grow. For those whose field is Renaissance culture,

however, the fact that the boundary that divides human from animal is neither
fixed nor stable in this period, but is in the process of being established, makes
it an especially fruitful field—not only can such scholars demonstrate that
"human" is a constructed category, manufactured at a specific historical moment, but they also seem to glimpse something beyond conceptual historicity,
some possible alternative version of the human-animal relationship that is
important to resurrect.

However, the authors I've cited above, like others working on early modern animals, have so far barely broached the subject of animal embodiment,
though all agree it would be a useful turn in the debate over the historical roots
of animals' status. For most critics concerned with animals, for example, the
influence of Cartesian thought on subsequent constructions of the distinction between human and animal is a crucial historical juncture. Descartes'
description of the "beast-machine" is a transformative concept responsible for
banishing animals from their prior, problematic, intimate equivalency with
humans. Human bodies and animal bodies, Descartes argues, are the same in
that they are composed of a collection of parts that operate in unison to produce observable actions. But only the human is endowed with language and
with the ability to adjust actions situationally, inspired by knowledge based
on reason: "for while reason is a universal instrument that is alike available
on every occasion, these organs, on the contrary, need a particular arrange-
ment for each particular action; whence it must be morally impossible that
there should exist in any machine a diversity of organs sufficient to enable
it to act in all the occurrences of life, in the way in which our reason enables
us to act."[8] To achieve this certainty, Descartes discards the sensory functions
of the body, like sight, or touch, or hearing, since all can be deceptive. If he
sees human beings passing by in the street, Descartes points out, he cannot
determine with any reliability their precise nature: "I do not fail to say that I
see the men themselves, just as I say that I see the wax; and yet what do I see
from the window beyond hats and cloaks that might cover artificial machines,
whose motions might be determined by springs?"[9] In other words, neither the
evidence of the body nor the presence of a body in another that resembles the
human can finally be relied on to establish the distinction between human and
nonhuman. Only thought can accomplish that.

Long before Descartes, of course, reason was also already an important
characteristic of the category "human." But as Fudge has convincingly shown,
before the Cartesian schema and the invention of the beast-machine, explanations of the divide between human and animal were beset by troubling

mind > body   interior > exterior

inconsistencies in the rational status of groups or individuals—a child, for instance, clearly was not yet fully rational, while adults could be bestialized by their irrational behaviors.[10] Boehrer has focused on how animal characteristics and categorizations conveyed early modern ideas about marginalized humans, or generated characterological discourses. Descartes, according to Boehrer, solved the problem of defining the human in distinction to the animal by "elevating human reason to the status of a first principle, requiring no proof outside the philosopher's own reference," but that skeptical turn inward constitutes, Boehrer argues, a form of character, "not an Aristotelian taxonomy of shared attributes, but rather a sense of personal identity as singular and doubtful, consisting in particularity and observation, privileging mind over body and interior over exterior."[11] Having charted the Cartesian moment, Boehrer turns to pre-Cartesian literary texts to mine them for alternatives to post-Enlightenment blindness to human-animal connections. Likewise, Fudge is committed to recovering a more complete and balanced (anti-Cartesian) history, and suggests that once animals were rendered objects in Cartesian discourse, they could be made invisible to scholarship and criticism. A Cartesian worldview is so encompassing that it can be difficult to discard: "In fact, many modern critics read the Cartesian human back onto pre-Cartesian writings, even while those critics are assessing the workings of Aristotelian psychology," writes Fudge, making their work anachronistic.[12] There is no study of the human, pre-Descartes, that can omit animals without being therefore incomplete, Fudge concludes.

Both of these critics clearly struggle against Descartes' legacy, but do so by returning to issues that seem destined to reproduce precisely the emphasis they wish to remedy. Boehrer's topic is the role of animals in creating "character," a subject thus bound up with identity in ways that naturally tend to privilege thought, behavior, and attitude. Fudge's work takes as its primary field of enquiry the complications and variations in what is recognized by early moderns as reason. Without discounting the important work that both have done (or the work of others like them), I want to note here that given Descartes' absolute rejection of the body as a locus of distinction, it might be more profitable to look to histories and narratives about embodiment for ways to accomplish an end run that fully subverts Cartesianism. As long as we fight over reason, we are stuck on Descartes' playing field.

The promise glimpsed in turning to the body has been acknowledged, if not always thoroughly pursued, in recent debates about animals. Jacques Derrida's ten-hour conference address on the subject of the animal (published

Descartes = Reason is the difference

posthumously as *The Animal That Therefore I Am*) investigates the absence of the animal from prior philosophical thought.[13] Gilles Deleuze and Felix Guattari have proposed "becoming animal" as part of an effort to establish the grounds of an ethics that does not exclude animals.[14] Steve Baker, Donna Haraway, and Cary Wolfe have not only continued to think critically about the consequences of dualism for both human and animal subjects, but have turned a critical eye on their philosophical precursors, often from the perspective of problems of embodiment: Haraway challenges Derrida for having avoided "seriously consider[ing] an alternative form of engagement . . . one that risked knowing something more about cats and how to look back, perhaps even scientifically, biologically, and therefore also philosophically and intimately."[15] Baker, Wolfe, and Haraway all differently question the degree to which animals for Deleuze and Guattari are any more than conceptual pieces in a philosophical game—as Steve Baker puts it, "Animals, for Deleuze and Guattari, seem to operate more as a device of writing . . . than as living beings whose conditions of life were of direct concern to the writers."[16] In Derrida's famous cat, which inspires his meditations, in Deleuze and Guattari's obsessive attention to parasitic insects, in Haraway's "knowing more," and in Baker's "living beings" subject to "conditions of life" we get glimpses of this constant but incomplete search for actual animals with actual bodies, animals that have more than just conceptual proximity, the search for a world in which we cannot remain insensible to their or our animal being.

In a forum that grew out of a conference panel on early modern studies and speciesism, Donna Landry and Cary Wolfe both indicated their belief in the primacy of the body in the more successful formulations of a historically informed anti-speciesist stance. The field of Renaissance animal studies is already diverse enough to include discussions of animals and national identity, bestiality, and experimental philosophy; authors have examined apes, horses, dogs, cats, bees, even rats, worms, and other vermin.[18] Yet the role of the body in discourses concerning animals has not yet taken center stage or been adequately explored in literary and cultural criticism, let alone in the more narrow historical field of early modern studies. Since much of the recent criticism in the field is materialist and broadly cultural in nature, borrowing heavily from other disciplines, it is the more surprising that this is the case. In literary and cultural studies per se, the history and representation of the human body has been an important recent feature of materialist work. Michel Foucault's groundbreaking work invited critics to take account of the body's construction in conjunction with changing cultural and historical regimes.[19]

"role of the body" → changes due to cultural history

One consequence of Foucault's influence was a revisionist reappraisal in literary studies of exactly how early moderns understood the link between identity and the body. Gail Kern Paster, Jonathan Sawday, Michael Schoenfeldt, and others have taken seriously early modern epistemological systems like Galenic humoralism, anatomical practice, and medicalized metaphors to explain early modern attitudes toward the self, others, disease, the mind, and so on.[20] Their work, like Foucault's before them, reminds us that it is almost impossible to overstate the significance of the body to almost every area of early modern life: from the nature of interiority to attitudes toward trade and city planning, the body is the bedrock of early modern conceptual organization—albeit one in flux because of seismic shifts in the biological sciences, the humanistic disciplines, theology, and other tools for interpreting the body's physiological and cultural functions.

Indeed, this flux is still with us. Philosophy and science converged in the twentieth century over the question of the body. Even as science was analyzing, codifying, and technologizing the body, revealing more and more of its internal machinery, critics, philosophers, and historians were considering the costs and advantages of scientific knowledge. From Maurice Merleau-Ponty to Alphonso Lingis and Michel Serres, the role of the flesh and sensation has seemed to require rescue from the tyranny of the cogito, from atomism, from erasure by the privileging of language and vision, and from the influence of late capitalism.[21] Donna Haraway, coming at the role of capitalism and nature/culture binarism in late twentieth-century feminism from a very different angle than Merleau-Ponty or Serres, sees in the cyborg an alternative to assumptions about the body's essentially organic constitution. I've already noted that science and psychology have joined up to evolve new answers to the question of what the "mind" is and how it works, answers that reject the same Cartesian dualism that is being dismantled in sensory theories and phenomenology. Models of the "extended mind" take as axiomatic that the mind is grounded in the body and so inseparable from it, as well as impossible to localize in a particular organ. Challenging twentieth-century trends in psychology, including behaviorism and cognitivism, philosophy and science cooperatively arrived at a variety of more flexible, socially and culturally nuanced models of mind. James J. Gibson's ecological psychology, as he delineates it in *The Ecological Approach to Visual Perception*, argues that animals and humans are radically situated and embodied, that information about what they perceive and how they will act based on their perceptions is entirely contingent upon the environment that delivers stimuli to systems of perception (not isolated

senses).[22] The idea of socially distributed cognition, first introduced by Edwin
Hutchins, proposes that cognition relies on the operations of social networks
and is shared across boundaries that separate individual minds; a certain kind
of thought can arise out of a group that resembles what we normally assume
is a thought process occurring within a single mind.[23] Andy Clark and David
Chalmers, in their essay "The Extended Mind," argue that versions of "mind"
or cognition can even happen outside the brain itself.[24] Clark and Chalmers
use the example of two people who "know" the way to a particular landmark,
one by having located and memorized it via past experience, and the other
who (having Alzheimer's) has written down the directions on a notepad. For
the latter individual, the notepad *is* his memory, just as for the former the
mind itself contains the memory-function. If we take all of these slightly di-
vergent but related theories together, we arrive at a version of the mind that
is not bounded by the operations of the brain itself, that is at times the product of—and entirely dependent on—interactions with others, that may be
displaced into other objects, and is always primarily dependent on complex
communication among many senses and the environment.

Now thinking about these several models, let's consider some of the most
ordinary, unremarkable, and unremarked experiences of early modern life:
using a dog to hunt or herd, petting a cat, riding a horse. The very common
nature of these working animals and pets leads us to overlook how extraordinary are the implications of early modern human activities involving them—
and how much they exemplify postmodern theories of ecological, extended,
or socially distributed mind. Normally if we were going to use theory to talk
about these animals, we might turn to theories like Wolfe's, which brands
most prior attempts to theorize the place of the pet as byproducts of humanism itself. We might alternately turn to Yi-Fu Tuan's influential writing on
pets, *Dominance and Affection*, which by its title announces its perspective on
the psychology of pet ownership and pet keeping.[25] Marc Shell, James Serpell,
and Donna Haraway have all also written crucial works on these domesticated
creatures, cited in most critical animal studies.[26] Wolfe and Tuan would unequivocally conclude that each activity involves a certain (humanist) domination and oppression of the animal; Shell would agree insofar as he sees pets'
inclusion in kinship networks as obscuring "the brutally inhumane reality of
the doctrine of universal (human) brotherhood."[27] Serpell and Haraway, in
contrast, would resist dismissing companion species out of hand, or the uniformly negative conclusions of the other scholars, perhaps balancing the conflicts and contradictions in our treatment of different species. Serpell would

most certainly observe the effects of petting a cat on human blood pressure, stress, and hormone levels, while Haraway would note the necessarily extraordinary human engagement with dogs or horses required during the training process.[28] What many of the critics I've named have not yet fully accounted for, I think, is the idea that each of these examples involves a violation of the generally assumed boundaries of perception and cognition. The stroked cat is not a passive object: cats demand attention in a cooperative and fluid relationship with humans, and a human-attuned cat can plant in a human mind the idea that stroking would be welcome and mutually beneficial.[29] Working with a dog requires a shared language that is not English, as does training a horse; as Merleau-Ponty insists, it is only because human and animal share a gestural repertoire that acts as language that the two groups can communicate at all.[30] "When you minde to helpe your Horse therewith, it must be with most milde & cheerful voice, as to say, hey hey: hola, hola: so boy, so, hap," writes Nicholas Morgan in *The Horseman's Honour*; the sound of the voice is supplemented with "a chirke with the tongue, which may be called clacking."[31] The hand adds "stroking" or "clawing" (scratching), and the leg applies subtly different forms of pressure. These "linguistic" and physical cues are not language per se; rather, they are mutually decipherable signals that let both creatures, human and horse, arrive at a shared set of references for both environmental and direct stimuli (this touch or sound means such a thing, that reaction in such circumstances is not permitted).[32] All three animals function at times as extensions of the human memory (the cat reminds its human that it needs feeding; its alertness indicates mice on the prowl), as part of the social network that creates thought (the dog understands it should flush game, the hunter follows to kill the creatures the dog will retrieve), and as part of the very body of the human that "thinks" as it performs actions (the horse creates the mutual embodied experience that we call "riding").

One instance of how extended mind theories intersect with animal embodiment arises in the case of flocks, herds, and schools. Certain animals function in aggregates in a fashion that has "capture[d] our imagination" historically, generating linguistic oddities that can be a kind of game to decipher.[33] Why a murder of crows? A shrewdness of apes? A pod of dolphins? Some of these terms seem to have obvious origins in associations with the animal's motion, character, or the form of its massing—an army of ants, a swarm of bees, a parliament of owls, a scurry of squirrels, a labor of moles—while others relate more to the animal group's social structure, as in packs and colonies of wolves or fox. Recently, flock movements have fascinated computer geeks and engineers interested in the complexities of collective movement. The thing about a herd or flock is that it moves with such precision, each animal keeping a place that is not cramped or dangerous within a huge, morphing unit. Studies of actual animals in aggregates have turned out to be only partially useful, since it is extremely difficult to follow individuals within the group, or to determine how group movements are carried out without chaos. Indeed, the remarkable waves and undulations of fish, birds, and some large mammals like cattle or wildebeest herds have inspired observers to believe that something like a shared mind must exist to account for their fluid and organized but sudden shifts and billows—but this impression is usually dismissed as practically impossible or fanciful. However, new computer modeling and other technologies have revealed the millions of negotiations of space, direction, motivation, force, and so forth that control group movement.

Take birds as one example: it turns out that it is impossible to account fully for the movement of a bird flock by normal individual reaction times. In 1984 Wayne Potts explained the nature of birds' superfast reaction time by analogizing it to chorus line movements, in which individuals are primed to react instantly to the movements of people on either side but do not necessarily decide or recognize the motivation for movement.[34] In 1986, Craig Reynolds examined computer-generated "boids" (birdlike computer artifacts programmed with simple commands) and determined a few general rules most flocking animals follow: separation, or steering to avoid crowding local flockmates; alignment, or steering toward the average heading of nearby flockmates; and cohesion, or steering to move toward the average position of nearby individuals. In fact, while our initial reaction to the idea that a herd is controlled by a single "mind" that has no individual embodiment might be to dismiss this as fantasy or error, the truth may be very close to that image after all. Our increasingly intricate understanding of herd movement suggests physiological responses and behaviors that do not arise from rational or thoughtful choice, but are what we usually call "kneejerk" reactions; yet the overall result is a logical, necessary, and functional movement that protects against predators and maximizes food gathering. In practical ways, human interaction with flocks, schools, and herds also requires that "we . . . think of the school as an animal itself, reacting with all its cells to stimuli."[35] Thus, when Temple Grandin designs a humane slaughterhouse, she takes into account the reactions not only of individual cows, but of the herd as a whole to each of its members, accounting for the ripple of anxiety or recognition of distress that can communicate instantly to the group; she treats the aggregate as if it had a single "mind."[36] Similarly, when a cowherd, shepherd, goatherd, or fisherman (in any century) moves a flock, he cannot lead from the front (no animal in its right mind follows a predator), but must be able to control and direct the myriad minds of a host of individuals making nanosecond decisions about where to turn, which way to move, often based on stimuli imperceptible to humans. Hence the use of the dog (who reacts with nearly equal speed), the horse (like the dog, more agile and responsive and able to cover ground), the motorcycle or helicopter (which drown out competing stimuli), the boat engine and the net (which impose uniform danger and a barrier), and other supplemental technologies that allow the herder to interact with the "mind" of the group. Ironically, to become effective herders, humans usually have to develop their own extensions of mind, whether animal or mechanical.

When the seventeenth-century Royalist poet Abraham Cowley wanted to credit Lord Falkland with the perfect melding of skills for his role, he used the image of the cohesiveness that marks the extended mind of flocks, herds, and schools:

England commits her Falkland to thy trust;
Return him safe; Learning would rather choose
Her Bodley or her Vatican to lose:
All things that are but writ or printed there,
In his unbounded breast engraven are.
There all the sciences together meet,
And every art does all her kindred greet,
Yet justle not, nor quarrel; but as well
Agree as in some common principle.
So in an Army govern'd right, we see
(Though out of several countries rais'd it be)
That all their order and their place maintain,
The English, Dutch, the Frenchman, and the Dane:
So thousand divers species fill the air,
Yet neither crowd nor mix confus'dly there;
Beasts, houses, trees, and men together lie,
Yet enter undisturb'd into the eye.[37]

The "kindred arts," that neither "justle nor quarrel" here, although initially compared to an army's organization, seem more closely allied with the "species," or nations, that share the earth, also defined by the parallel phrasing

"neither crowd nor mix confus'dly." Fascination with the orderliness that
would define a flock or herd, with its ability to include diversity yet behave as
if it were one organism, clearly is not limited to postmoderns, but can be deployed to describe a person, an army, and the mingled elements of a landscape.
Falkland's world, in Cowley's description, is a kind of early "boid."

What Questions Do We Ask?

I am no zoologist or biologist: I know very particular things about some
animals and their behaviors, but nothing about many others. However, in
each and every instance in which an animal appears in scholarly discussions,
whether postmodern or premodern, it is my "instinct" to consider that animal's physical characteristics, reactions, and engagements, whether they are
explicitly written about or not—and usually they are not. Animals are being
exhumed from oblivion in the scholarship of nearly every historical period;
they are being charted and explained by modern science in unexpected ways.
Yet animal embodiment is still incompletely available in the critical literature,
including—perhaps especially—that which deals specifically with animals in
early modern culture.

   There are some exceptions to this general absence of animal bodies: Gail
Paster, for instance, has written on the extension of humoral theory to animals, and Laurie Shannon has begun useful work on shared corporeality.[38]
Older historical works on bestiality, like E. P. Evans's, for instance, provide
the case studies that influence Bruce Boehrer and Dympna Callaghan, both of
whom find in the sexualization of human-animal relationships a fundamental
problem for early moderns concerned with drawing distinctions between species.[39] Histories of livestock, horses, and wild animals in the period naturally
entertain animals' physical characteristics, as do histories of veterinary medicine. However, Paster's one essay on animal humoralism is primarily designed
to explain Shakespearean references associated with characters like Falstaff
and Shylock, rather than pursue the implications of a shared humoral system
for the problem of the human-animal bodily relationship, and Shannon's is
oriented toward her perception of animals as part of a broad "zoopolitical"
spectrum in the early modern world. Evans collects bestiality cases as a legal
oddity, while Boehrer and Callaghan draw conclusions that rely more on abstract or fictional erotics than actual bodily encounters; and historians of livestock and veterinary medicine are usually less interested in the implications

for cultural assumptions and representational strategies when humans interact with animals' bodies.

There is, then, both a gap in scholarship here and a clear incentive to fill it. I borrow from a number of discourses to do so: literary works, livestock manuals, medical treatises, vermin-killing manuals, and anatomy books all make their appearances as primary focal texts, but I also draw on architectural theory, studies of urban geography, legal and philosophical debates, biological and zoological studies (early modern and postmodern), and a number of other relevant fields. Just as it is impossible to put together a complete picture of any particular animal, real or imagined, without having recourse to many sources of information in our own moment, it is equally impossible to do so with past representations of animals. My overarching argument is that *animal bodies* were as troubling to the emergent early modern divide between animal and human as was *animal reason*; in fact, the division of reason from the body is, I would say, an erroneous step influenced a posteriori by Cartesianism's pervasive influence in the sciences and the humanities. In fact, there is a rapprochement happening in both those domains that provides a useful template for exhuming the Renaissance animal body. "Science" once dismissed animals for being unworthy of study; the idea that animals might have verifiable moral reason or ethics, that they might be capable of abstract thinking, or that their DNA was relevant to anyone but breed enthusiasts, was once mocked. But in recent years, animal ethologists like Mark Bekoff have demonstrated sophisticated systems of moral behavior governing some animals' actions;[40] the DNA of Boxer dogs has been coded and used to help isolate the source of heart disease in both dogs and humans; experiments with animals as diverse as parrots, dogs, cats, and dolphins suggest degrees of cooperative intelligence unmatched even by chimpanzees and other human relatives.[41] Animal ethology was only invented in the twentieth century, and as the field has grown it has contributed to the understanding of human-animal relationships with scientific backing for what has often been dismissed as anthropomorphism, poetic enthusiasm, dewy-eyed sentimentality, or simple wishful thinking when expressed by nonscientists.

What once seemed like silly claims—dogs "read" human emotions, or cats manipulate their owners' behavior, or animals grieve lost animal or human partners—have in recent decades garnered their own scientific proofs. These discoveries, relying on the analysis of bodily responses through information from brain physiology, psychology, evolution, and ecology, test the limits of human willingness to surrender exceptionalism: for instance, Irene

Pepperberg's famous experiments with her parrot Alex, who learned to "speak" English, or similar experiments with chimpanzee and gorilla sign language, have provoked endless debate, some of it furious and angry, about the degree to which animals can ever be said to "have" language that conveys original thought, rather than the repetition of rote learning enhanced by human-delivered cues. (So does the chimp sign its own real desire, or does it respond to microscopic hints in the body language of its human interlocutor? Does the parrot really "know" what its phrases mean to it or its human partner, or is it just being trained to give the appearance of interaction?) On the other side of the argument are human beings for whom Alex and Koko the "talking gorilla" are confirmation that there is little or no difference between humans and animals.

These debates, ironically, replay an old scenario familiar to some early modern scholars: the case of "Bankes's" horse, Morocco, which traveled in England and Europe in the sixteenth century demonstrating its ability to count, read minds, and "speak" back to and about human viewers (Figure 1). Thomas Nashe, Richard Brathwaite, Thomas Bastard, George Peele, Thomas Morton, Thomas Heywood, Ben Jonson, William Prynne, and John Taylor all reference the horse, according to Erica Fudge's detailed research on the subject.[42] Morocco is a fine example of both human resistance to and celebration of displays of animal intelligence, as well as of the crucial role of the body in what we tend to think of as "mental" functions like reason, logic, and language. Fudge has detailed Morocco's "infamy," the dozens (perhaps hundreds) of references to him in the literature of the period, while framing his activity in terms of the challenge an apparently rational animal presented to Renaissance thought. Morocco was able to recognize individual members of his audience, count the coins in their purses or the marks on dice, dance, and generally earn a good living for himself and his owner with his tricks. As Fudge points out, efforts to explain away Morocco's performances (he was unnatural, a demon; he was exceptionally well trained; he was merely a performer, a juggler and crowd pleaser) did not defuse the implication that an intelligent animal threatened human superiority in reason:

> To state that animals are inferior to humans is to state something
> that, within a Christian, Aristotelian framework, appears to require
> no further explanation. . . . However, what is clear in numerous
> texts available in early modern England is that such a statement of
> animal inferiority is not always present—not only because of the

breakdown in the logic of the discourse itself or the reemergence of a lost philosophical tradition, but because all the complications of humans' everyday existences alongside animals challenge it. In this sense, Morocco comes to represent what was already known. Animals are not the same as humans, but that does not mean that they are incapable, or that they are not in themselves subjects. . . . Animals think.[43]

For centuries after Descartes, however, the implications of a Morocco seemed clearly different: the animal was merely mechanically generating actions based on training and a close reading of its owner's physiological behaviors. In 1907, Clever Hans, another "intelligent horse" was exposed as a fraud: like Morocco, Clever Hans made money for his owner, a German named Wilhelm van Osten, by performing higher intellectual tasks, including mathematical calculations, keeping time and dates, and reading and understanding German. The psychologist Oskar Pfungst, however, examined Osten and his horse, and concluded that the animal was not independently arriving at the answers to questions posed it, but was instead "reading" the unconscious behavior of his owner and trainer. The phenomenon is now called the "Clever Hans effect," and it surfaces most often now in those debates about parrots, primates, and language. Pfungst found that having learned the cues himself, he could not repress them sufficiently to prevent Clever Hans from reacting to them—that is, human reason and consciousness were defeated first by the human body's need to express what the mind holds, and second by the horse's extraordinary sensitivity to the most minute physical reflexes of a human. Indeed, as Vinciane Despret puts it, "Who influences and who is influenced, in this story, are questions that can no longer receive a clear answer. Both, human and horse, are cause and effect of each other's movements. Both induce and are induced. . . . Both embody each other's mind. . . . If we can see, according to Pfungst's hypothesis, how human bodies influence the horse's answer through his peculiar sensitivity and talent, shouldn't we also imagine the converse situation: the horse has taught the humans, without their knowledge, the right gestures to (involuntarily) perform."[44] Morocco and Clever Hans were not "intelligent" in having human-defined reason and ability; they were geniuses *as horses* in being physically attuned beyond human comprehension to environmental cues provided by their partners.[45] In fact, neither horse probably had much more equine skill than the average horse, now or then, who must sort out a confusing and changing vocabulary of signals from its trainers and

Figure 1. Woodcut of Marocco (Morocco), from John Dando's *Maroccus Extaticus, or Banks Bay Horse in a Trance* (1595). The baton in the horse's mouth indicates his mastery, comparable to his owner's.

riders, and perform feats of athleticism on command. Such skills, ethologists are beginning to inform us, may in the end amount to as significant a kind of genius as human intellect ever has.

The Human-Animal Sensorium

One of the principal ways that early moderns interacted with animals (or each other) was through their bodily senses. This seems so obvious it is hardly worth mentioning. But recent scholarship on the way sensory experiences intersect with cultural expectations and beliefs, as well as that on early modern senses in particular, suggests it is not so self-evident that we understand what such a fact meant to early moderns. Early modern defenses of human superiority often assert reason as the sole proof and justification of such a hierarchy because they must concede (as we have seen Crooke does, for instance) that animals have far better senses: not even the most committed apologist would claim that people can smell scents better than can dogs, or hear sounds better than can cats, or see better than can birds. In the sensory domain, humans *animals are far better @ sensory tasks.*

are clearly challenged, dull, thinly endowed; they assume the right to control and exploit animals based on their ability to outthink most animals in most circumstances. In fact, human utilization of animals in various occupations only confirms human sensory deprivation. What need is there for a hunting hound except to smell out game that no human would perceive? What need for a household cat but that it hears so much better the tiny sounds of mice and rats, the better to stalk and capture them, and so on. The stupidest animal still outperforms the smartest human in these tasks.

But each sense has attached to it a whole spectrum of cultural associations and implications. Take, for instance, a cat's ability to hear, which is the basis of its hunting skills. William Baldwin's *Beware the Cat*, a sixteenth-century narrative meant to be a thinly disguised attack on Catholicism, capitalizes on the cat's extraordinary abilities by giving its various felines a rich world of discourse usually inaccessible to humans, and then by using the idea that cats somehow communicate outside normal human ranges to create anxiety about their access to the world of their human cohabitors.[46] Baldwin's protagonist takes a magical potion that enables him to understand feline "speech," and what he discovers is not just that cat screeches mean something, but that cats have a developed, far-reaching system of communication, as well as their own history, politics and laws, morals, and so on. Now, by analogy this is meant to suggest that Catholics exist not just sub rosa, but sub audio. But it relies on actual human observation of cats' sensitivity to sounds that humans cannot perceive, alongside what naturalists like Edward Topsell call their shrieking, wailing "speech."[47] Ultimately, *Beware the Cat* testifies not just to Protestant fears about Catholics, but to human fears about inferiorities in their "rational" perception of the creatures (human and animal) around them. We may not hear what they hear, and so what they "say," or we may hear, yet not understand. Baldwin's attack on Catholics is thus reminiscent of the suspicion and hostility so many harbor toward human groups who speak different languages—those too are sometimes portrayed as sounding like the inarticulate cries and screeches of animals, but the awareness that they are language makes the listener the more anxious about her or his lack of perfect perception or comprehension.

Franz Wolfgang mounts another kind of attack on cats in his *History of Brutes* of 1672. Although Wolfgang credits the cat with extreme cleanliness, he nevertheless accuses it several times of bad smell: "The breath of a Cat is very unwholsome, and the smell of his urine is very strong, and therefore we use to say, that a Cat alwaies leaveth a stink behind him; he is naturally very hot, his skin is very warm, he being alwaies so hot, hath a bad scent about him. His breath is exceeding strong and unwholsome (as we said before) and therefore those that let them lye with them in bed are seldome free from diseases."[48] Now it is true that male cats who mark their territories can carry that scent on their fur for a time, and the marking itself is pungent; however, Wolfgang is unique in finding this scent to be extraordinary, extrapolating it to all cats (females do not mark or smell) and finding it the cause of diseases for those who keep cats as pets. It is actually a bit difficult to imagine that cats are any more notably stinky than their other companion-species peers, or than humans for that matter, given standards for bodily cleanliness in the period.

A previous account of cats in a similar compendium, Topsell's *History of Four-Footed Beasts*, includes numerous identical "facts" about cats (suggesting that Wolfgang cribbed from Topsell), among them the story that their eyes shine like carbuncles, an account of their resemblances to lions, and their distinction from dogs in loving places over people. Topsell also gives accounts of cats' "breath" poisoning or causing diseases in those who sleep with cats.[49] But Topsell means "breath" to reflect the cat's actual exhalations, while Wolfgang's account seems to blur "breath" with "smell"—in the quote above, it is actually unclear whether breath means respiration or the odor breathed in by the pet owner, the "stink" a cat "alwaies leaveth behind him." Nowhere, however, does Topsell mention that cats create bad odors or "stink," so we may assume that aspect of cats is Wolfgang's own preoccupation.

Constance Classen David Howes, and Anthony Synnott outline one reason for Wolfgang's peculiar move: "Smell is *cultural*, hence a social and historical phenomenon. Odours are invested with cultural values and employed by societies as a means of and model for defining and interacting with the world. The intimate, emotionally charged nature of the olfactory experience ensures that such value-coded odours are interiorized by the members of a society in a deeply personal way."[50] Smells, good and bad, are both social and biological markers; in fact, the two domains overlapped in the early modern world. Bad odors were considered pathogenic—plagues were believed to be caused by putrid smells. At the same time, foul odor was associated with sin, whether as a reminder of its presence in all humans, or to distinguish certain individuals or groups of humans from others, to hierarchize them, and to attach moral or other meanings to their existence. Classen, Howes and Synott, and Alain Corbin all argue that early moderns were just beginning to create the conceptual systems of distinctions and regimes of hygiene that would find their ultimate expression in today's bias against odorous bodies, witnessed in advertisements for soaps, deodorants, and home sanitizers.[51] Ethnic and racial groups are now sometimes ascribed inherent odors, one part of a network of assumed "essential" characteristics used to marginalize or exploit certain groups.[52] I would suggest we can find in Wolfgang's harping on cat odors an expression of this cultural use of smell: in Wolfgang's account, the cat is clearly a lecherous, duplicitous, repellent animal—and so it must smell bad, even pathogenically foul, as well.

If the social is produced from the interactions of perceptive senses with the environment, it turns out that the senses are in turn always already socially determined. And yet, the senses are inescapable encounter zones between species. Excavating the social significance of sensory interaction, however, can be difficult. When early modern texts discuss cats, they rarely if ever dwell on the haptic zone that for postmoderns may be the most significant source of pleasure for both parties: petting cats simply does not figure in early modern texts or cultural artifacts, although we must assume that it happened. Not until the early eighteenth century were cats in paintings depicted as lap cats, being held—and presumably petted—by their owners.[53] Thus we are missing a core sensory experience in any attempt to reconstruct the encounters of cats and humans, along with the social meanings that experience conveyed. We are left with cats who speak, who smell, but who have no tactile being, an inversion of our modern encounters with the species.

In contrast, the flea was the inhabitant of, and even a kind of ambassador on the human body's haptic zone. Like scholarship on cats, which is more often than not dismissed as hobby history, too cutesy to be serious, work on the common insect life of the early modern social world is lacking. But the shared sensorium of early modern humans and animals includes, in far more overt ways than we might always appreciate, the tiniest creatures—fleas, lice, flies, bedbugs, gnats, and so on. Not only do domestic and other animals share pest insects with human hosts (and vice versa), but many of those insects may be keys to human success as a species.[54] The idea that we actually share our bodies with nonhuman life has reemerged with a vengeance in the early twenty-first century: almost 90 percent of the cells within the human body are microbes, not human cells at all, and we literally crawl with microscopic organisms, some of which we could not survive without. Internal parasites are now so unusual in Western countries that their occupation of our organs is considered a momentous and awful event. Fleas and lice are somewhat more common, but they are often categorized as the pests of children or pet owners, not of the general populace. Granted nobody writes love poetry like they used

to, but surely no one these days would address to his beloved a poem about a
flea; yet, of course, Donne's little gem "The Flea" testifies to the absolute ubiquity of fleas on even the most elevated human corpuses and belongs to a recognized subgenre of early modern poetry. Lice and fleas were leveling influences
in early modern life: commoners and royalty were equally subject to both head
and pubic lice, according to the recent examination of the mummy of Ferdinand II of Aragon.[55] Nearly every human body in the period, like every cat,
dog, or rat body, was thoroughly explored and colonized by tiny life-forms.
And the flea or louse was credited with a kind of knowledge unavailable to
fellow humans: the flurry of flea-poems of the seventeenth century, including
Donne's, relied on the idea that where the flea could travel, the lover wished to
go, but couldn't. Intimate, yet alien, the flea occupied the body of its host like
a tiny explorer searching its fleshly world like a cornucopia, the most secret or
taboo places wide open to its small hairy feet.

A social history of fleas and lice might trace their gradual removal from
the explanatory discourses of religion, according to which they are evidence
of the flesh's corruption and a tribulation that can elevate the soul by re-
minding the suffering individual of her or his body's transience. Fleas and
lice mortified the body for some zealous Christians. Hans Zinsser repeats
the tale of Thomas Becket's dead body, laid in state, and found to be wear-
ing layers of clothing that included a hair shirt, infested with scores of lice
and fleas: "As the body grew cold, the vermin that were living in this multiple
covering started to crawl out, and, as MacArthur quotes the chronicler: 'The
vermin boiled over like water in a simmering cauldron. . . .'"[56] Since he wore
the hair shirt under his rich vestments, and since he clearly must have suffered
the discomfort of constant biting from the vermin in it, Becket's infestation
was taken as a sign of his real piety. Whether his embrace of the itching and
misery of bites was really intended as a form of penance is impossible to determine, although there was a rich tradition of such use for tiny creatures that
devoured flesh and blood (for instance, Francis of Assisi considered the flea
the "pearl of poverty").[57]

But by the sixteenth and seventeenth centuries, vermin like fleas and lice
had acquired a different significance. As Linda Woodbridge points out, beggars and vagabonds were associated with their vermin, so that not only was
their filth subject for condemnation, but "beggars themselves seemed like lice,
parasitic on the body politic."[58] Piero Camporesi likewise finds that disease
and vermin become compelling images for the poor, who are characterized
as hordes of "human insects" who threaten the prosperity and integrity of a

nation.[59] Suffering the touch of vermin like lice and fleas was, by the late seventeenth century, more a marker of personal failing than of sanctity. Dutch art depicting flea hunts is, for instance, meant to convey the idea that hygiene is the path to spirituality—cleanliness next to godliness. To have one's skin crawl with the touch of tiny insects is no longer occasion to meditate on God, but a source of shame. The sensory message of infestation has done an about-face in the space of a century or two.

Robert N. Watson has written brilliantly on the early modern approach to the body as a cornucopia of life, taking literally and literarily Thomas Browne's remark in *Religio Medici* that the self is "a Microcosm, or little world," a digest of the teeming, diverse forms of life that comprise creation.[60] Watson observes that the deconstruction of discrete selfhood implied in Browne's image is omnipresent in Shakespeare's *A Midsummer Night's Dream*, suggesting that early modern models of a nonautonomous, ecologically embedded "self" are worth recuperating and align remarkably well with current scientific understanding of the body.[61] The "hidden symbiotic universe" Watson describes included a human haptic system that was never closed, never sanitized, constantly under assault by tiny invaders that swarmed regions of the flesh that few humans ever saw, creatures that took up persistent residence on the human body, making it their globe and horizon. Interior and exterior, cleanliness and filth, corrupt and sanctified—binaries and boundaries fall prey to these miniscule mortifiers.

Restoring the Animal Body

The animals that populate the chapters that follow this introduction are the ordinary creatures of early modern daily life—horses, sheep, dogs, cats, moles, rats, worms. I have not chosen a particular group or set of animals, but rather representative cases in which animal bodies become suddenly crucially important in specific literary or cultural discourses. Thus, both the first and second chapters revolve around horses: in the first chapter, I look at the implications of early modern horse anatomies, consciously constructed to mirror human anatomies like Vesalius's *De Humani Corporis Fabrica*, while in the second I revisit the limitations of arguments about animal-human eroticism that collapse into discussions of bestiality, taking as my texts both the poetry about horse love and the literature of horsemanship. My third and fourth chapters deal with mammalian and invertebrate parasites: I discuss cats and dogs in the context of early modern architecture in *Romeo and Juliet*, and rats, mice, worms, and other tiny vermin as they inform early modern attitudes toward the problem of interiority as it is explored in *Hamlet*. Finally, my fifth chapter examines two examples of animals caught up in discourses of property: *Hamlet*'s mole and the sheep of Thomas More's *Utopia*. If the material of the individual chapters does not pretend to be comprehensive, the domains of animal embodiment addressed—how animals figure in the discovery of the body's material functions, how they participate in erotic life, how they influence external human structures, how they in turn inhabit human bodies, and how they alter ideas of property—seek to be fairly broad and complete.

I begin and continue with the assumption that there is no such thing as a "human" without animals, not entirely in the manner that recent theory has affirmed that proposition as a philosophical problem (although I am happy to entertain that theory), but rather in the material sense that there is no such thing as human identity, history, *culture*, without the prior cooperation, collaboration, habitation, ideological appropriation, consumption of animals, without animals as the "always already" of both materiality and culture itself. That is the larger argument of this book. Raymond Williams reminded us of this long ago: "Society, economy, culture: each of these 'areas' now tagged by a concept is a comparatively recent historical formulation. . . . 'Culture,' before these transitions, was the growth and tending of crops and animals, and by extension the growth and tending of human faculties."[62] When early moderns turned inward, looking for Hamlet's "that within which passeth show," when they sought the essence of the self that distinguished them from all other mammals (and all other human beings), they not only found the potential for self-fashioning understood as regulation of the body's material condition, they found animals dwelling there, aiding or resisting (or simply ignoring) their efforts at self-discipline.[63] No one in early modern Europe lived without a load of parasites; what it meant, therefore, to be an "individual" was highly contingent upon interanimality, the shared experience of bodily existence.[64] Indeed, where early sciences like anatomy converged with everyday experiences of multitudes was on the subject of the body's inevitable openness to its environment, a fact that precluded its absolute conceptual or physical division from animal creation.

I also question the idea that erotic encounters with animals are a one-way street, or that the erotics of human encounters with animals are reducible to genital sexuality. As the etymology of "pet" suggests, physical contact with an animal is always something of an erotic encounter; the process of riding a horse (at least, riding one *well* according to Renaissance horsemanship treatises), because it more completely engages the body, is that much more of one. Although many early modern horsemanship treatises begin and end by asserting human dominance, they cannot escape the consequences of the physical process they attempt to shape—indeed, their efforts to encourage sensitivity in the aspiring horseman require that they harp on moments when pleasure arises from the process of exploring bodies, a mutual process that can't exclude the agency of the animal involved. Scholarship that reads only for examples of bestiality misses a great range of early modern emotions, experiences, and exchanges; and the politics of speciesism, which dictates that bestialization necessarily involves the victimization of the abject animal, misses the more interesting problem of cooperative erotics that marks some of the most canonical works of Renaissance literature. Again, the erotic landscape laid out in horsemanship manuals, as well as in literary references to horses, tends to confirm that both human *and* animal bodies are open to an erotics of contact, a pleasure in union, even the pleasure of a collapse in individuated identity.

Humans and animals share architectural spaces and geographical places like the rural farm, city streets and squares, the urban household. Humans traditionally see themselves as sole creators, builders, labelers of these domains. But Renaissance theories of architecture, and the material processes of city planning, do not cooperate in making humans solely responsible for these things. Given the array of complex social and cultural ideas based on the division of space, expressed through binaries like inside/outside, wild/tame, barbaric/civilized, urban/rural, the question of who or what controls and directs the construction of architectural spaces is crucial. Not only do animals play a fundamental role in architectural divisions, but individual species of animals in early modern Europe—horses, cats, dogs—had specific and concrete influence over both the material nature of built environments and the ideological uses to which versions of the environment could be put.

Finally, it may have appeared to later readers and theorists that the exclusion of animals from concepts like property ownership was simple and straightforward fact; however, if the basis of ownership begins with the body itself—that is, a human being owns a thing because the labor of his body, which he unequivocally owns, has improved it—then animals again interrupt and problematize such confident logic. Locke tries to solve that dilemma by invoking biblical fiat: "The earth, and all that is therein, is *given to men* for the support and comfort of their being. And tho' all the fruits it naturally produces, and beasts it feeds, *belong to mankind* in common, as they are produced by the spontaneous hand of nature; and no body has originally a private dominion, exclusive of the rest of mankind, in any of them, as they are thus in their natural state: yet *being given for the use of men*, there must of necessity be a means to appropriate them some way or other, before they can be of any use, or at all beneficial to any particular man."[65] However, the theological argument about dominion created points of tension. The earth feeds beasts and humans alike, but God gave animals to Adam and his offspring to use as he saw fit; individuals may appropriate the fruits of the earth, including beasts, with their labor. Yet God also gave animals the ability to create, to labor, to seize, and to make territorial claims. Can the consequences of these attributes always be so easily contained? And when mankind labors for his beasts, and not the other way around, who then "owns" the labor—indeed, who owns whom, the man his beast, or the beast "his" man? Reconsidering the role of animal bodies in constructing theories of labor and property not only in Renaissance texts but also in subsequent economic models like Marx's might give us a new way of conceiving the repressed links between human and animal production, labor, and ownership.

In my view, when current criticism focuses on the faculty of reason as the weak point in the construction (and therefore the best point at which to engage in deconstruction) of the human-animal divide, it goes exactly wrong. Humans are remarkably consistent in insisting on or reverting to difference, even when those humans call themselves "animals" and agitate for a posthuman world.[66] Exploring problems of human and animal embodiment in Renaissance culture, however, lets us demonstrate that where the body is concerned differences are and have always been simply impossible to maintain. Again, rather than join Ulysses in endless debates about reason, I would instead imitate the majority of Gelli's talking animals and argue that the body is a site of shared (but not necessarily identical) experience, a site of shared consciousness, a kind of zone of exchange where we can come together with animals and comprehend them as ourselves—literally, as part of ourselves, indistinguishable from the supposedly individuated "selves" that we believe we have.

The body allows us
(animals & humans) to
come together

Chapter 1

Resisting Bodies:
Renaissance Animal Anatomies

If we are going to talk of bodies, there is no more fitting place to begin than with early modern medicine's advances in, and continuing obsession with, anatomy. Andreas Vesalius's monumental *De Humani Corporis Fabrica* (1543), published with dozens of carefully created illustrations, inspired decades, even centuries of imitators whose volumes joined Vesalius's in revealing the secrets of the human body. Jonathan Sawday calls the post-Vesalian period of 1540–1640 "the age of dissection" and the "period of the discovery of the Vesalian body," a period that can be distinguished by its aura of wonder, as well as it analogical approach to human form.[1] Vesalius and his heirs saw themselves exploring the miniature of God's divine cosmos, extending mankind's dominion over creation to his own internal landscape. However, that landscape was produced through a process of "partition," since dissection involved the separation of a coherent whole into its constituent parts, which functioned in tension with the idea that the human individual was an organic whole. This troubling implication of dissection may have eventually been recuperated in the creation of a new scientific order with its unified rational "body" of order, but for early moderns the "dialectic of unity and partition" was a source of constant anxiety, given that the "spatially imagined body . . . [was] the most common vehicle for the making of social and cosmic metaphors in early modern Europe."[2] In undertaking to confirm the proposition that the human being was a "Microcosm, or little world," Vesalian anatomy in fact began the process of deconstructing such a model.

For a time, the body's complex role in post-Vesalian thought was obscured in the critical scholarship by triumphal narratives of individualism, or by retroactive application of Cartesian versions of the mechanistic body.[3]

In the last decade or so, cultural and literary criticism has rediscovered the human body and plumbed its secrets anew, finding in it the primary locus of Renaissance ideas about interiority, reading it for the somatics of religious experience, analyzing its inspiration of anxiety about integrity versus fragmentation, and making it a central agent in social and political discourse. On the whole, however, this new age of discovery has restricted itself entirely to discussions of the *human* body, as if human organs, bones, nerves, skin, joints somehow have nothing to do with those of nonhuman animals, and as if the condition of being distinctively human, rather than animal, were unproblematically established a priori in the anatomies under examination.

Anatomies of animals are generally consigned to the prehistory of veterinary medicine, categorized according to a division of professional and academic practices that is the result of exactly the process scholars of human anatomy pretend to expose as an ideologically charged historical fiction. Yet, scholars in early modern animal studies have repeatedly established that in this period the boundary between human and animal was fluid, inconsistent, and fraught with its own anxiety-producing contradictions.[4] Marching forward without reference to the context of animal anatomy, scholars newly interested in the human body ignore the many questions their own work raises about how that problematic human-animal boundary influences, or is influenced by, their arguments. If we accept that anatomies created a sense of "inwardness" that grounded human subjectivity, as Michael Schoenfeldt argues, which in turn made possible a sense that the individual was a separated self, do we also imagine that dissecting animals did the same for ideas about animals' inward selves?[5] Did the shift from imagining the human body as porous and open to imagining it as a closed and defined system—one therefore capable of supporting an entire edifice of ideas about individuality—similarly affect the way humans thought about animals? If so, what did an *animal individual* look like, inside and out?

To illustrate how his method led him to the conclusion that God instilled the rational soul only in mankind, Descartes begins the fifth part of his *Discourse on Method* with "the motion of the heart and arteries."[6] In fact he advises the reader not versed in anatomy to "take the trouble of having dissected in their presence the heart of some large animal possessed of lungs" to locate the veins, arteries, ventricles of the heart, and other physical attributes that animals and humans share.[7] Descartes concludes, however, that the body, a marvelous machine, is animated by "animal spirits," not by reason. As I pointed out at length in the introduction, even recent critics have fallen into

the trap of following his lead in disenfranchising the body by privileging issues
of behavior, thought, or sympathy. Early modern critical analysis aimed at sav-
ing the animal from Cartesian dualism that ignores Descartes' own location
of anatomy at the root of his method may, as I've noted, have overlooked the
real remedy to that dualism.[8]

In this chapter I attempt instead to restore the presence of animals to discussions of anatomies of the body. To do so, I focus first on the imagery used
in Vesalian anatomies, especially in their title pages, and on the few examples
of animal anatomies from the same period. While dogs, apes, pigs, and other
animals were most commonly dissected, through the social and institutional
conditions that applied to publication of nonhuman medical treatises, they
did not merit full texts themselves. Instead, the only major animal anatomies before the late seventeenth century and the advent of the Royal Society
are anatomies of horses. In addition to locating representations of animals in
human anatomies, therefore, I also examine in depth two of the most significant animal anatomies published during the century and a half following the
appearance of Vesalius's *Fabrica*, Carlo Ruini's *Anatomia del Cavallo, Infermità
e Suoi Rimedii* (1598), and Andrew Snape's *Anatomy of an Horse* (1683).[9] Because each of these texts responds directly in some fashion either to the Vesalian model of dissection or to its transformation of scientific discourse, I read
them against a variety of human anatomy texts, including Vesalius's *Fabrica*,
instead of situating them in traditions of horse-leeching or horsemanship and
husbandry manuals, as has often been the case. In fact, it is my sense that there
is no such thing as "human anatomy," full stop; animals cannot be banished
from the literature of bodily discovery since they undergird that project in
ways large and small. Laurie Shannon reminds us that all anatomy is by definition comparative, relying on the fact of what she calls shared "creatureliness":
anatomical methodology relies on a "zoo-analogical conundrum" that led to
"a crisis of authority" in Renaissance medical knowledge, which looked less
and less to classical and biblical sources, and more to cross-species bodily resemblances.[10] The historical trajectory bears out her assertion: from comparisons of humans with animals in medieval question books, where animals were
present to demonstrate the superiority of God's creation in the human form,
to Darwinian evolution, which is based specifically in the tradition of comparative anatomy as it was professionalized during the eighteenth and nineteenth centuries, animals remain the ground on which epistemological and
ontological understandings of the human body are constructed. The animal in
these cases is, however, often indecorous, occasionally resistant toward fictions of

bodily compliance evident in human anatomies. The partition-unity dialectic that
emerges in animal anatomies is grosser, its implications more difficult to control or
alleviate with the usual amelioratory rhetorical and visual devices, especially in the
case of the horse anatomies with their enormous, vigorous subjects and their attendant traditions and mythologies. In what follows, I track the persistence of the
animal, particularly animal bodies, their occasional coy opacities, even the simple
threat posed by their sheer mass to the anatomist's epistemology.

Animal Comparisons

When Andreas Vesalius published his *De Humani Corporis Fabrica*, he as-
serted that its improvement on Galenic anatomy hinged on his experience
with the dissection of human bodies, rather than animals; unlike Galen, who
was "deceived by his apes" and dogs, Vesalius had verified his own discoveries
in dissections of actual human corpses.[11] He corrects numerous Galenic errors
in the identification of organs, bones, and other structures and advocates an
empirical, scientific, intimate, rational approach to the human body over any
system that sets classical, textual authority above the individual faculties of
observation. For instance, Vesalius first notices that the human breastbone is
segmented into three portions, not seven as Galen had argued, an error traced
to animal physiology. Describing the membrane that rests beneath the skin,
possibly the superficial fascia, Vesalius defends himself against detractors:

> Others, even though they have seen me demonstrate that this
> membrane covers the whole body, are so stupid that they will not
> admit that this is what Galen refers to very frequently elsewhere . . .
> simply because I point to fat . . . between the skin and this mem-
> brane, often as much as three inches thick, and because in man
> this membrane always stands apart from the skin by the amount
> of the thickness of the fat. These people, born solely to decorate a
> professional chair, should have realized that Galen was speaking of
> his apes and not of man; for in apes no fat intervenes between the
> membrane and the skin. (2: 144)

Those "decorative people," other academic anatomists, refuse to dirty their
hands with the work of dissection and so remain ignorant of the differences
between man and ape. While Vesalius does not discard Galen—indeed, the

project of the *Fabrica* is rather cooperative with Galen's—he considers those who adhere unquestioningly to Galen's teachings to be irrelevant aesthetes. If the mantra of anatomists is *nosce te ipsum*, know thyself, then Vesalius proposes that the self in question must not be approached indirectly or comparatively, but must submit itself directly to the probing gaze and hands of the physician. Indeed, the self that was the subject of scientific knowledge was in part grounded in the whole spatial and conceptual existence of an "inside" to the human that is as much corporeal as it is philosophical or spiritual. It could therefore be assumed that it would be pointless to plumb the depths of animals, which supposedly lack both reason and spirit, for evidence of selfhood.

According to Erica Fudge's analysis of Bacon and the new science, however, the project was compromised by its inescapably analogical, comparative nature. The premise of the animal experimentation that drove the empirical investigations of the anatomists was the religious goal of knowing God by knowing His works in nature, of which the human body was the most complex, glorious, and revelatory—it was, in effect, the temple of God, of the soul that was a piece of godhead.[12] Yet as Fudge points out, "The temple of God is supported by the anatomists' endeavor to know[,] but as soon as the animal is placed in the debate the temple, based as it is on a notion of the separation of human and animal, crumbles." Anatomists and the new science inevitably "destroyed the most important myth of all," namely the myth of absolute difference between human and beast.[13] And it was simply impossible to build the temple without animals. Even Vesalius, it turns out, could not function without animals to bolster his work, and he freely refers to dissections of pigs, dogs, apes, and other creatures, at some moments for comparison to explain Galen's errors, but at others simply as material for insights into the human form. Indeed, at times his own work is as guilty of being "deceived" by animals as was Galen's: for example, his illustrations of the hyoid and the tongue are animal in origin. It is, it turns out for Vesalius as for other anatomists and scientists, entirely impossible to avoid being a comparatist—but being a comparatist ultimately makes it difficult to assert the human as specially qualified to embody God's perfection.[14]

Bacon and presumably other anatomists and scientists experimenting on animals discover an alternate basis for an anthropocentric worldview, suggests Fudge, in the power of the scientist to name what he observes. The ability to call the animal an animal, to see "insides and outsides" at the same time becomes the foundation of the mythmaking that we call science.[15] But, as I will argue here, such a triumphalist attitude among anatomists, an attitude that is

often expressed most eloquently in the artistic images that decorate their otherwise relatively unpoetic published texts, is not complete or inevitable, nor
is the ability to "see inside" the animal any more absolute and unproblematic
than is the venture to see inside the human.

Frontispieces and illustrations to anatomy books involved the collaboration of the artist and the scientist, sometimes even establishing the conjunction of these two roles in the skills of the anatomist himself. Vesalius's *Fabrica*
may have been illustrated by students in Titian's studio, possibly Stephan van
Calcar, who is credited with creating its frontispiece.[16] But most historians believe Vesalius also did some of his own illustrating, at the very least diagraming
the results of his dissections as a template for the engravers. Several images in
his volume involve animals, including most famously that frontispiece (Figure
2), and the illustration of a human skull resting on a dog's (see Figure 6 later
in this chapter).

As Andrea Carlino remarks, the title pages to anatomy books illustrated
the process of the "ceremony" of dissection: "By means of a figurative language
made up of both explicit and more hermetic elements, the title pages reveal
some of the action and some of the relationships that come into being while
the ritual of the anatomy lesson is played out."[17] They are, in other words,
ancillary texts in which cultural or iconographic material that cannot be included in the anatomical descriptions themselves can be presented. Vesalius's
title page is a rich display of the new state of the anatomist's art, expressing its
author's relationships to tradition, to Galen, his principal precursor and the
main target of his corrective arguments, to the religious and scholastic communities in which he moved, and so on. It is a manifesto, a defense, and a
celebration all at once.[18]

The animals that appear in the *Fabrica*'s frontispiece are clearly marginal,
even antagonistic to the central activity focused on Vesalius, who is shown dissecting a female cadaver. His right hand is "thrust" into her abdomen, while
the other points upward as he lectures the throng of observers gathered around
him.[19] The engraving celebrates the superiority of Vesalius's method in nearly
every aspect: the very fact that he is pictured touching a body distinguishes
him from his contemporaries who ordered dissections from a raised podium,
leaving the actual cutting to illiterate barber-surgeons. Vesalius describes such
physicians "croak[ing] away with consummate arrogance like jackdaws about
things they have never done themselves" (1: li). "A butcher in a shambles," he
concludes, "could teach a practitioner more than the spectators are shown
amidst all this racket" (1: li). In the crowd that attends Vesalius, nearly every

Figure 2. Title page of Andreas Vesalius's *De Humani Corporis Fabrica* (1543). Bibliothéque de l'Académie de Médicine, Paris. Photo: Marc Charmet/The Art Archive at Art Resource (AA526088).

eye is on him; only a few look away. Among these are the figures associated with the engraving's animals. At the left, a monkey climbs onto a table, distracting a boy below and a man above; at the lower right, a goat and a dog are being controlled by a male figure, attracting the attention of one of the engraving's most prominent audience members, a full-length heavily robed "sage" apparently calming the beasts, whose hand redirects the reader's gaze back to the anatomy lesson in progress. This figure may be Marcantonio Genua, a supporter of Vesalius, or it could possibly be Galen himself.[20] Whichever is the case, the relative weight and force of this figure's authority in the engraving are meant to convey the authority of his real-life status, while his behavior in containing the chaos the animals could incite cooperates with the message that here in Vesalius's dissection theater, humans, not animals are the main subject.[21]

The presence of the monkey, dog, and goat in the image are generally assumed to be a rebuke to Galen—as one writer puts it, "it is not their turn on the table."[22] But the abundance of animals in similar frontispieces of many other anatomy books could suggest a rather different reading even for these that appear in the *Fabrica*. In the collected works of Galen of 1565 animals likewise populate the lower portions of the frontispiece (Figure 3). The central scene shows Galen about to be interrupted in dissecting a pig by the philosopher Alexander Damascenus. Ranged on the opposite side are a collection of figures, one carrying a trussed pig to the dissecting table, while two sheep lie just behind him ready to be slaughtered or cut open alive. Since the two groups are deliberate mirror images of each other, I can only conclude that the scene suggests Galen will eviscerate his philosophical opponents with the same alacrity he dispatches the next pig and the sheep thereafter. The human-animal analogy here undercuts any notion that rational or philosophical endeavors divide man from beast. Rather, in the age of anatomy, the body and control over its secrets is everything. Galen, the master of the process, stands hunched over his pig, back to the viewer—as if oblivious to the commotion on either side (although he stands to the right, closer to his animals), while the ranks of viewers face us from behind the table. We are on Galen's side, literally, in this image, and so our relationship is with the dauntingly heavy pig (the man carrying it stoops under its weight, just as Galen stoops over his dead animal on the table), not the quibbling theorists. Where Vesalius's title page is assumed to speak for the marginalization of the animal in anatomizing, Galen's work, which remained a powerful influence on Vesalius and other writers, asserts the centrality of the animal to what were at the time "modern" regimes of knowledge.

Figure 3. Galen, *Opera Omnia* (1565). Dissection of a pig. Courtesy of the Wellcome Library.

Felix Plater's *De Corporis Humani Structura et Usu* (1583) includes a frontispiece that surrounds the image of the author with animals, living and dead. Plater's portrait rests at the center of a set of classical columns, featuring male and female forms, but these are almost obscured by the profusion of animals, living and dead, that populate the image's margins. On the left, the male figure rests a hand on a monkey's head, while on the right the female figure stands above a live eagle. Beneath each, the skeletons of the two animals appear again, the monkey holding an apple; above, a dog and a squirrel play with a cherub; on the right, next to the male form, a fleshed fish hangs suspended; on the left, hanging beside the female human body, is a fish skeleton. Below the author's image, a table with anatomical instruments tops a motto and a coat of arms, the text a traditional reference to the wonder of God's creation, the arms organized around a dove.[23] This veritable zoo appears to confirm the omnipresence of animals in the work of anatomy; in its iterations of live and skeletonized creatures, it establishes the animal as an object in the hands of the dissector. It also, however, puts into question its own suggestion of the superiority of human investigation of the world. The apple in the monkey's hand belongs to a medieval and Renaissance tradition that reads the monkey as the devil, or as the emblem for the fall of humanity; the apple, the fruit of the tree of knowledge, reminds the viewer that knowledge in the fallen world is of good and evil, and requires the ability to distinguish the two. Anatomizing the monkey, baring its secrets with its bones, achieves knowledge, yes, but always attended by the reminder that knowledge of the fallen world is also knowledge of humanity's sin and its ultimate end in death. Like the eagle, human aspiration soars in the medical arts; like the eagle, its flight is truncated (the mark of its fallenness confirmed) by the achievement of its own ends. In contrast, the cherub above seems to beg us to read the squirrel and the dog as innocents who rise above the complicated muck of the anatomist's "art." While this title page's religious anti-triumphalism is conventional, it is not less powerful because of that, blending scientific and theological skepticism to destabilize the anthropocentric view.

Adrian Spigelius's *Opera Omnia* (1645) offers animals as the building blocks of anatomical science—literally, a monkey and a dog appear in the base portions of the two columns that rise on either side of his frontispiece (Figure 4). And the frontispiece to the *Miscellanea Anatomica* of Gerard Blasius stages a dog, a goose, a rabbit, turtle and rat in its lower foreground, while through a window behind the author the viewer sees first a monkey, and beyond it in the landscape outside, a pig, a fox, an ox, a sheep, and even ducks and geese in a pond (Figure 5). As do Galen's, Spigelius's and Plater's, Blasius's title page acknowledges that a menagerie of animal bodies is the necessary material by which the anatomist produces his body of knowledge; without animals, the human remains always partially opaque, and anatomies of the human body are always incomplete. On the corpses of animals by the hundreds and thousands rises the edifice of human understanding: appropriately, then, both Regnier de Graaf (*Opera Omnia*, 1678) and Bartholomeo Eustachi (*Tabulae Anatomicae*, 1714) choose to litter their frontispieces with dead animals, instead of living ones.

These many images beg the question of what it means to place animals at the margins, inferior to or beneath the supposed primary object of study, the human form. A plate from the *Fabrica* illustrates the paradox in the animal that is sub-mitted, laid low: one of the more familiar skeletal images from the text is of a human skull resting on a dog's ("man bites dog," as one scholar subtitles it) (Figure 6): "This figure depicts the frontal aspect of the skull, in order to reveal the bones of the upper jaw with the greatest possible accuracy. We have portrayed the dog's skull beneath the human one so that Galen's description of the bones of the upper jaw may the more easily be understood by

Figure 4. Title page, *Opera Quae Extant Omnia* by Adrianus Spigelius (1645). Beneath each human form in columns on the right and left are an ape and a pig. Courtesy of the Wellcome Library.

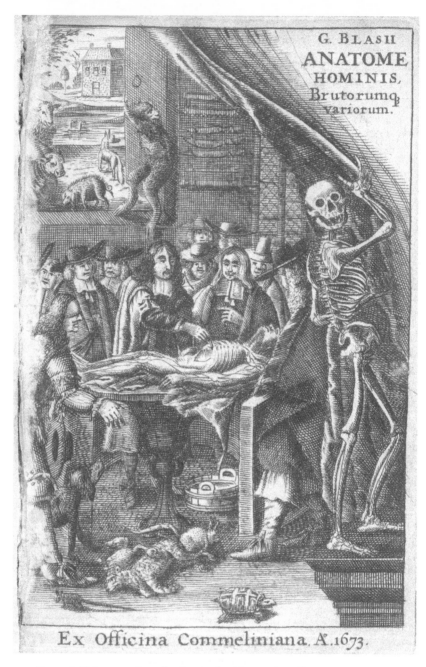

Figure 5. Title page, Gerardus Leonardus Blasius, *Miscellanea Anatomica Hominis, Brutorumque Variorum Fabricam Diversam Magna Parte Exhibentia* (1673). Mimicking the skeleton in the foreground, an ape (top left) reveals a scene filled with animals through the window at the rear of a dissection room. Courtesy of the Wellcome Library.

anyone. In addition, in order that the eye sockets and the bones and sutures within them might be visible as far as possible, it was necessary for the human skull to rest upon its occiput with its anterior surface lifted above the canine skull."[24]

At first glance, and for most critics at second and third glance, this image indicates the supremacy of the (skeletal) human over the animal, again marking the advance for which Vesalius is credited so often—dissecting the proper subject of anatomy, the human body and not the animal one. However, this human skull lacks its lower mandible; the dog's half-skull on which it rests elevates it, holds it in place, and substitutes for the jaw that is missing. The joke, for the discriminating reader, is that Vesalius has staged a "complete" skull that would fulfill Galen's mistaken attribution of the dog's mandible structure to a human.[25] Vesalius later remarks again that Galen's version of the skull "favor[s] his apes too much," and decides to "agree with Celsius . . . who, showing scant respect for dogs in general, and Galen in particular, taught that the jaw consists of a single bone."[26]

The image is thus part of Vesalius's ridicule of Galen and his self-justification as a human anatomist. Laurie Shannon, for instance, takes the image this way, pointing out that it illustrates that "the proper object of learning is *the human*," not Galen's animals or hybrid errors, which Vesalius's methods surpassed.[27] Shannon's point is well taken. But I think a bit more pressure on the image also suggests why animals can never be surpassed or even marginalized despite the image's clear attempt to do so. The ultimate joke in this image may be on Vesalius, as much as on Galen: although Vesalius did not yet practice rigorously what would come to be called comparative anatomy, just such an approach to the human body emerges, if unintentionally, from the placement of human and animal in his illustration.[28] How do you know what is human? By contrast with what is animal. These skull parts are being asked to "speak" eloquently for the unique power of human over animal: the image brings together the jaws, instruments of language and of vocalization, in order to express human dominion, enacted in the anatomist's practice through the vivisection and dissection of animals. But without the dog jaw, would the body, or the image speak? Surely not, at least not to enforce any of the messages Vesalius wished to send. The dog's jaw is erroneous, yes, but literally this image leaves the human re-lying on his companion animal for the power to articulate the "truth" of human supremacy.

The justification for human-animal comparisons in anatomies is established in Aristotle's *Historia Animalum*, where confirmation of the *scala*

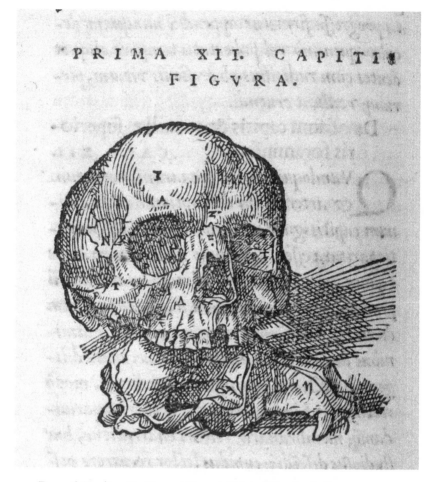

Figure 6. Vesalius, *De Humani Corporis Fabrica*. Human skull resting on canine jawbone. Courtesy of the Wellcome Library.

naturae relies on the recognition that humans and animals can be classified according to the same system. Unable to dissect humans, Aristotle used animal anatomy to extrapolate about categories that included humans: "The inner parts of man are uncertain and unknown, wherefore we must consider those parts of other animals which bear any similarity to those of man."[29] His work inspired Albertus Magnus, who was also curious about animal species and form. It may seem inevitable that investigations of human biology would happen in the context of comparisons to animals, and irrelevant that they did: as F. J. Cole points out, animals were used in these cases merely as substitutes for the missing human subject at the heart of anatomical study and were not of interest in themselves.[30] It is worth thinking more carefully about the consequences of comparative approaches to human and animal anatomy, however, since as I am insisting they tend inevitably to blur the human-animal boundary that elevates the human and devalues the animal. While the ultimate goal of early comparatists was the more thorough establishment of human preeminence, this was not the only possible outcome. Andrew Snape's late seventeenth-century horse anatomy, for instance, inverts the usually hierarchy in which medical and anatomical information about animals extends or bolsters investigations of human physiology: Snape repeatedly cites Thomas Willis and Helkiah Crooke, both important sources for seventeenth-century *human* medical knowledge, to bolster his descriptions of equine anatomical function.[31] That human and animal anatomies would cross-pollinate was to be expected; that human bodies and information about human physiologies would illustrate and illuminate *animal* discoveries was a reversal that did not fully accord with the anthropocentrism of human anatomical science.

Other early anatomists, unencumbered by Vesalius's need to distinguish his work from Galen's, were more willing to embrace the idea of comparison, even to celebrate themselves for their achievements in animal dissection and physiology, as much as for those in human medical knowledge. Nicolaes Tulp, the subject of Rembrandt's famous painting of an anatomy lesson, unapologetically places a chimpanzee front and center in his own frontispiece simply because he was the first to give an anatomical description of the creature. In works like Giulio Casserio's *Pentaesthesion* (1610), which includes plates comparing human and animal ears, or Volcher Coiter's commentary on Gabriele Fallopio's work, *Lectiones Gabrielis Falloppii de Partitus Simularibus Humani* (1575), which compares human skulls with those of mammals and other animals, the comparatist approach dominates, even though no scientific "genre" yet exists for such analogizing anatomies. By the end of the seventeenth century, William Harvey was working by analogy from animal to human, and vice versa; M. A. Severino, who likewise believed in the universality of certain physiological processes and structures, illustrated his *Zootomia Democritea* with side-by-side illustrations of a bird's skeleton and a man's.[32] Of course the drive of all of these comparatist ventures is to advance *human* knowledge, which in turn justifies the death and dismemberment of animal subjects, but they shatter the fiction of the univocality of matter, ceding space, and occasionally, we might suggest, a degree of superiority, even independent value to the animal.

Sovereign Equines

An early example of Vesalius's influence on animal anatomy, the foundation of comparatist medicine, is Carlo Ruini's *Anatomia del Cavallo*, a handsome, complete, and lavishly illustrated volume the figures for which are very much in the mode of the *Fabrica*—but, of course, with figures that feature horses, not humans. Ruini's is a medical compendium, easily recognizable as part of the tradition of horsemanship and husbandry manuals stretching from the sixteenth century through the nineteenth, and as such it includes everything from advice on choosing a sound mount to diagnosing and dosing illnesses. But the volume was also published with more than thirty images, all representing the dissected parts of the horse, as in the example in Figure 7 of the horse's belly. These clearly follow closely the model set by Vesalius, even imitating specific details of the *Fabrica*'s plates—positions of skeletons, techniques for displaying organs, and so on. Ruini was an educated Bolognese layman, possibly a lawyer and a senator with no special training in medicine, and so could clearly not participate directly in the human medical revolution of his generation as a physician or human anatomist.[33] He was, however, tutored by the Aristotelian philosopher Claudio Betti, and had a large "collection" of horses; thus, "although lacking membership in the university," he was "able to conduct the studies reflected in his early and only masterpiece."[34] His ambitious volume suggests that he was inspired both by his education and his exposure to Vesalius's text to write on a topic about which he was well qualified. *Anatomia del Cavallo* is the first full-length exposition of a species other than the human—Singer comments that it did for the horse what Vesalius did for the human body, and its "truly magnificent figures" can be set beside those of Vesalius and Eustachius.[35] For F. J. Cole, the text is "the direct logical outcome of the Vesalian tradition," taking up each type of system for exhaustive treatment with few tangents.[36] Ruini's preface makes it clear that he has searched for a way to engage with the lofty philosophical ideas of his age: "the divine mysteries and deep secrets of wise and provident common Nature" are the worthiest subjects for human investigation because through "the delightful knowledge of all natural things" men come to "perfect consciousness . . . of God's creation." The soul of humans "feeds and is nourished on the knowledge of these things as if from real food"; in the search for knowledge, humans recognize within themselves that which is like God, and thus they are "rationally eager and driven."[37] Ruini's text would become a kind of *Fabrica* for the field of horse-leeching, translated into several languages, widely read throughout Europe, and garnering a number of imitators or plagiarizers over the next century and a half. Cole notes that Ruini's book "must have been well known and its influence considerable" not only at the time of its publication, but long after, when its figures circulated anew without attribution.[38] Andrew Snape's *The Anatomy of an Horse* (1683) uses many of Ruini's plates (some slightly modified). The influence of both texts extends through the next century, probably inspiring George Stubbs to set a new anatomical standard for his generation with his *Anatomy of a Horse* (1766). What Ruini's plates reveal, however, is a more recalcitrant subject than Vesalius's cooperative écorchés, his self-displaying or classicized figures. The dissection of the horse turns out to resist in provocative ways the methods for visually manipulating human bodies perfected in the *Fabrica*. And the partitioning of the body, the violation of unity through its rendering as mere parts, has some unexpected consequences in Ruini's plates.

The artist who designed the figures for Ruini may have been from the same Titian workshop that Vesalius used; at the very least, they show the same attention to detail, realism, and dynamism as those in the *Fabrica*. A side-by-side comparison of images from both texts confirms how deliberate were Ruini's replications. For example, he offers an écorché head in Figure 8 that approximates those we find in the *Fabrica*, as well as in other contemporary human anatomies. His horses give up their anatomical secrets while in motion, or awkwardly elongated for the convenience of the observer, or are portrayed in static poses "suspended" by ribbons or ropes (perhaps an ironic twist on Vesalius's propped de-muscled skeletons). Ruini's diagrams of nerves and blood vessels resemble similar pictures for various of the human anatomies, some in full abstraction from the body, others in the context of the horse's full physical form (Figure 9).

Most medieval anatomies used a "frog-like" positioning of the body under study, and this is occasionally replicated in Ruini's images; however, the splayed illustrations of medieval texts largely lack the vast *presence* of later figures in both the human and the animal anatomies. Animals shown spread-eagled and restrained for the vivisector are also a convention in early modern anatomies: Vesalius includes a plate to demonstrate the proper position and restraint for a pig to be vivisected. Another well-known image from Jean Pecquet's *Experimenta Nova Anatomica* (1651) is a drawing of a dog cut open and splayed to display the thoracic duct he discovered. But Pecquet's dog and Vesalius's pig are conspicuously tied at all four limbs, and Pecquet's dog is even

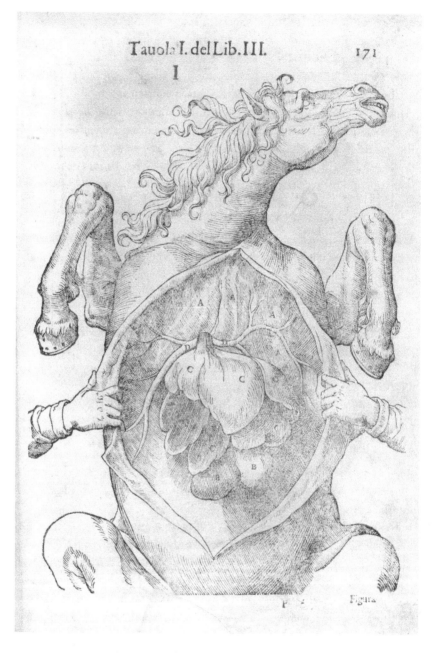

Figure 7. Carlo Ruini, *Anatomia del Cavallo, Infermità et Suoi Rimedii* (1618). Engraving showing the horse's internal organs. Image courtesy of the Cornell University Library.

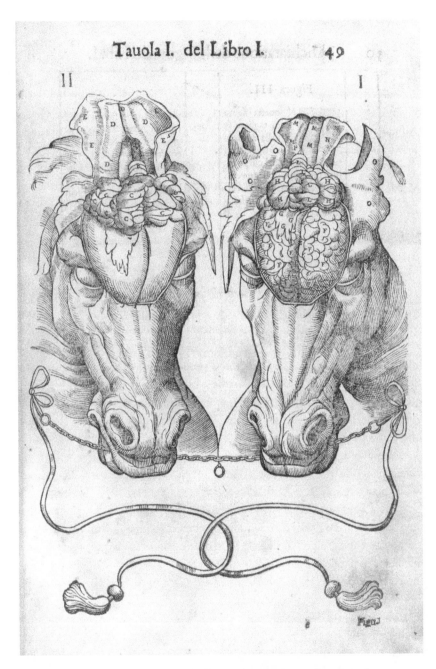

Figure 8. Carlo Ruini, *Anatomia del Cavallo, Infermità et Suoi Rimedii* (1618). Ecorché head of horse. Image courtesy of the Cornell University Library.

shown muzzled with rope, since live animals being dissected are obviously going to struggle. Despite their living condition, however, and in contrast to Ruini's horses, these and other images of dissected animals are impersonal, enchained to the process of the anatomy, their agency explicitly limited in favor of the dissector's quest for knowledge about the body's interior workings. Ruini's animals instead seem engaged in their own revelation, aware of the action and participants in it, if not always entirely cooperative.

In the image of the opened abdomen we saw above from Ruini's volume (Figure 7), two hands reach in from either side, orienting the viewer to imagine that the animal depicted might be lying or propped on its back end—a position that is physically impossible to maintain in a creature as large as a horse, or in one with its physical attributes, without stringing the animal up in a rig to prevent it rolling to either side.[39] Instead of a rig, or any other kind of ropes, pulleys, or machinery, we have a horse with a vigorous set of legs curled away from its abdomen to provide a better view, its head turned away, neck outstretched, mane flowing, teeth bared. It is equally possible to believe this horse must be rearing to allow the angle and the scope of the illustration, or that the artist is positioned below the animal, while two different helpers reach in from either side to expose the viscera. A second "belly" figure from the *Anatomia*, depicts a similar posture of the horse to that which we found in Figure 7, with the horse twisted into a posture that is impossible in life; yet once again, in Ruini's illustration the animal remains in motion—the mane, the contracted legs, the view of the hooves from the bottom again contain a kinetic potential that Pecquet's dog or Vesalius's pig simply do not. In two different plates, then, Ruini's horses confirm their vigorous, active character even while being dissected.

Why would an animal anatomy, and specifically one of the horse, have merited such an elaborate and beautifully illustrated volume as Ruini's? And if an author were determined to create one of an animal species, why not an anatomy of the ape, or the dog, or the pig, all of which are far closer in physiology to humans and more commonly dissected by anatomists?[40] Indeed, the horse is quite distant, anatomically speaking, from humans, and its physiology has little bearing on knowledge of human bodies. It would seem an anomalous undertaking, given the importance of Vesalius and the human anatomists for Ruini's project. The obvious reason has to do with the horse's traditional position in a hierarchy of creatures as a "noble" beast. "When I consider the wonderful work of God in the creation of this beast," writes Edward Topsell, "enduing it with a singular body and a Noble spirit, the principal whereof is a loving and dutifull

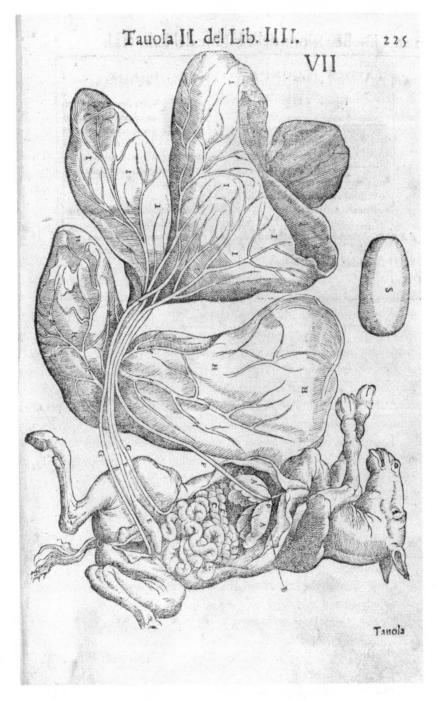

Figure 9. Carlo Ruini, *Anatomia del Cavallo, Infermità et Suoi Rimedii* (1618). Organs removed and enlarged. Image courtesy of Cornell University Library.

inclination to the service of man: Wherein he never faileth in peace nor Warre, being every way more neare unto him for labour and travel: and therefore more deare (the food of man onely excepted:) we must needs account it the most noble and necessary creature of all foure-footed beasts, before whom no one for multitude and generality of good qualities is to be preferred, compared or equaled. . . ."[41] For Ruini, the horse is "endowed with so many both commendable and rare qualities that one does not find in any other being deprived of reason."[42] Andrew Snape begins his *Anatomy of an Horse* with the following tribute: "In Fields nor Pastures, Woods nor Forests, wide, / Does any Beast so Noble as this Reside."[43] Giambattista della Porta's *De Humana Physiognomia* (1586) carries to an extreme this identification of the horse as the most noble and worthy of animals (Figure 10). Della Porta's work proposed a variety of analogies between humans and animals, and humans and plants, extending from physiological characteristics of face, form, and posture to humoral interconnections. A noble man is expected to stand upright, proudly, so as to resemble the upright neck and head of a horse—and clearly not just any horse, but one used for the martial disciplines. Such a resemblance confers status on the horse and draws on specific associations between horses, aristocracy, and war. In Ruini's estimation, the horse combines "great love of man" with natural docility and is so celebrated for its many ways to bring "pleasure and assistance" to man that it is everywhere commemorated in monuments, tombs, poetry, and paintings.[44]

The martial passions of otherwise sanguine equids were supposed to mirror their riders', making the horse a sympathetic extension, as well as instrument, of human warlike aggression. From the Bible, to da Vinci's studies of "rage horses" for his Battle of Anghieri (Figure 11), the horse is most commonly anthropomorphized as a warrior in his own right:

> Hast thou given the horse strength? hast thou clothed his neck with thunder?
> Canst thou make him afraid as a grasshopper? the glory of his nostrils *is* terrible.
> He paweth in the valley, and rejoiceth in *his* strength: he goeth on to meet the armed men.
> He mocketh at fear, and is not affrighted; neither turneth he back from the sword.
> The quiver rattleth against him, the glittering spear and the shield.
> He swalloweth the ground with fierceness and rage: neither believeth he that *it is* the sound of the trumpet. (KJV, Job 33:9–24)

LIBER   SECUNDVS.   *83*

A *LIBI vero. Patulæ nares, & resimæ iracundos demonstrant, & referuntur ad passionem, quæ sit in ira, & ad generosos equos. Et in figura iracundi concauas nares ei tribuit. Adamantius. Expansæ aures iracundiæ, & ferociæ testes sunt. Suetonius C.Cæsarem spumante rictu, & humentibus naribus fuisse scribit, & fuit præcipitis iræ.*

Obstructæ nares

Figure 10. Giambattista della Porta, horse and human, from *De Humana Physiognomonia Libri IIII* (1586). Courtesy of the Wellcome Library.

Ruini again concurs: "one can perceive in it an immense boldness, a great love of man," "and what should I also say about its valor, which is fully attested by continuous and long experience and the ample evidence shown by the illustrious deeds of many horses, which the wisest kings and greatest emperors hold in the highest esteem?"[45] Even Snape's title page horse is described in quasi-martial language, although it seems most pacific in its person (Figure 12): "His Nostrils raise a Tempest when he blows: / His Feet produce an Earthquake when he goes. / Runs he? the Swiftest winds behind retire, / Whilst from his Eyes flow streams of flaming fire."[46] Snape's horse blends natural competitiveness with anthropomorphic aggression, creating a horse that is a superior elemental, expressive of human aspiration to exceed the most frightening phenomena of nature.

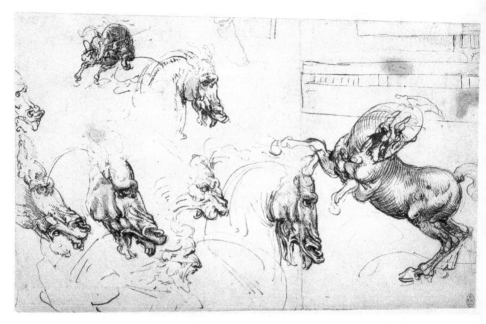

Figure 11. Leonardo da Vinci (1452-1519), study of a horse. Uffizi Museum, Florence, Italy. Photo: Scala, Art Resource (ART89949).

Another possible explanation for his choice of species derives from Ruini's social and educational position vis-à-vis the medical establishment. Clearly he was an enthusiast of the horse; and he was also, as we've noted, clearly not part of the professions that regularly attend dissections or that study the arts of medical anatomy. This combination of factors placed Ruini at the nexus of a variety of conflicting social and intellectual ideologies. One of the advances that Vesalius's *Fabrica* and other anatomy texts effected was the extension of new forms and domains of knowledge through printed sources to those with an interest in them and the wealth to purchase them. The actual practice of anatomy and dissection of humans, however, was limited to those in professional training, something a gentleman like Ruini would not attempt. But the concept of amassing medical knowledge and contributing to the burgeoning field of anatomical study was both seductive and available to a well-educated and wealthy gentleman like Ruini; being tutored by an expert in natural philosophy made Ruini a budding scientist himself, an aspirant whose gentlemanly status would not be compromised by amateur writing on a related field. We see hints of the conflict among these imperatives in Ruini's preface: having discussed the fact that investigations of nature fulfill a human need to seek God within its mysteries, he translates that

In Feilds nor Pastures, Woods nor Forests wide,   Runs he? the Swiftest Winds behind retire.
Does any Beast So Noble as this Reside.~   whilst from his Eyes flow streams of flaming fire.
His Nostrills raise a Tempest when he blows;   Wouldst know his Parts? the following Book peruse,
His Feet produce an Earthquake when he goes.   which Shews of each the Figure, Seat and Use.

Figure 12. Andrew Snape, *Anatomy of an Horse* (1683), title page
illustration. Courtesy of the Wellcome Library.

desire, perhaps oddly, into a desire to be of service to the horse, by illuminating
its particular secrets for those in whose care it rests:

> Therefore, since this happened to my soul . . . for the sweetness
> and delight that springs from desiring to know, I thought to myself

about how I could achieve the duty of every gentleman. . . . I finally
decided that I could best realize my honest desire by turning my
reflections toward the artful instruction of the horse's anatomy. . . .
An intense desire has pushed me since I always wanted to be of use
to such a noble animal, which I have always enjoyed. . . . Believing
that many would be interested in this subject and would profit from
it, I could also show them a new knowledge of its bodily parts, and
the way to address the illnesses of such an essential, generous, and
so useful animal . . . since this method has until now (from what I
can observe) been hidden to mankind.[47]

This passage (and the text generally) plays with both democratizing elements
and hierarchy: Ruini has "new knowledge" of anatomy presumably garnered
through experimentation that will allow him to reveal truths previously hidden, rather like Vesalius, whose human dissections explored a new territory
formerly hidden to human eyes. But Ruini channels his claims to advance this
new knowledge through a humble submission to *the horse's* needs, which in
turn will preserve the animal's ability to give further pleasure and service to
mankind.

The uneasy balance of humility and hubris in Ruini's brief justification
characterizes many examples in the field of manuals on the horse, mainly because they are a domain in which competing class agendas converge. On the
one hand, horsemanship and husbandry manuals make arcane information
widely available to the otherwise excluded or uneducated; on the other, their
subject matter is an exclusive kind of possession, and knowledge of it is un-
likely to translate far beyond a privileged class. Previous volumes on horses in
the late sixteenth century were mainly guides for riders, breeders, and trainers.
The Naples school of Federigo Grisone was famous for producing the elite of
European equestrians during the sixteenth century; horse masters like Grisone
published their own treatises during a period when the nature and hierarchy
of "professional" trainers was in flux, which meant that writing and publishing in their subject was a means to establish their own rules and standards,
simultaneously claiming their own authority to judge what was or was not
good horsemanship. Sixteenth- and seventeenth-century farriery manuals in
England and Europe achieved similar ends for their authors, signaling their
status as gentleman, but also their mastery of a still-noble field of knowledge.[48] Even members of the academic community, humanists who struggled
to solidify the status of their own bodies of knowledge, often appropriated

the genre of horsemanship or training manuals, most of which
medical compendium like that we find in Ruini. Pia Cuneo poin
the horse as subject served this class of writers as well, linking then
a literary-intellectual tradition extending back to Xenophon: "hippological"
texts provided an "arena to demonstrate their specialized knowledge and skill"
in history, languages, and ancient literatures.[49] Ruini's choice to write a medical text on horses participates in both these lines of justification.

Ruini's are not carthorses or workhorses, however "useful" they are to
their owner. Their eviscerated bodies carry the signs of equine nobility—
they are the prized animals belonging to a horseman not a farmer; they are
baroque animals with rounded haunches, arched necks, and elegant slightly
dished faces most likely from Neapolitan or Spanish stock.[50] Elite animals
like these are markers of their owners' own status, authority, and wealth. They
are the property of a *gentleman*, as Ruini names himself in his preface; the
gentlemanly art of riding will, through his *Anatomia*, be enhanced by the art
of the newly popular practice of dissection. The professional interests of the
medical community are thus adapted, denatured, and translated for the aristocratic nature of well-born Italians through the medium of the noble horse.
Ruini is ennobled, medical dissection is ennobled, and his readers will be
enlightened—and ennobled by his discoveries.

Like his model, Ruini's work relies on a budding genre in art, the anatomical illustration. Vesalius's *Fabrica* is unquestionably one of the most visually
rewarding of the early modern anatomy texts, filled with artistic techniques
to enhance the reader's appreciation of the human body's complexity. Martin
Kemp observes that "Vesalius recognized the potential of veridical illustrations as a tool in a way that was integral to his reform of anatomical science."[51]
Critics have commented extensively on the *Fabrica*'s impressively characterful
skeletons, while its muscle men and écorchés have attracted critical attention
in their own right. At least one scholar has traced the intensely visual experience of reading the *Fabrica* to Vesalius's own highly visual orientation.[52] Early
in his career, during his first public dissection, Vesalius found himself in a dispute with the Bologna faculty's elder statesman of anatomy, Curtius; during
the debate over the results of their simultaneous anatomies, Vesalius insisted
on the visual confirmation of some structures that Galen wrote of, to the con-
sternation of Curtius, who defended their existence by way of reason (that is,
they must exist because Galen said so and because the function he described
is necessary to the body). Vesalius specifically challenged Curtius to point to
the disputed structures: "Where, I ask? Vesalius said, *Show them to me.*"[53] The

pressure to show unites the project of the *Fabrica* with Vesalius's many demonstrations to others of his skill; the frontispiece to the *Fabrica* includes dozens
of figures looking into the body of the corpse in Vesalius's hands, merely a
fraction of the numbers who were probably present at most of his actual dissections. He writes in his introduction that he is encouraged by a slight shift
among his peers, who are now willing to consider the evidence of their "own
not ineffective eyes" (1: liv) even when these reveal Galen's errors. The whole
purpose of the *Fabrica* is "virtually to set a dissected body before the eyes of
students" (1: iv) even if they cannot dissect one themselves.

It is possible to link the *Fabrica* to a regime of sight, in which visual
evidence trumps textual authority, making it not only an early example of
a gradual privileging of sight among the senses that characterizes European
history of the sixteenth and seventeenth centuries,[54] but also a forerunner to
the new science of Bacon, Harvey, and others.[54] Yet the faculty of sight in
Vesalius's work cannot be extracted from the faculty of touch: he repeatedly
advises students to "feel" for themselves the structures of the body, to come
to their own conclusions. Asked during the vivisection of a dog whether the
heart and arteries have distinct motion, he answers "you yourselves should feel
with your own hands, and trust them."[55] While cutting into a sheep's eye to
display the various fluids within, Vesalius comments: "All these anybody can
see for himself at home; for surely . . . you can learn only a little from a mere
demonstration if you yourselves have not *taken the object in your own hands*."[56]
To see is to touch; to touch is to see more effectively. To know the eye, one
must hold it in one's hand, touch it, feel it for oneself. The text is merely a
supplement to the application of the senses both visual and tactile, and does
not replace the experience of the dissector, or of the observer/reader, in a hierarchy of modes of knowledge.[57]

The many exquisitely detailed and oddly animated figures Vesalius includes testify to the conjunction of sight and touch. Kemp observes that the
need for so many illustrations arises from "the primacy of direct, sensory
knowledge in the exposition of the physical world."[58] However, the premise
of the *Fabrica* is that the visual can somehow connect the reader to the tactile
almost seamlessly. As we've seen, its frontispiece rebukes anatomists for their
removal from the hands-on process of dissection by placing one of Vesalius's
hands directly into the viscera of the corpse. That gesture creates a physically
intimate connection between one body and another, the living, probing hand
of the dissector exploring the secrets of the body as it cuts dead flesh. The
anatomist's hand is thus as critical to Vesalius's project as are the eyes of his

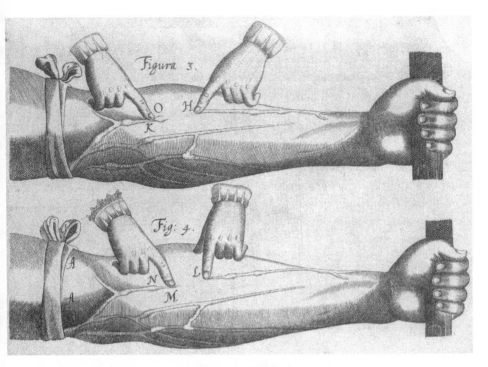

Figure 13. William Harvey, *Exercitatio Anatomica de Motu Cordis et Sanguinis in Animalibus* (1620). Valves in the forearm, showing the use of pointing hands common in anatomical illustrations. Courtesy of the Wellcome Library.

observers. This may explain why the portrait that accompanies the first editions of the *Fabrica* portrays Vesalius demonstrating the dissection of a hand and forearm, as if announcing the particular advantage his method confers in knowing details of its creator's most subtle invention, a gesture repeated in so many subsequent anatomy texts (Figure 13).

Among all the parts of the body, the hand has special weight in early modern natural philosophy, weight that makes it the equal of the eyes, to elevate which the human frame was supposedly created upright. God has endowed humans with "two wondrous weapons," explains Helkiah Crooke, "which he hath denied to all other living creatures, Reason and the hand."[59] The language of hands is, in John Bulwer's *Chirologia* (1644), as much a part of language as speech: "for as the Tongue speaketh to the Eare, so Gesture speaketh to the Eye."[60] In fact, the hand acts as a second "fountain of discourse," with detailed principles that can be recorded and understood by anyone, whatever his or her native tongue. In his introduction, Vesalius advocates "hands-on" medicine, combining all the various disciplines, not least surgery, which had been ceded to the "barbers": "It therefore follows that beginners in the art must be urged in every way to take no notice of the whisperings of the physicians . . . but to use their hands as well in treating, as the Greeks did and as the essence of the art demands, lest they convert a crippled system of learning into a curse on the whole of human life" (1: l). The monkey at the lower left of the *Fabrica*'s title page illustration appears to be biting the hand of the man who is sitting near him. Carlino imagines that this signifies the monkey's "essential feral qualities," but it is just as likely that the monkey's bite stages an attack on the organ of human superiority, the one the primates nearly—but not quite—share: an opposable thumb is the only thing missing from a primate's otherwise most human hand, as Renaissance anatomists were well aware.[61]

In light of the relationship between vision and touch, and the centrality of the anatomist's hand to the new conditions of anatomical practice, we might look again at those hands grasping the sides of Ruini's horse's abdomen in Figure 7; why, after all, represent such an intimate touch in such an anatomically impossible moment if not to encourage the "feeling eye" of the viewer, to render the visual tactile? They do the same work that Vesalius's pointing hand and exploring hand do in his frontispiece, they demand our attention and draw us into the knowledge of the horse's gut: to point, according to Bulwer, is to declare knowledge of something, with a gesture of command that others recognize that knowledge.[62] Through the image of those hands, the reader becomes part of the dissection, "viscerally" identifies with the process of exploring the horse's body. Any man, every man with hands *and eyes* can now paddle around in the secret spaces of that noble creature, the horse. Further, these hands are themselves disembodied, establishing a more generalized human control and authority over the horse under examination; they peel away its interfering mass to give the viewer both literal and figurative *insight* as well as the proxy experience of opening the otherwise unassailable body of this large mammal. But the separation of these hands from the body or bodies that might own them, their partition from the human, results in some odd potential interpretations of them that problematize their use in this moment.

Katherine Rowe has argued that hands in Renaissance anatomies and other texts are vehicles of agency, complicated by the hand's simultaneous status as conveyor of interior will and its ability to grasp, wrest, assault, or create beauty and reveal God's design in nature.[63] Likewise, Bernard F. Scholz finds severed hands, arms, and legs used in the emblem tradition to signify disembodied will, ambiguously belonging either to God or to humans.[64] The *Anatomia*'s hands should thus confer the abstracted agency of the anatomist, their creative and destructive power, on the visually/tactilely connected reader of his book, while freeing the reader from any contamination by the actual blood and viscera that would attend a horse dissection. The hands in Ruini's image of the horse's abdomen opened are certainly intended to participate in all the conventions and significations that lead to this conclusion; however, to me they look remarkably *uncomfortable* in comparison to the disembodied hands that populate human anatomies (or emblem books or other sources of severed hands). They do not really indicate anything (that is, they do not point to anything): they struggle to open the animal; they seem futile, puny, even a bit irrelevant to the process. These fundamental differences from other disembodied hands beg a series of questions one doesn't normally think to ask: Do they in fact belong to the anatomist himself? Do they both belong to the same person? Do they refer at all to a singular, coherent human form in control of the moment of display? It's impossible to think that the answer to any of these questions is an unequivocal yes—the dissection of a horse makes a mockery of questions that would be perfectly intelligible in a human anatomy drawing. The horse, in fact, won't submit to the kind of unitary authority that Vesalius, for instance, asserts for the new human anatomist, who no longer needs his lector or his barber-surgeons to contribute their labor—one genuinely can't imagine dissecting a horse without *many* hands helping.

Imagine for a moment that the two hands spreading the horse's abdomen in Figure 7 are indeed the hands of Ruini, rather than of two workmen: he would either have to be standing in the very position of the reader/viewer, or he would have to be embracing the whole body of the horse. Either option is fascinating in its implications, since on the one hand the consequence might be to affirm the intellectual and social alignment or overlap of anatomist and reader, on the other to testify to the more vast, totalizing control of the dissector over such a monumental subject.

But the meaning and impact of these hands, I would suggest, is finally unstable because the body to which they are applied is a horse. Whatever authority they attempt to establish is finally also demolished by the intense atmosphere of dangerous mobility in this horse's position—whoever owns those hands is at risk of this animal's thrashing mass. Following the *Fabrica*'s method of using moving muscle men, posing skeletons and bodies variously situated against classical backgrounds or props, *Anatomia del Cavallo* includes images of horses in motion, in classical poses, accompanied by props or set against landscapes. Figure 14, for example, has its partially dissected horse in parade trot, a motion that allows it to helpfully expose its front right and back left legs; Figure 15 depicts a muscle horse against an Italian landscape replete with castle; and Figure 16 has its horse posing for a rear view. In all these scenes, the horses seem placid, unmoved, even cooperative. Jonathan Sawday argues that when such classicizing conventions appear in human anatomies, they sacralize the work of the anatomist in order to negotiate the shift from a theological understanding to a scientific understanding of the body's secrets. The *Fabrica*'s woodcuts juxtapose its corpses with classical scenes or pose its skeletons and muscle men in poses reminiscent of classical statuary to contribute to "sho[w] us a body as though it were alive (which it cannot be) and, at the same time, as though it were no more than carved stone," allowing reference to two simultaneous frameworks, the discourse of classical art and that of the new science.[65] Why a "living" dissected corpse? Why one that is blithely unconcerned with the process to which its component parts are being subjected? Sawday finds in these images bodies that are "acquiescent" in the surrender of knowledge, participating in their own rendering by the anatomist's hand, even "conspiring with [their] own demonstration[s]."[66] The result is twofold: first, the violence and horror of the dissection itself is elided, and the many forms of assault to which the body's flesh is—sometimes resistingly—subjected in being flayed for an audience, and second, classical references introduce the element of time, a reminder of the death that awaits all living human bodies, transcended with through the process of dissection. The anatomist's art speaks through the artistic transformations of the dissection to defend itself from charges of irreligion or hubris.

The *Anatomia*'s various figures largely continue the discourses established in the *Fabrica*. But the opened abdominal cavity of the horse in Figure 7 emphatically does *not* cooperate. This is a horse in distress. It is indeed in motion, but its expression is far from serene, and it does not appear to be blithely accepting its fate. While its eyes are dead, its other features suggest thrashing and flailing, not discrete or subdued submission. In fact, I think the reason the two hands opening its belly demand explanation is precisely because they are rendered so fragile, so vulnerable by this enraged animal's posture. What are we to make of this in light of Sawday's analysis? I would suggest that Ruini's woodcut, having invoked the "rage" tradition of the warhorse to justify the author's venture generally, cannot then foreclose on the further implications of raging battle mounts identified with their rider's aggression.[67] Ruini's martial beast, like its noble rider, will not be dominated by an enemy in battle, even

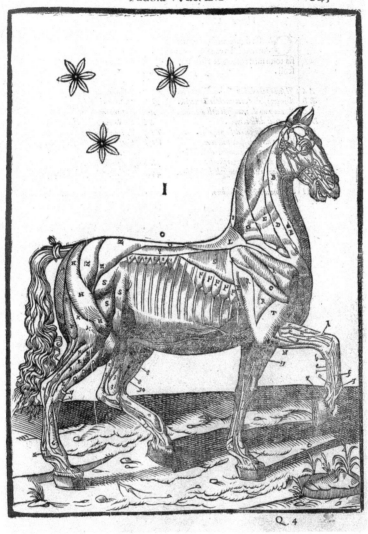

Figure 14. Carlo Ruini, *Anatomia del Cavallo, Infermità et Suoi Rimedii* (1618). Side view. Courtesy of the Wellcome Library.

Figure 15. Carlo Ruini, *Anatomia del Cavallo, Infermità et Suoi Rimedii* (1618). Muscles of the horse from the front; background shows landscape with castle. Courtesy of the Wellcome Library.

Figure 16. Carlo Ruini, *Anatomia del Cavallo, Infermità et Suoi Rimedii* (1618). Muscles of the horse from the rear. Courtesy of the Wellcome Library.

if that fact undermines the epistemological imperative of the similar splayed figures in Vesalius's text.

Animal anatomy, unlike human anatomy, does not uniformly hide the violence of the dissector's hand. Lurking in this image is a cultural history of vivisection, of animals wrestling with their dissectors to hold on to the secret truths of their inside spaces. There is extensive information on the difficulties in producing sanitized human anatomies: Vesalius himself grubbed in graveyards for bodies and remarked to his audiences on the rapid decomposition of the corpses he dissected: during the third demonstration recorded by Baldesar Heselar, the anatomist remarks that he cannot complete a dissection of a human omentum because "it is already stinking," and in the fourth demonstration he again notes the rotting of the corpse.[68] The moral ambiguity of anatomizing in Vesalius's hands-on method arose out of the demand for dead bodies, which generated a voracious appetite for criminals fresh from the scaffold (not to mention indecorous observations like that Vesalius makes in his first lecture at Bologna: "if we can get a man drowned or killed any other way but not beheaded or hanged, it would be better"), and required all the labors of the artist to obscure in favor of sanitized, sanctified imagery.[69] But anatomists were further suspected of longing to vivisect a human as they did animals; and their stories are replete with the unsavory details that come from working with dead bodies—smells, fluids, receding flesh, flies, maggots, the threat of infection. On all fronts, the actual work of the anatomist was gruesome and had to be effaced in the art of his textual record.

Where the anatomy of the horse is concerned, however, the grisly nature of the process is magnified a hundredfold. From a later venture in horse anatomy we gain some insight into the possible logistics in opening Ruini's spread-eagled animal—and what the consequences were for the dissector in turn. In the 1750s George Stubbs undertook his own dissection of a horse in a "remote farmhouse" in North Lincolnshire. The remote location was intended to spare anyone association with Stubbs's research, or its miasmas, effluvia, and potential opprobrium. The painter Ozias Humphry described the dissection as follows: the horse was bled to death by the jugular vein (a thousand-pound horse has about thirteen gallons of blood in it, ten times as much as the average human), and the arteries and veins injected with wax. The animal was then suspended from a rig that Stubbs probably had devised himself:

> The Horse was suspended from the Bar of Iron by the above mentioned Hooks, which were fastened into the opposite side of the

Horse to that which was intended to be designed; by passing the
Hooks through the ribs and fastening them under the Backbone
and by these means the Horse was fixed in the attitude which these
prints represent and continued hanging in this posture six or seven
weeks. . . . He first began by dissecting and designing the muscles of
the abdomen—proceeding through five different layers of muscles
till he came to the peritoneum and the pleura through which appeared the lungs and the Intestines—after which the Bowels were
taken out and cast away.[70]

The dissection goes on in stages for the whole "six or seven weeks," without disinfectants, fly spray, refrigeration, or other modern ameliorants. Aside
from the incredible stench and mess that Stubbs must have faced, or Ruini
before him, what stands out from this description is the sheer complexity of
arranging a large equine carcass for examination and illustration ("design," as
Humphry puts it). Stubbs's plates, like Ruini's, or Snape's before him, erase
the evidence of all this labor, filth, and struggle in favor of a "serene" animal
placidly revealing its anatomical features (Figure 17). Only Ruini, in these few
abdominal plates, seems to allow us to appreciate the staggering dimensions of
his undertaking, and the defiant nature of the body under his knife.

A war horse is clearly never likely to be the subject of a vivisection, expen-
sive and unrestrainable as it must be (in contrast to the legions of dogs and
pigs who were neatly trussed for experimentation), but Ruini's horse enacts a
kind of bizarre expression of fellow-feeling for both the human and animal
subjects silenced in the process of creating human anatomy manuals. In fact,
the poised weight of this agitated horse, its motion only partially arrested, its
position one that is anatomically impossible for a real animal, hardly seems
to submit to the revealing hands of human dissection at all. Whatever the insight here, it is gained at the cost of a sense that the animal looms beyond our
full ability to contain its agency—it is more of a nightmare than a quiescent
subject of study.

Vesalius's woodcuts often manipulate the posture of a human body to
better expose portions of interior organs; they are "carefully rearranged, with
structures removed, or pushed to one side, or 'fractured' to enable art to intervene within the body cavity."[71] Ruini too has several images of equine ab-
domens from which some organs are removed, or which tumble the intestines
and other parts outward for a better view. If even a huge animal like a horse
requires the distortion of the artist's imagination for its secrets to be fully

Figure 17. George Stubbs, engraving from *The Anatomy of the Horse* (1766). Side view of first stage of dissection. 37.9 x 48 cm. British Museum, London. Trustees of the British Museum/Art Resource (ART306923).

revealed, surely the much less gross and visible interior of the human corpse will be a far greater challenge to portray realistically. Vesalius's *Fabrica* uses art to subtly decode human matter for science; Ruini's *Anatomia* explodes the fiction that the illustrative art of the anatomies is realistic at all. Ruini's gutted horse thus challenges the representations of human anatomies that elide the violence of dissection, that assert abstract, disciplinary authority through their disembodied hands, and that purport to deliver truths about the body's interior spaces with a confidence that is undermined by the need for artistic interventions in even this grossest version of gross anatomy.

But I think yet one more possible explanation of the identity of those intruding anatomists' hands is worth mentioning. When Andrew Snape borrows Ruini's figures for his *Anatomy of an Horse*, he omits the plate that includes the disembodied hands in preference for rather more abstract, if sometimes more enormously exploded equine forms. Why leave the hands out if what they accomplish is a simple, reductive symbolic conquest of the animal body by human skill? Snape's choice might be random or it might be a sign that Ruini's hands are too unstable in their meaning and need to be dismissed in the interests of a more absolute authority available in the abstract, invisible hand Snape apparently prefers. Without the intervening hands, the horse in Snape's version struggles against no one and no thing—it no longer speaks anything intelligibly as it thrashes against an invisible force (Figure 18).

Human Horses

Ruini and Snape both include a number of less intensely resistant images of horses, including some that are thoroughly stately. These are mainly muscle horses and skeleton horses, depicting the equine subject in mid-trot to better demonstrate muscles and joints in flexion and in extension. Again, like Vesalius's muscle men and skeletonized figures, Ruini's and Snape's horses remain lifelike and in motion to obfuscate their status as stinking corpses, allowing them agency in cooperating with their own dismemberment. I want to use these illustrations, however, to explore another context for the early modern horse anatomy and its relationship to human anatomies—a context that again classicizes, but with rather different results than the antique statuary of the *Fabrica*.

In what seems an almost impossibly happy accident of myth and literature, the tale of Chiron the centaur links the man-horse hybrid with the "skills of the hand," with medicine, specifically surgery, and with the distortions forced by the agendas of humanism. Chiron was born of the union between Chronos, who took the form of a horse, and Philyra. Unlike his fellow drunken and violent centaurs, products of the union of Ixion and Nephele (or sun and cloud), Chiron was a paradigm of humane learning, skilled in music, astrology, and medicine; he became the tutor to many of the Greek heroes, including Hercules, Achilles, Pelamon, Theseus, and Asclepius, the god of medicine. Indeed, Chiron's name means "hand" in Greek (*cheiron* or *kheiron*), and he shares the root of that name with the discipline of chirurgy (*cheirourgia*), or surgery, stressing Chiron's association with civilized human values, rather than the chaotic natural impulses that drove other centaurs. So humanized is Chiron that early Greek portraits often show him with a full human torso and legs, inexplicably attached to a horse's rump.

In general, early modern centaurs are representatives of the wild, of rapaciousness, random aggression, and the confusion of bestial qualities with human ones that leads to the degradation of the human. Ovid's account in

TAB XIII *page* 75

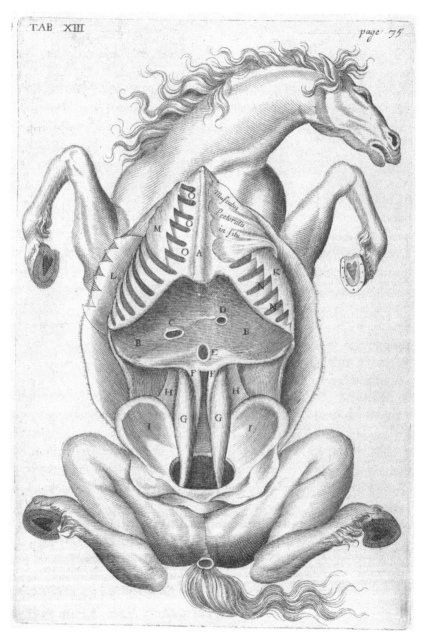

Figure 18. Andrew Snape, *Anatomy of an Horse* (1683). Variation on Ruini's illustration of horse's abdomen. Courtesy of the Wellcome Library.

Metamorphoses 12 of the centaurs' drunken and lustful violence at the wedding of the king of the Lapiths is rendered in a memorable painting by Piero di Cosimo (ca. 1510); Dante's centaurs guard the river of blood in the seventh circle (*Inferno* XII) to which those suffering bestial wrath are consigned: "O blind cupidity and insane wrath" observes the narrator, "*spurring* us on through our short life on earth."[72] Chiron (to whom Dante's Virgil chooses to speak first, bypassing the more warlike Nessus, who was responsible for Hercules' death) is distinguished from other centaurs, used for instance by Machiavelli to instruct the prince in the nuances of his requisite hybrid nature:

> You must recognize that there are two ways of fighting: by means
> of law, and by means of force. The first belongs properly to man,
> the second to animals; but since the first is often insufficient, it is
> necessary to resort to the second. Therefore a prince must know
> how to use both what is proper to a man, and what is proper to
> beasts. The writers of antiquity taught rulers this lesson allegorically
> when they told how Achilles and many ancient princes were sent
> to be nurtured by Chiron the centaur, so that he would train them
> in his discipline. Their having a creature half-man and half-beast as
> tutor only means that a prince must know how to use both the one
> and the other nature, and that the one without the other cannot
> endure.[73]

The successful prince will further combine the beastly qualities of the fox and the lion, but the strategies involved will require the subtlety to dissemble with the "discipline" of a Chiron.[74]

Douglas Stewart has puzzled over the origins of Chiron's exceptional status among Centaurs. He traces them to misinterpretations of the early Greek accounts of Chiron; in Stewart's reading, the possibility that a centaur was as wild, dangerous, and uncivilized as his peers yet had something crucial to offer the great heroes as a teacher was unfathomable to early writers, who simply "embroidered" the myth by turning Chiron into an "anti-Centaur" with an unthreatening curriculum of talents.[75] For Stewart, however, retaining Chiron's centaur qualities makes better sense: lacking father figures, the Greek heroes needed a substitute paternal deity, who could not be merely human, and who possessed the kinds of esoteric knowledge of nature and the cosmos that all centaurs shared.[76] Restoring Chiron to his role as "counterforce to civilization" allows Stewart to borrow the myth in the service of interpreting Hal's relationship to Falstaff in Shakespeare's second tetralogy.

What we have, then, is a centaur who is ambiguously—perhaps even erroneously—defined as wise and civilized in contrast to the species to which he belongs, which is in turn defined as uncivilized and dangerous to human institutions (like marriage) or values (like sobriety). We should add to these dimensions of the Chiron myth the use of the horse-human hybrid in Renaissance poetry and prose, where skilled horsemanship achieves the union of beast and human, subordinating the fury and power of the beast to human control in such a fashion that both are enhanced beyond their individual abilities. Philip Sidney is probably the best touchstone for such an image, given his persistent identification with both great horsemanship and great humanist ideals. Consider this description of Musidorus in *The Countess of Pembroke's Arcadia*: "But he, as if centaur-like he had been one piece with the horse, was no more moved than one is with the going of his own legs; and in effect so he did command him as his own limbs; for though he had both spurs and wand they seemed rather marks of sovereignty than instruments of punishment, his hand and leg with most pleasing grace commanding without threatening, and rather remembering that chastising . . . nor the horse did with any change complain of it; he ever going so just with the horse, either forthright or turning, that it seemed as he borrowed the horse's body, so he lent the horse his mind."[77]

But nearly every painting or statue of a nobleman on horseback attempts to evoke just this blending of horse and human, reason and passion, to emulate Chiron, rather than Nessus or other centaurs in mythology.[78] The compliance of the horse, here, its submission to the intellect of the human, and the human appropriation of the horse's muscularity, speed, and agility, should remind us of the Neapolitan coursers Ruini chose to represent in the *Anatomia del Cavallo*, but should also resonate with Vesalius's compliant corpses, in their antique poses, helping the anatomist establish his dominance over the unruly bodies of his criminals and vagrants via their apparently autonomous, vital, and self-surrendering gestures.

Chiron, the centaur-god of surgery, is thus the avatar of the anatomist as well, establishing the hand's (literally the *kheiron's*) authority in plumbing the secrets of human physiology. Ruini's pleasingly mobile muscle- and skeleton-horses are his Chirons, set in opposition to their wilder, flailing abdominal horses who escape the disciplining authority of the human hands sent to rein them in. Look again at Ruini's decorous horses performing parade trot in medial and posterior views (Figures 15, 17) or standing majestically in an Italian landscape (Figure 16). Each of these images dispels entirely the potential revelations of the abdominal figures, of the violence of dissection, of the incomplete or missing control of the anatomist, of the professional compromises made necessary by the size of the animal under the knife. They cooperate entirely, gracefully with the illustrator. And this, I would argue, is because of the positions in which they are portrayed—not merely that they are self-mobilizing because on their feet (or hooves), but because they are *up-right*, a position that physiological texts agree signifies the elevation of reason. Humans, writers like Crooke tell us, are upright for a variety of reasons that have to do with the eye and the mind: "As the soul of man is of all sublunary forms the most noble, so his Body, the house of the soul, doth so far excel, . . . the measure of all other bodies. . . the frame and composition which is *upright and mounting toward heaven*."[79] Crooke argues several reasons for human uprightness, including the need for a clear visual field and the heat that is generated by the human body; but above all, the soul, he notes, has built herself a "mansion" that "is mindfull of her Originall" (God), and so soars toward the sky.[80] Now horses are not quite as upright, but they can clearly, given Ruini's extremely vertical horse postures, be more or less so; and these horses approximate as much as possible the "mounting toward heaven" of which Crooke speaks. If the equine language ("mounting") is an accident, it nonetheless affords us a glimpse of how horse and rider could interconnect and share or swap qualities of nobility and transcendent wisdom.

Ruini's graceful trotting horses are intelligent: several of them seem to gaze knowingly out of the drawing toward the viewer; their gait and self-disciplined carriage demonstrate that they have internalized their education as proud parade or war horses. Without riders, they are self-governing, with agency—but what makes such agency possible is their commitment to the human search for knowledge, their performance on behalf of Ruini's anatomical project. Returning once more to Giambattista della Porta's illustration of comparative nobility in horse and human (Figure 10), we might consider how far this image goes toward suggesting a degree a mutual substitutability, even of transposability in its two figures. Horses that can look as intelligent, as rational, as proud, and as self-aware as a human—both della Porta's horse and Ruini's trotting horses achieve a blending that approaches the hybridity of the centaur. If they are not all Chirons, they are good analogs. There is, however, a paradox embodied in Ruini's trotting horses: to become his own version of Chiron, to achieve the insights of anatomy, Ruini must purge his subjects of the more obvious forms of human command, like hands, and instead endow them with *an interior* "humanity."

In addition to medicine and philosophy, the mythic Chiron instructed his heroes in the secrets of the hunt, an aristocratic pastime in which human and animal must decipher one another's nature and intentions. Suzanne Walker has argued that stag-hunting treatises of the Renaissance are "meditation[s] on the nature of the limits and dangers of subjectivity."[81] Itemizing the stag's useful body parts, hunting treatises create a kind of animal blazon, a poetic accounting of the creature's noble qualities; the fractured stag's whole bodily presence, necessary if the chase is to rise to the standards of aristocratic warfare (which the hunt was supposed to resemble), must then be constituted or manufactured by the hunter who can piece together tiny clues in nature—hoof prints, scat, glimpses of a fleet form in the mist—and out of them fashion a single stag. Having singled out that one individual from the herd, preferably the cleverest and most difficult to chase, the hunt proceeds to do battle with this worthy opponent. So compelling is the creation of the stag's interior identity in the hunt that participants might end up meditating on the animal's point of view, as well as its "cunning" strategies for escape. Jacques' mournful identification with the pursued stag in Shakespeare's *As You Like It* takes such a response to an extreme, but it is one that is explicit throughout these treatises. So dangerous is this process of constructing and then recognizing the internal and individual selfhood of the stag that it must be thoroughly undone by the hunters who, immediately upon killing the deer, *dissect* it, and distribute its parts to one another by rank.[82]

In a reversal of the hunt's trajectory, made possible by the conventions of Vesalian anatomical illustration, Ruini's and Snape's horses *gain* subjectivity through dissection, through the requirement that they obscure the violence of the fragmentation that dissection enacts. Without consciousness, without individuality, without interiority and rational understanding, their compliance wouldn't work. Perhaps we should not be surprised that a side effect of a horse anatomy, otherwise occasionally revelatory of dissection's obscured violence, is that it confers interiority, even subjectivity on the body whose depths it plumbs. Anatomies, medical regimes, dietary treatments, humoral balances—critics have identified all these as contributing to the creation of early modern ideas about identity and selfhood. And all are part of Ruini's and Snape's texts as well.

Chapter 2

Erotic Bodies: Loving Horses

The myth of Chiron, the rational hybrid horse-human, haunts Renaissance anatomy texts, as we saw in Chapter 1, but that is not the creature's sole domain. In examples like Philip Sidney's Musidorus, the more generalized image of the rider-as-centaur shows up in chivalric romance, where the centaur's hybrid nature expresses human triumph in appropriating and exploiting animal power and grace through the aristocratic arts of horsemanship. But other uses of the centaur myth in Renaissance literature register the fragility of the supremacy of human reason, most often undermined by the bodily assaults of lust, gluttony, and rage. The centaurs of Thessaly famously violated their peace with the Lapiths when they became drunk at the wedding of Perithous and attempted to rape the Lapith women; Nessus raped Heracles' wife, and was the eventual cause of the hero's death, while Pholus, despite behavior as "civilized" as Chiron's, breached his fellow centaurs' communal wine at Heracles' insistence, leading to an attempt on Heracles' life.[1] It is thus no surprise that Renaissance authors often seized on the image of the centaur to express the tendency of human beings to degenerate into beasts when under the influence of drink or high emotion.

That is the origin of one mythological strain in depictions of the centaur, but it does not fully explain the physiological and psychic sources and influences that made the centaur myth so widely relevant to the Renaissance in a way that it could not be, for instance, to a postmodern world. To understand those origins and influences, we would have to resurrect the physical, embodied experience of contact with horses, elaborated in some literature but more thoroughly in the dozens of early modern horsemanship manuals that instruct aspiring gentlemen in how to become imitators of Musidorus—to become noble hybrids with their mounts. To be a centaur is to be poised between absolute assimilation of the body of another, an animal, into one's own bodily consciousness and riding the knife's edge of losing oneself *to* another, enveloped by and transformed by the union. That is the "oneness" of horse and human that the centaur epitomizes. For postmoderns, such knowledge is not usually available—we are largely uncomprehending of the details, the nuances, the transcendent pleasures, the somatic sympathies, and the reflexes involved in the experience of riding because horses have disappeared from everyday life. Early moderns of any class, however, would have had a glimmering of this ideal through the cultural saturation of horsemanship imagery and discourse. Resurrecting dead horses in anatomies requires merely a good eye and some knowledge of the genre; resurrecting the human-horse relationship in terms of the centaur's unification of bodies is a little more difficult.

There is, however, one common and entirely obvious early modern experience that approximates just such an ontological confusion that is still relevant and widespread today, an experience involving the potential loss of individual identity during an act of physical and emotional excess: sexual intercourse.[2] In fact, Renaissance drama and poetry often borrow various dimensions of centaur imagery to celebrate, deplore, or register the social anxiety caused by the experience of ecstasy and self-transcendence that marks sexual union. Take, for instance, Sidney's sonnet 49 from *Astrophel and Stella*:

> I on my horse, and Love on me doth trie
> Our horsemanships, while by strange worke I prove
> A horseman to my horse, a horse to Love;
> And now man's wrongs in me, poor beast, descrie.
> The raines wherewith my Rider doth me tie,
> Are humbled thoughts, which bit of Reverence move,
> Curb'd in with Feare, but with guilt bosse above
> Of Hope which makes it seeme faire to the eye.
> The Wand is Will, thou, Fancie, saddle art,
> Girt fast by Memorie, and while I spurre
> My horse, he spurres with sharpe desire my hart:
> He sits me fast, how ever I do sturre:
> And now hath made me to his hand so right,
> That in the Manage I do take delight.[3]

The poem's conceit has its speaker practicing his training of his horse, while love performs the same arts on him: he is saddled and bridled with the effects of his own passion, made a "poor beast" instead of a "horse*man*" by his own desire. Overthrown by his love for Stella, Astrophel degenerates into something less than human—indeed, the poem teasingly posits a series of subject-position inversions via "bosse," "spur," "sturre," being "made [right] to *his* hand." The rider, otherwise masculinized through his pursuit of the manège (the high schooling of the horse), an art associated with male authority, is here ridden, controlled, and so effeminized as well as bestialized by lust's erasure of will and self-control. His new position as mount mimics the position in which women are traditionally placed, bearing the weight of a man, sexually dominated, tamed, taught to accept, even revel in their inferiority.

Astrophel thus comes to resemble the many female characters associated with horses, bits, bridles, and acts of taming throughout the period's literature about women, love, and marriage. For instance, *The Taming of the Shrew*'s Kate is named by Petruchio "my horse, my ox, my ass, my anything" (3.2.232) and is "curb[ed]" (4.1.4), or forced to submit to Petruchio's training techniques;[4] ultimately like Astrophel, she internalizes his teaching, to proclaim the doctrine of obedience in Act 5 as if it were her own—that is, in the end "in the Manège she takes delight." Cleopatra apostrophizes Antony's mount: "O happy horse to bear the weight of Antony" (*Antony and Cleopatra*, 1.5.21); while *Love's Labor's Lost* (3.1.30–32) and *The Winter's Tale* (1.2.276) exploit the sexual meaning of "hobby-horse," slang for a prostitute or sexually available woman. Lear's condemnation of his daughters' lust and treachery references the association between women and centaurs, comparing their "riotous appetite" to that of "the soiled horse" (*King Lear* 4.6.122–23): "Down from the waist they are Centaurs, / Though women all above" (4.6.124–25).[5] Women and/as horses are thus the dangerous alternative referent informing the centaur imagery, complicating Sidney's use of it to express heteronormative, heterosexual desire.

Shakespeare's Sonnet 51 treats a similar theme with the same imagery:

Thus can my love excuse the slow offense
Of my dull bearer, when from thee I speed:
From where thou art why should I haste me thence?
Till I return, of posting is no need.
O, what excuse will my poor beast then find
When swift extremity can seem but slow?
Then should I spur, though mounted on the wind,
In winged speed no motion shall I know.

Then can no horse with my desire keep pace:
Therefore desire, of perfect'st love being made,
Shall neigh, no dull flesh in his fiery race;
But love, for love, thus shall excuse my jade;
  Since from thee going he went willful slow,
  Towards thee I'll run and give him leave to go.

Whereas the trick of Sidney's poem is slippage of the speaker's position between rider and mount, Shakespeare's derives from the embodiment of the
lover's desire in the horse that carries him to and from his beloved, so that
desire "neighs" as it sprints ahead of his "dull bearer." Sidney's sonnet bestializes its speaker, placing him in the position of feminine sexual partner;
Shakespeare's first grossly materializes, then de-materializes its narrator, who
becomes a horse of desire—but one of wind, not flesh.

Even John Donne, who rarely uses images of horses or horsemanship,
turns to them at the conclusion of Elegy 7, in which the male lover reproaches
his protégé, now educated in the skills of love, but married to another:

Must I alas
Frame and enamel plate, and drink in Glass?
Chafe wax for others' seals? Break a colt's force
And leave him then, being made a ready horse?[6]

Sidney, Shakespeare, and Donne all borrow images of horses, horse breaking,
riding, and good or bad horsemanship to convey aspects of wooing, winning,
and losing a sexual object. None of these examples would make sense, nor
would these metaphors have currency, however, were not the visceral experience of a human on horseback memorably linked to a confusion of bodies that
underwrites the shift in horse/rider positions each poem articulates. All three
poems also rely on a prior understanding among its readership of the *pleasures*
of riding, pleasures associated with that confusion of bodily boundaries that
are physical and even erotic, but again, in ways not entirely clear to a modern
audience unfamiliar with the arts and skills of riding.

This chapter focuses on cases of human-horse eroticism. Its argument is
also intended to resonate with the material on embodiment that comprises
the next chapter—to call attention to the many and varied contexts in which
Renaissance human and animal bodies mingle, in pursuits like riding and sex,
or as we will see in Chapter 3, in the remedies for both humans and animals

prescribed by husbandry and medical manuals, and in mutual acts of consumption. All of these instances involve a reciprocal confusion of identities in which human and animal trade places, merge, or inhabit one another's defenseless, porous bodies. Through these exemplary moments, I argue that early modern human bodies were shared with, invaded by, occupied by, and colonized by animal bodies. This was both an unremarkable fact of everyday Renaissance life and a specter that threatened to dismantle efforts to distinguish the human self from its licit and illicit cohabitants.

The particular case of horse-human erotics, however, raises the issue of animal *sexual* agency in a way that other examples of shared or mutual embodiment do not. When most critics approach Renaissance examples of eroticized human-animal relationships, they tend to instantly translate them into cases of bestial sexuality.[7] This, perhaps, is both a byproduct of the legacy of the centaur—its lustful sexual predation returns to color even sidelong references to bestial love—and a result of critical resistance to anthropomorphic readings that would seem to endow what we prefer to view as victimized creatures with quasi-human abilities to choose, engage, or resist what is assumed to be a specifically human form of violation. In the analysis of human-equine bodily erotics that I offer here, I hope to nudge the discussion toward a more flexible, less defensive understanding of human-animal intersexualities. While the chapter focuses specifically on horse imagery and horsemanship manuals, I would suggest that some of its arguments apply just as well to the erotics of other interspecies relationships.

Bestial Sex

Renaissance literature offers an embarrassment of riches to anyone seeking examples of horsey sex. Shakespeare is, as we've already begun to observe, a goldmine. When Hotspur teases his own Kate, rebuking her for questioning him about his love for her, he imitates Petruchio's association of women with horses, coyly hinting at the kinds of "riding" that men may do with women, as well as horses: "Come, wilt thou see me ride? / And when I am a-horseback, I will swear / I love thee infinitely" (*1 Henry IV*, 2.3.99–101). The distance he means to put between himself and his wife guarantees that he will "love" her, but of course the lines also invoke the idea that he loves her most when *she* is being ridden by him (remaining silent like a good beast of burden, instead of quizzing him on the eve of battle): "But hark you Kate: I must not henceforth have you question me" (2.3.103). Like other shrew tamers, Hotspur longs for a well-managed, or well-manèged mount (the manège being the correct training, or dressage, of the horse), of the sort that the Dauphin lauds in *Henry V:* "I once writ a sonnet in his praise and began thus: 'Wonder of nature!' . . . I had rather have my horse to my mistress" (3.4.40–41, 60). "Having good judgment in horsemanship" as Orleans mockingly credits, lets the Dauphin substitute a willing "Prince of Palfreys" for an "unbridled" mistress. The Dauphin and Hotspur, like Sidney and Donne, and a host of other Renaissance writers, consider sex and horsemanship analogous activities.

Excellent work has been done on the kinds of links between sexuality and bestiality that we find in the examples above. Bruce Boehrer, Dympna Callaghan, Jeanne Roberts, and others have plumbed the literary and philosophical nuances and sociocultural implications in the language of bestial desire.[8] But critics have generally read the use of horsemanship metaphors in describing sexual acts as if the only thing at stake is the sexuality of humans essentially interacting with other humans. Thus, for Boehrer, cases of "bestial buggery" manifest anxiety that once women have been characterized as less than human, all acts of heterosexual copulation, including those sanctioned by marriage, are acts of bestial sex. Roberts, on the contrary, sees in *The Taming of the Shrew*'s language of animality evidence of Ovidian metamorphosis that allows dissimilar human beings to transform through marriage into something more equal—equus, she notes, may derive from the same root as equal.[9] The result is nevertheless the privileging of human sexual behavior over any "real" interspecies relationship. Dympna Callaghan does address the manner in which sexuality challenges the boundary that supposedly divides species: in her reading of Shakespeare's *Venus and Adonis*, "the fundamental distinction between the human and the animal, whose articulation is undergirded by the ostensible sexual integrity of the human species, also depends on what threatens to undermine it, namely sex itself."[10] Yet even her reading does not confer much equivalent agency on the nonhuman.

These critics chart the broader discursive field in which sexual relations between humans and animals are constructed, a field that must include pets, various sorts of animals, and even plants. However, all work from a model in which the main, indeed the only significant sexual act at stake is clearly an *act of bestiality*—sexual congress with an animal. Noting Renaissance obsessions with the crime of bestiality, Callaghan characterizes Adonis's choice as one between two versions of criminality: either he must mate with the incestuously maternal Venus, or "mate" with the violent boar and its sharp tusk.

Like Boehrer, Callaghan finds that the identification of women with animals reveals "the fragile cultural membrane that separates the feminine from animal sexuality and the taxonomic confusion that ties them together."[11] Venus threatens to turn Adonis into a pet, inappropriately inverting the power structure that makes acts of "petting" (which Callaghan defines as "the fondling of both dependent animals and people, but especially children") aberrant, capable of generating monstrous births. Staving off the threat of degenerate sex by impaling himself on the boar's tusk, Adonis safely ends the poem in the realm of vegetable art and aesthetics, "A purple flower . . . chequer'd with white, / Resembling well his pale cheeks and the blood / Which in round drops upon their whiteness stood."

Callaghan's interest, then, is in how Shakespeare's poem participates in discourses of bestiality, incest, and art: "By repeatedly transgressing the discrete taxonomies of human and animal, nature and culture, the poem's images render them demonstrably artificial categories."[12] I wonder, though, whether a different poem would arise from a more thorough reading of an episode Callaghan barely mentions, the long interlude that dominates the poem's first third involving the courtship of two horses, the famous jennet and courser. Instead of triangulating desire among a woman, a man, and various animals (and plants), the courser-jennet episode channels erotic energies among a man and two horses. Does this make a difference? And how would a detour through the popular horsemanship treatises of the period elucidate further the content and implications of this episode?

When horses appear in Renaissance texts they usually represent the need for reason to control the (bodily) passions. It is because they establish a hierarchy of mind over matter that horses make perfect substitutes or metaphoric analogues for women, especially, as we have seen, for uncompromising lovers or shrewish wives. Whether they appear in texts devoted to civil government or in comedies about spousal rebellion, horses are there to represent the appetites that should properly or "naturally" be subjected to (masculine) containment in the interests of social or political order. To invoke the centaurs once more, the bestial lusts of the body are either harnessed to social good, as in Chiron's case, or range free threatening to destroy civilization, as in the case of the battle with the Lapiths. Horses thus provide the bodies through which regimes of self-control are exercised, or by which various forms of hegemony are justified.

Shakespeare, for instance, complexly transposes Venus's fantasy of fulfilled desire onto Adonis's "trampling courser," who woos and then escapes with the "breeding jennet" he discovers in a nearby copse. Betraying Adonis at a moment of crisis, when the besieged hunter tries to flee Venus's clinging embrace, the animal bursts the bounds of discipline—literally, the bonds that hold his gear together—when "his woven girths he breaks asunder" and "the iron bit he crusheth 'tween his teeth / Controlling what he was controlled with." Such a loss of control is typically a projection of his *rider*'s inadequacies. In Spenser's *Faerie Queene*, for instance, when Guyon loses his horse to Braggadochio, his unfitness for the task of razing Acrasia's bower and his need for Alma's healing treatment are exposed; Braggadochio, meanwhile, cannot hide from Guyon's mount his own lack of merit, demonstrated by his "burn[ing] in filthy lust" for Belphoebe:

> So to his steed he got, and gan to ride,
> As one vnfit therefore, that all might see
> He had not trayned bene in cheualree.
> Which well that valiant courser did discerne;
> For he despysd to tread in dew degree,
> But chaufd and fom'd, with courage fierce and sterne,
> And to be easd of that base burden still did erne.[13]

Shakespeare likewise often deploys references to the "manage" or training of the horse to denote moral authority. Richard III's unhorsing at the battle of Bosworth Field not only presages his defeat at Henry VII's hands but reflects his moral unfitness to rule; similarly, Richard II's loss of authority is expressed through the image of Phaethon's chariot horses, "Down, down I come, like glist'ring Phaethon, / Wanting the manage of unruly jades" (3.3.177–78). In other contexts, the association of women with horses, needing bridling and "manage" is, as Roberts points out, well established: she cites the example of "A Merry Jeste of a Shrewde and Curst Wife Dress'd in Morel's Skin" (1580) in which the henpecked husband flays his old, decrepit horse, Morel, beats his wife mercilessly, and then clothes his wife in the horse's skin in order to enforce her to the same faithful service that his horse provided for so many years:

> For this I trow will make her shrinke.
> And bow at my pleasure, when I her bed,
> And obay my commaundementes both lowde and still,
> Or else I will make her body bleede,
> And with sharp roddes beate her my fill.[14]

Whether enforcing gender hierarchy and sexual compliance, exposing moral failings in its rider, or acting out fantasies of bestial lust, literary uses of the horse disseminate the imperative that regimes of discipline and control must triumph over chaotic passion to preserve civil order. But the constant renewal of such images suggests that the imperative is never finally fulfilled. Boehrer finds bestiality's "ultimate source in the institutions that ostensibly oppose it," like marriage, which "yokes" together two beings of vastly unequal status—the human male and the dubiously human female, who is, as we've noted, most often compared to a recalcitrant horse.[15]

It is easy to read the courser and the jennet in Shakespeare's poem as a simple case of transposed lustfulness overthrowing the bonds of social and cultural discipline to engage in bestial sex, in the tradition of the examples above. In such a reading, however, the problematics of identification the poem introduces are lost: after all, which is which? That is, does the jennet stand in for Venus, the "breeding" goddess, or is the (female) jennet a substitute for the effeminized Adonis, who would have to submit to a rather macho dictatorial supernatural lover? Is the violently out-of-control (male) courser instead the violently loving Venus, who later defends the horse's behavior? Or both, since the lusts of Venus threaten Adonis's hold on masculine superiority? Is the courser's lust a sign of "nature," and if so, is Adonis somehow blameworthy (that is, tempted by Venus and what she represents) in failing to control his mount? The binaries seem to stack up: Venus's lust versus Adonis's masculine desire for control; the courser's explosion from the bounds set by his rider versus proper and disciplined use in the hunt; nature versus culture; love of a woman versus love of masculine pursuits; sex versus riding. Yet it is difficult to stabilize the vehicles of these binaries in any meaningful way—the courser and jennet tend to violate the containment of their bodily genders, to burst out of their stalls and run from the orderly boxes of their "stable."

When Adonis moans, "My day's delight is past, my horse is gone, / And 'tis your fault I am bereft him so," he characterizes Venus's intrusion, and the loss of his mount, as a kind of love affair in which the mount is his first source of pleasure—an erotic pleasure with sexual content, of course, since clearly that is what is at stake between Venus and Adonis himself, as well as between the courser and the jennet; but not *purely* a sexual pleasure, in that the erotics of the rider-mount relationship do not reduce to a simple sexual act. Indeed, Adonis's language seems nicely framed to resonate with Renaissance interpretations of Platonic *eros* as the *recognition of a lack* that provokes a certain kind of desire; clearly, Adonis does not "lack" anything Venus has to offer, but without *his horse* he is "bereft."

If there is a hint of Platonic *eros* in this otherwise sexually explicit episode in a sexually explicit poem, it comes as a corrective, not a corollary, to the otherwise genitally oriented sexual pleasures rampant throughout. When Adonis chooses the boar over Venus, the animal over the woman, he is not merely preferring bestial sex, he is choosing a specific type of penetrative pleasure—one that is *not* available in either heterosexual or homosexual sex with a human. Platonic love, the kind that Adonis might enjoy with his courser, is composed of erotic energies, yes, but it realizes a drive to union that transcends the genital expression of that union. Adonis, to put it briefly, wants to be conjoined with his lovely horse, to be corporeally interpenetrative with a creature that makes him feel complete, instead of united sexually with a woman, even if she is a goddess.

Here, then, we have the crux of my problem with readings that simply elide pleasure with sex. They leave no room to ask what *kind* of pleasure is at stake in loving an animal. Even the apparently clear example of "buggery," an act with legal and religious content that is specifically sexual, isn't so clear when we put some pressure on its emotional and pleasure-giving components: does the human participant find in it purely sexual release? Is there a specific erotics of the animal's body that engages human interest? Is there some indefinable loneliness that only a relationship with animals, and not people, can redress? Would any critic be willing to risk entertaining the notion that the animal is in any way a participating agent in acts of bestial pleasure? Surely not: such a suggestion would disrupt the social coding of bestiality in the twentieth century as a peculiarly human act of dominance, power, and abuse enacted on a silent, passive victim.[16] To indicate otherwise would shuffle off some of the responsibility onto that victim, a double violation; but it is convenient that the assignment of eternal victimhood to the animal enforces a degree of denial of agency, of reciprocity, of mutuality.

Yet both the Renaissance love literature that relies on horse imagery and the literature that describes the training of a horse like Adonis's courser agree that there is a particular kind of pleasure at stake in "riding," and they entertain the possibility, raised precisely by their conjunction and by the fact that pleasure is at the heart of horse-human interactions in both genres, that the horse may itself have an erotic connection to the rider and may actively participate in creating the gratifications involved in the experience of "riding." Indeed, when we look more particularly at horsemanship manuals designed to instruct humans in how to create the actual or non-mythological centaur—that is, the horse and rider who, like Musidorus, appear to be one—we discover the pervasiveness of this boundary collapse. Anxieties over patriarchal hierarchy and order are as much at stake in the horsemanship manuals as in the literature of the period; yet in their language of pleasure, training manuals repeatedly posit a kind of eroticized commingling of bodies and an actively mutual source of pleasure in the experience of riding that reverses the love literature's bias toward human genital erotics. In other words, the riding manuals articulate an erotics that is sexualized but not only sexual; unlike the love literature, which cannot escape its investment in a final sexual act, training manuals describe a human-animal eroticism that escapes binarism—one that we might identify as profoundly queer.[17] These manuals also leave room for the appreciation of the animal's beauty, its nobility, its generosity, which in turn justify the passion of the rider for his mount in ways not available in the love literature. And they insist upon the possibility that the horse can equally invest in pleasures of participation, mutuality, and the creation of beauty. With a detour through those manuals, then, we will return newly informed to our reading of *Venus and Adonis* to identify further its queer pleasures.

[handwritten annotation: riding a horse is a mutual pleasure, not only sexual though]

Pleasuring the Animal

Riding a horse is a unique experience for human beings, an experience that is now the domain of a very limited, elite group of people who continue to practice an entirely obsolete art. Horsemen and women have consistently, even obsessively, expressed the nature of this experience in one compelling image: when riding rises to the level of high art, the experience is counted as the union of two distinct bodies and intellects (in Renaissance literature, sometimes spirits or souls) so that they move, think, and act as one—exactly the formulation we have seen in Sidney's description of Musidorus on horseback. Such oneness is not merely the product of severe and punitive techniques, since union requires the willing cooperation of a creature that Renaissance texts repeatedly assert has its own agenda, its own sensations, and its own character. Elizabeth LeGuin compares the training of the horse to the higher levels of manège or dressage to the education of pupils in music or dance. But she emphasizes that the same one-way channel between master and student we find in dialogues about these human arts does not work for horsemanship manuals: "Horses, however, demand another sort of dialogue altogether:

even as they exhibit extraordinary ability to adapt to human purposes, they challenge human methods through their sheer Otherness."[18] To produce the "harmony" that so often is invoked in horsemanship treatises, that which makes a Musidorus "one" with his horse, requires tremendous investment in deciphering the physical, as well as the mental, "intelligence" of the horse. As John Astley puts it in his work *The Art of Riding* (1580), horsemanship allows "these two severall bodies [to] seem in all their actions and motions to be as it were but one onlie bodie."[19] The horse is, Astley proclaims, a "sensible creature" who is moved to cooperate "by sense and feeling," but will "shunne such things as annoy him, and . . . like all such things as do delight him."[20]

This harmony is at the heart of the new training methods that arise with the rediscovery of Xenophon's *Art of Horsemanship* and its translation, redaction, or inclusion in texts of every language throughout the late sixteenth and seventeenth centuries. Punishment, as LeGuin makes clear, is "a delicate business" for the true horseman in these texts, since to crush the horse's spirit makes it useless for the arts of the manège.[21] Rather, a gentle, gradual disciplining of the body of the horse takes place once the body of the rider has adapted to its own subtle task. Most horsemanship treatises advise riders to have great care to reward their mounts, whether or not they also simultaneously advocate draconian punitive measures. Past scholarship on these texts has focused on their imposition of discipline, not unnaturally given some of the outrageous methods they include for chastising animals. The Italian master Federigo Grisone, for instance, recommends plenty of beatings about the head and shoulders for unmanageable horses, and gives instructions for using a cat on a pole or a hedgehog tied to the tail to inspire stubborn horses to go forward.[22] However, it is entirely possible that past critics, myself included, have taken at face value a tactic that has little to do with actual training methods from the sixteenth and seventeenth centuries; it is as likely that these included "training techniques" are purely rhetorical gestures meant either to assure readers that the author has a remarkable new system not available from other competing texts or to impress readers with the lengths to which the trainer is willing to go to impose discipline on unruly beasts. It is also possible that the language of extreme discipline, given the degree of mutuality, of interpenetration of horse and rider, represents the degree of effort needed to recuperate the distinction of human and animal, which should not surprise us, but should instead attest to the degree of anxiety such collapse arouses. Whatever the explanation, it is clear that by the end of the sixteenth century, many trainers were far more concerned with gentle methods for coercion than with spectacular displays of cruelty.

We see this trend especially in the description of rider contact with the horse's mouth, that especially sensitive part through which a great deal of communication must take place. Thomas Blundeville, whose *The Four Chiefest Offices of Horsemanshippe* is a redaction of Grisone, nevertheless scolds his English audience for having the reputation for creating "jades," or hard-mouthed mounts. They should take care to introduce the colt to the bit in a happier fashion by anointing it with honey and salt, to "make him the more to delight in it, and to be always champing the iron, and to staie his mouth more temperately."[23] Gervase Markham advises giving the horse "kinde words, as ho boy, ho boy, or holla love, so my nagge, and such like tearmes, till he have won him to his will" and "carry[ing] a gentle hand, so as you may have a feeling of the Colte, and the Colte no more but a perfect say of your hand, unless extreamitie compel you."[24]

The great French equerry, Antoine Pluvinel, describes in *Le Maneige Royal* (1623, 1626) the posture that the graceful and judicious rider must adopt in order to be effective: *approach & mant horse w/ care*

He must sit only in the centre of the saddle, taking care not to
touch the cantle out of fear of falling. At all times must he sit
straight in the saddle as if he were standing on the ground. His two
shoulders must be bent slightly and equally forward, his stomach
thrust forward, making a slight hollow at the waist. His two elbows
must, at all times, be placed parallel, and without constraint,
slightly away from the body. The right fist must be close to the left
one, at a distance of about four or five fingers from each other. . . .
The legs must be thrust forward, the end of the foot pressing firmly
in the stirrup; the knees must, as always, be squeezed with all one's
strength so that, should the horse become animated, he does not
throw my ass [*mon âne*], I mean my man, to the ground.[25]

So ideal is this posture that it can be charted within a rectangle, outlined in the engraved plate for the reader's easy appreciation (Figure 19). With such a seat, notes Pluvinel, the rider will remain in exact communion with the horse's motion, always ready to correct errors and produce the greatest response to spur and thigh; the rider must thus never deviate even an iota from this posture precisely because he has such extreme instruments of control, or "the horse as well as the Horseman, would be thrown out of balance due to the great sensitivity of the horse's mouth and his belly." Astley notes that battle horses "teach a man to sit surelie, comelie, and stronglie in his seat," in the manner required by Pluvinel; likewise, William Cavendish claims "a good seat is of such importance . . . that the regular movement of a horse entirely depends upon it, which is preferable to any other assistance [that is, of bit, spur, or whip]; therefore, let it not be despised. Moreover I dare to venture to affirm, that he who does not sit genteely upon a horse, will never be a good horseman."[26] These authors agree that the control of a horse's extraordinary power, which is combined with such extraordinary responsiveness to the touch of human limbs and instruments, can only be achieved through the complete control of one's own body; those who fail in this self-discipline of bodily movement will be, like Pluvinel's "man," an ass (âne), demoted, grounded—denied the superior and gentlemanly pleasures of riding.

For the rider, the pleasure of riding comes in part from the physical experience of rhythmic or explosive motions generated by a body outside of oneself, a body more powerful and agile than oneself, whose efforts fleetingly register as if they nonetheless were one's own. This pleasure can be both exhilarating and dangerous to the rider's sense of self. Recent studies on how tactile-kinaesthetic systems contribute to the perception of selfhood in humans suggest that what we call the "self" is more fluid and transposable than is allowed for in most versions of bodily identity. In one study, participants were seated with their left arms resting on a table but screened from their view. Meanwhile a life-sized rubber model of a left arm and hand was placed on the table directly in front of the subject. Participants watched the artificial hand and arm, while two small brushes were used to stroke both the rubber hand and the subject's hidden hand, "synchronizing the timing of the brushing as closely as possible." After only a short while, participants had the distinct sensation that they experienced the stroking and tapping of the artificial hand, when in fact it was their own fleshly hand that was being manipulated. That is, the tactile stimulus was received as if it came from the artificial hand. "Further tests revealed that if the experimenters asked participants, with eyes closed, to point to the left hand with the hidden hand, their pointing, after experience of the illusion, were [sic] displaced toward the rubber hand."[27] For the researchers, this experiment suggests that "our sense of our bodies as our own depends less on their differentiation from other objects and bodies than on their participation in specific forms of intermodal correlation." But the experiment also suggests that humans can, through certain kinds of kinaesthetic experiences, either proprioceptively incorporate body parts that are not their own or extend their consciousness into inanimate objects. This is precisely

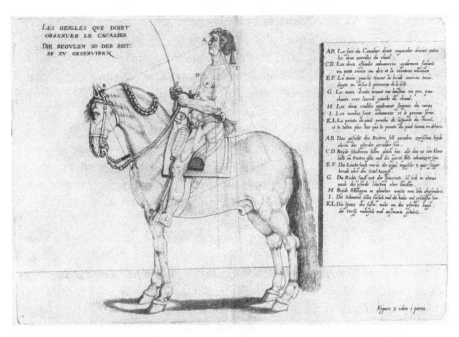

Figure 19. Antoine Pluvinel's *L'Instruction du Roy* (1625). Illustration of the rider's position. Herzog August Bibliothek Wolfenbüttel, A: 8.4 Bell.2.

what riding a horse accomplishes when done well, with the additional complication that proprioception of the human rider can extend to include the complete body of an animate, conscious, and wholly other being.

Current research into the experience of riding by those interested in animal-human communication emphasizes the uniqueness of the horse-rider bond, which relies on a created language of the body. Horses and riders "speak" to one another with their bodies—literally, they communicate through "body language," albeit in a way that is foreign to most humans because this body language must intersect with equine models of behavior and responses to stimuli. Keri Brandt has noted that one consequence of learning this difficult new grammar is that horse owners and riders become hyper-aware of their movements around their horses because movement always has some meaning for the equine partner; they become, like Pluvinel, Astley, or Cavendish, more thoroughly self-disciplined in the pursuit of a purer language.[28] Psychologists, cultural anthropologists, and animal ethicists have coined a number of terms to convey this kind of bodily communication: Kenneth Shapiro calls it "kinesthetic empathy," while Thomas Csordas brands it a form of "somatic attention."[29] Maurice Merleau-Ponty was perhaps the first to identify it as a "kinetic melody" of body and behavior, a phrase that LeGuin evokes in her work on "harmony" and her comparison of horsemanship with musical study, as well as one that clarifies the role of music in horsemanship performances from the Renaissance through the twenty-first century.[30] The French ethologist and equestrian Jean-Claude Barrey notes that the most infinitesimal and involuntary motion of the rider generates a response in the horse, through "isopraxis": "The human's right hand imitates (and anticipates) what the horse's right front leg will do, the bottom of the back of the rider makes a jerk which is exactly the movement the horse will do to begin to canter, and so on. In other words, according to Barrey, talented riders behave and move like horses."[31]

Since this bodily communication stands outside the language of human speech, it requires its own rhetoric and vocabulary if it is to be taught to another human: a sensitive mouth on a horse (that is, a horse that is instantly responsive to the most minute movements of the bit) is "soft," a bad mouth (a horse that ignores the bit) is "hard;" a horse that is confident in its posture and is pushing forward to the rider's hand instead of backing away from it is called "through," while one that is well-educated enough to be constantly balanced is in "self-carriage" (that is, it does not need as much the support of a rider's hand or leg). Indeed, new terms are being invented and applied all the time: recently, dressage language embraced the German *schwung* to describe the impulsion or forward movement in self-carriage of the more advanced horse (hence *schwung* because the result is the swinging relaxed back of the horse); a vigorous debate rages now in the international dressage community over the use of *rollkur* or the forced extreme flexion of the horse's mouth, head, and neck. The strangeness of these terms and others belonging to the world of horsemanship signal the difficulty in finding appropriate spoken vessels for the experience.

Natural horsemanship, a recent fad in training circles, often associated with famous practitioners like Monty Roberts, Buck Brannaman, and Vicky Hearne, has its own distinct language, as Paul Patton observes, one that privileges concepts of voluntary and mutual association. While Patton accepts that the aesthetico-moral justifications for training an animal are "corrupt" (citing Vicky Hearne citing Nietzsche's *Genealogy of Morals*), he concludes that the inequality and anthropocentrism of the human-animal relationship that characterize even natural training techniques do not preclude ethical treatment of animals: "what we learn from the disciplines of animal training is that

hierarchical forms of society between unequals are by no means incompatible
with ethical relations and obligations toward other beings."[32] While the language of partnering, of equality, of mutuality is often assumed to conceal a
relationship of dominance, obedience, and even slavery, Patton concludes that
what natural training does well is to establish "a form of language that closes
that gap," which is another way of saying that it enables a form of interaction
that enhances the power and the feeling of power of both horse and rider."[33]
I would contend, however, that training has always done just this, even in
the historical past where we expect to find only techniques for repression and
dominance. Thus we find in early modern horsemanship manuals the same
effort to develop a language to further the horse-human bond.

Renaissance treatises on riding, literature on horses, and images of great
feats of horsemanship often struggle to express exactly the same range of
phenomena of "softness," of "speaking through the reins" that we encounter
in modern training techniques, indicating willing partnership and mingled
proprioception. But few take the subject as far as does Astley, whose treatise
focuses on "the true use of the hand" with extensive discussion of the pleasures the horse may take from a well-educated rider's manipulation of the bit.
Indeed, perhaps the most common term Astley uses throughout his treatise is
"pleasure," almost always referring to the *horse's* response to its rider. Ignorant
riders, whose "intemperate hand[s]" can be compared to the gross failures of
the intemperate drinker, turn this "sensible" creature into a "senseless block"
who feels neither hand nor spur; violence in the use of the bit, "which Nature
abhorreth," amounts to a kind of rape of the horse's mouth, as far as Astley
is concerned.[34] Educating the hand to the reins is, according to Astley, comparable to teaching penmanship, and the influence of a master can always be
read in his pupil's hand.[35] He gives detailed descriptions of the mechanics of
the bit's movement and force in the horse's mouth and constantly reminds his
readers that the horse should have a "sweet mouth," be "champing at the bit
with great pleasure," and "take pleasure of the bit" with a soft and "temperate
hand."[36] Astley emphasizes that the rider will not succeed if he tries to enforce
his will on the horse through the bit, "pressing" the animal with it so "that
thereby he be put to despaire of libertie." Only with the freedom to believe
himself an equal part of the man-horse centaur does the mount show himself
at his best: "Therefore with certain quiet signes provoke him to shew himself
lustie and comelie in everie part . . . for he will by this most easily and willinglie
doe and perform those things wherewith he himself is chieflie delighted, and
wherein he pleaseth himself most. And that he doth take pleasure in those

things aforesaid, let this be a good witnesse." The horse, then, becomes the most beautiful he is able to be in the most natural fashion.[37] Freedom, liberty, pleasure, delight: Astley's horse is wooed by its rider with "gentle and courteous dealing," "allure[d] and entice[d]" rather than oppressed or abused.[38] The good rider, the treatises agree, inspires and invites the horse to do what "delights" and "pleases" it, maintaining the horse's agency in the partnership.

What the horsemanship manuals construct, then, is a relationship between horse and rider that revolves around bodily habituation to a balanced position upon the horse, with gentle and loving manipulation of the soft insides of the animal's mouth with the bit, in order to generate pleasure in horse, rider, and spectators. As LeGuin points out, training the rider (and horse) is most akin to training the musician or dancer: Monsieur le Grande indeed compliments Pluvinel on the stillness of the master's position for its "perfect harmony," which when applied in producing a great performance on his Barb, La Bonnitte, results in "the sarabande of La Bonnitte."[39] In this dance, bodies move in unison, rhythmically; the centaur engages in heart-stopping physical feats, achieving the elevation of an ordinary act, riding, into an aesthetic triumph.

Erotic Confusions

Sidney's sonnet 42 relies on all the traditional associations we've drawn so far, between horses and women, horses and lust, horses and the courtship of the considerate chevalier. The rhythms of riding that mimic the thrust of sexual passion, the comingling of two bodies that dissolve into union, the penetration of the soft inward secret places of the beloved, the desire to give as well as receive pleasure, all underwrite the sonnet's use of the manège as its dominant metaphor. They also inform the episode of the courser and the jennet in Shakespeare's *Venus and Adonis*, where the possibilities of the conjoined uses of horses and horsemanship imagery in the manuals and in the love poetry lead to the countenancing of the *horse's* pleasures as much as the human's. Acts of sexuality are figured in Shakespeare's poem as acts of incorporation, or minglings of bodies whose identity is indeterminate or inverted: despite his resistance, Venus's embrace of Adonis nonetheless makes the two "incorporate," while her fantasies insist that "although he mount her" Adonis "will not manage her" (540; 598, punning on the manège). Riding is a kind of sex, requiring the kind of skills applied to sexual encounters, and sex involves the skills of riding. The training

of the horse inflects the use of horsemanship metaphors with connotations of
mental and physical discipline; but in *Venus and Adonis*, the subject who seeks
to master her beloved, who appropriates the pleasures of being ridden as if they
were identical to acts of riding, is the female goddess, not the warlike male partner. The threat implicit in the connections between horses and horsemanship as
they are used in erotic poetry, and the construction of the horse in the training
treatises as a potentially erotic subject and equal participant in the pleasures of
riding, is thus realized in Shakespeare's poem: the mount seizes the reins of pleasure, rises to the top, and masters its/his/her master.

If we bring to Shakespeare's episode of the courser and the jennet some of
what we have learned from the horsemanship treatises, new tensions emerge.
Although its ostensible purpose is the traditional demonstration of lust released from rational control, the passage's descriptive details eroticize the
courser in provocative and unpredictably fluid ways. The poem mobilizes the
kind of confusion of horse/rider subject positions that we saw in the horsemanship manuals, along with confusions over the gender of the participants,
and the sources and direction of the episode's erotic content:

Round-hoofed, short-jointed, fetlocks shag and long,
Broad breast, full eye, small head, and nostril wide,
High crest, short ears, straight legs and passing strong,
Thin mane, thick tail, broad buttock, tender hide:
  Look what a horse should have he did not lack,
  Save a proud rider on so proud a back.

Sometimes he scuds far off, and there he stares;
Anon he starts at stirring of feather.
To bid the wind a base he now prepares,
And whe'r he run or fly they know not whether,
    For through his mane and tail the high wind sings,
    Fanning the hairs, who wave like feath'red wings.

He looks upon his love and neighs unto her;
She answers him, as if she knew his mind.
Being proud, as females are, to see him woo her,
She puts on outward strangeness, seems unkind,
    Spurns at his love and scorns the heat he feels,
    Beating his kind embracements with her heels.

Then, like a melancholy malcontent,
He vails his tail, that, like a falling plume,
Cool shadow to his melting buttock lent;
He stamps, and bites the poor flies in his fume.
　　His love perceiving how he was enraged,
　　Grew kinder, and his fury was assuaged. (295–318)

The courser is the paragon of horses, whose every part is the epitome of physical virtue in a horse; that he "lack[s]" only "a proud rider on so proud a back" would seem to confirm the need for his lusty behavior to submit to the reins of reason. But to end a poetic blazon of the animal's physical beauties, a blazon comparable to that anatomizing a woman in the vast array of sonnets and love poems, with the image of the rider on his back contributes an erotic charge to the act of riding that defeats its exclusive association with reason. What would a "rider" ride, in this instance, but a beauteous body, a sexualized hybrid creature, who would submit his "thick tail, broad buttock[, and] and tender hide" to the rider's caresses?

Meanwhile the jennet leads this courser a merry dance—literally, making him hop, bow, leap, and spin—performing the expected coy resistance of love poetry's scornful lady. She "beats" "his kind embracements" with her heels, and "spurns *at*" him, as if fully self-aware about her performance as a performance. The "beats" of her hooves become the measure of the dance; the distance between spurning his advances and *spurning at* his advances marks the distinction between reality and representation. This jennet is a self-conscious, musically trained, disciplined, and cooperative partner in the best tradition of the horsemanship treatises.

Finally, at the point of the fair lady's capitulation, the courser is portrayed with his tail "vailed," so that it falls like a "plume" over his "melting buttock." The double reference in such a short space to the courser's buttocks bestializes this encounter (apparently "appropriately," in the sense that it is a courtship between two beasts, but also metaphorically casting Venus's wooing as equally bestial, which is proper to the poem's gender politics), but also draws attention to the species of sexual attention being negotiated. When the jennet waxes "kinder" the pun is on kind as categorization by species, which undergirds her welcoming posture—she is more like a horse (or a woman?) when she stops performing resistance and submits. But what would the act she allows look like? As a horse, the courser would naturally mount his "fair breeder" from behind. But to "vail" his tail, that is to let its hair cascade over his buttocks,

requires that the courser first lift the dock of his tail. That gesture is characteristic of any horse in an excited state, regardless of gender. The dock is the
fleshy extension of the spine from which the tail grows; it is usually carried at
rest low, settled between the two flanks, lifted only for defecating. However,
in copulation, raising the dock of the tail is the signal given *by the mare* that
she is ready to mate, because it grants access by revealing the vulva. So a stallion "vailing" his tail confuses the gendering of the participants and inflects
this passage, I would argue, with a slippery erotic energy that does not resolve
to any clear sexual (and therefore human or even human-horse) binary. And
for whom might that stallion's tail be raised? The courser "rides" his mare; but
he is also ridden by a rider, who is at this juncture the only thing he "lacks," a
rider who desperately loves him. The fact that the poem doubles Adonis's lack
of his horse, of whom he is "bereft," with the courser's lack of its rider suggests
not merely a failure of control and reason, but mutual erotic desire. Finally,
whose is the gaze that appreciates this performance? That receives and enjoys
the image of the courser's erotically beautiful and noble physique? Adonis?
Venus? The jennet? The reader? In sum, this courser becomes a supremely
confused and confusing object and agent of erotic desire. So too the identity
of his jennet, and the desire expressed migrates from one subject position
to another until it is difficult to discern absolutely which participant in the
poem is the "masculine" aggressor, which the "feminine" pursued, or who
loves whom, who wants whom. Of course, that is exactly the poem's drama,
since its primary characters shift positions with equal fluidity, until its climax
in the goring of Adonis by the boar: "And muzzling in his flank, the loving
swine / Sheathed unaware the tusk in his soft groin."

   In fact, the poem does not stop at the species barrier of the equine in
its description. The courser's flighty actions, startling at a feather, lead to his
characterization as another kind of animal, a bird: "For through his mane and
tail the high wind sings, / Fanning the hairs, who wave like feath'red wings."
The hints of animate nature even in the wind's song, the tendency toward
species mobility in the courser's own motions, suggest a horse that is always
something else, somewhere else, impossible to pin down. Whereas Callaghan
reads the poem's references to the vegetable world for their ability to reinstall
poetic control over the implications of bestiality and hybridity in Adonis's
union with the boar, I would read the courser and jennet as examples that
the poem cannot establish any stable set of divisions that would make species
categories possible, something that is true long before the boar appears, and
long after Adonis is dead.

Beautiful Beasts

Shakespeare's treatment of the courser and jennet is as much a commentary on aesthetics as on animal love or human sexuality. The consequence of the jennet's performance of love, and of the blazon of the courser's beautiful body, is to emphasize the role of the reader-observer, whose appreciation of these carefully staged poetic moments knits them together with the rest of this very visual poem. Shakespeare's loving description of the animals' bodies, his celebration of the courser's speed and power, evokes and probably derives from the visual record of equine subjects in the art of the period.

Horses rarely appear either in horsemanship treatises or in poetry without inspiring awe at their unique blend of power and grace. Much of the great art of the Renaissance and the baroque period features the horse, whose form can be manipulated to demonstrate elements of its rider's character, or to manifest an artist's skill with anatomy, or to confirm ideologies of nobility, good governance, military authority, and so on. Leon Battista Alberti, otherwise best known for his theories of painting and architecture (and for his writing on family structure), penned *Il Cavallo Vivo*, which blends commentary on the horse's extraordinary beauty with analysis of the ethical obligations of leadership. Juliana Schiesari points out that Alberti's discussion of the horse as an aesthetic object, albeit a living one, relies on classical models—"in order to take up the technical aspects of formal beauty, beauty must first be understood as the realization of the 'natural inclinations' of horses."[40] Because the horse is a privileged "servant" among domesticated creatures (which, Schiesari notes, include women or wives, other animals, and even vegetation), given its unique combination "of a pleasing physique that combines great power housed within a fiery soul with a sweet and potentially docile disposition," its rider's actions are the more magnified, for better or worse: a worthy rider who governs in the interests of expressing the "nature" of his mount will be accepted, even loved by his animal, while a poor rider, who cannot modulate his methods in accordance with the horse's needs and capabilities, will "fail to live up to his own 'nature' and obligation to rule effectively."[41]

Alberti's concept of beauty as the realization of a thing's soul or nature, however, tends to shift the emphasis we find in other texts and images of horses away from the physicality of the animal toward an abstraction that purports to express that physicality better than the thing itself. Most equine art refuses to adopt this paradigm; the massive *materiality* of the horse is what is at stake in equine aesthetics, much as we observed it was in the Renaissance anatomy texts. Take, for instance, Albrecht Durer's two images of a soldier and his mount (Figures 20 and 21). Although one is supposedly "large" and one "small" (they are called simply "Large Horse" and "Small Horse" in the critical literature), both are massively fleshed with muscle and fat. The larger of the two, shown from the rear, is especially extravagant in its depiction of the animal's buttocks, which are disproportionately large in part because its hind end is raised on a dais.

Since we just witnessed Shakespeare's rather involved contemplation of his courser's back end in *Venus and Adonis*, this attention to a horse's ass should not be so surprising. But it does raise the question of what aesthetics is involved in painting a horse's anatomy with such a perspective. Kenneth Clark believes that there are fewer horses painted in medieval art because they have too many curves for the limited techniques of medieval painters, which are precisely what instead fascinate more expert Renaissance artists: "The splendid curves of energy—the neck and rump, united by the passive curve of the belly, and capable of infinite variations, from calm to furious strength—are without question the most satisfying piece of formal relationship in nature."[42] Advances in the knowledge of anatomy naturally enhanced the representation of the horse in art, something Clark notes is most evident in Leonardo da Vinci's studies of the animal. However, the aesthetic appeal of the horse rests in the confusion of visual, tactile, and ethical domains registered in Clark's words. While equine subjects may have had special status for Alberti as aesthetic animals because of their ability to convey moral and social ideology, they "satisfy" in most art and literature because of the plasticity of their physical embodiment, "capable of infinite variations." Erotically mobile, equine subjects prove to be also aesthetically fluid. Passive/active, docile/enraged, hard/soft, submissive/assertive—the horse slides between these binaries, confusing them as it does the compartmentalization of hetero/homoerotic.

Eat Me

"Come," declaims Hotspur in *1 Henry IV*,

> "Let me taste my horse,"
> Who is to bear me like a thunderbolt
> Against the bosom of the Prince of Wales.
> Harry to Harry shall, hot horse to horse,
> Meet, and ne'er part till one drop down a corse. (4.1.119–23)

Figure 20. Albrecht Durer (1471–1528), *Large Horse* (1505). Trustees of the British Museum.

Figure 21. Albrecht Dürer (1471–1528), *Small Horse* (1505). Trustees of the British Museum.

Having analyzed the horsemanship manuals with their appreciation for the sensitivity of the animal, combined with their fluid eroticism of the art of riding, we should find that this passage sounds far less odd than it might otherwise. Hotspur, true to his name, is here champing at the bit to slaughter Prince Harry in battle; "tasting" seems obviously to signify that Hotspur savors the rush to arms, rather than that he intends to slaughter and fricassee his horse. In the Renaissance, tasting still carried its original meaning of touching or feeling with the hands, so it is appropriately used to suggest Hotspur's gentle and gentlemanly caressing of his mount's sides (rather than an abrupt or crude use of spurs, rejected by the horsemanship manuals). However, its more common usage was obviously associated with eating, and therefore with the mouth, so Shakespeare is surely inviting his audience to consider other implications in Hotspur's choice of words.[43]

After all, putting such a word in the mouth of *this character*, who claims to love his wife never more than when he is on horseback, begs us to read in this brief passage another conflation of eroticized acts involving a horse, this time involving gustatory processes.[44] Hotspur's thighs, we might imagine, will kiss his horse's flanks, as he relishes the sensation of pounding across a field toward Hal: the opened thighs of a man astride a powerful beast are thus implicitly figured as a mouth around a piece of food. The moment belongs in the same tradition of the centaur-horseman that makes horse and rider incorporate, one flesh, exemplified by Musidorus and other idealized riders. But it does so via a new point of communion, the mouth, which I would argue is an important shift of bodily emphasis. This is also a moment when Hotspur's identificatory confusion extends through his and Hal's "hot horses" to their own fusion, "Harry to Harry," which will result in the erasure of one of the two in combat. Hotspur fantasizes that having physically merged with his horse, he will strike Hal's "bosom," and the resulting heat of their mutual (passionate) union will dissolve two bodies into one, until death parts them.

Hotspur's character, more than any other in the literary tradition, seems addicted to the physic of riding—he must satisfy his impulsive need for action, his lust for battle, and so must resort to tasting his steed from time to time. Unlike the Norman in *Hamlet*, for instance, another Shakespearean character who is "incorpsed" with his mount (4.7.81–88), and who figuratively dies only in order to become "deminatured / With the brave beast," Hotspur is very nearly too full of life and lust, too "hot" from excessive spurring of his mount and himself.[45] Using up his mount this way does not produce a philosophical Chiron, but rather a raging, appetitive centaur bent on murder. Eating, riding, and sex: in Hotspur's case, these actions align in a peculiar way to convey the culmination of fiery pleasure in riding a powerful beast that surges between one's thighs, a horse that carries one through the bloodletting of war and the assault on a fellow rider who shares one's own name, a horse that facilitates the absorption of the hated-beloved. The result is the mastication of the equid as well as of the enemy. His gluttonous appetite for war leads Hotspur to swallow a succulent, eroticized "hot horse."

It is not, however, that great a distance to travel from the horsemanship treatises' analysis of the means by which horse and rider become "one" to Hotspur's consumption of his mount in a frenzy of identity exchanges, and finally a thorough destruction of self. As the next chapter illustrates, losing oneself in the bodily pleasures of riding brings some literary characters into a far closer alimentary relationship with the equine Other than is comfortable for modern and postmodern readers. Eating your horse, or parts of it or its excreta, while you ride it into battle is, it turns out, a relatively tame version of the digestive exchanges Renaissance medical and husbandry texts recount. As we will see, for at least one famous Shakespearean character mutual consumption loses its promise of "physic" and instead completely expresses the kind of mutual annihilation hinted at in Hotspur's lines.

Chapter 3

Mutual Consumption: The Animal Within

In Shakespeare's *Antony and Cleopatra*, Octavius tells the tale of Antony's desperate foraging during the retreat from Modena to Gaul:

> When thou once
> Wast beaten from Modena, where thou slew'st
> Hirtius and Pansa, consuls, at thy heel
> Did famine follow; whom thou fought'st against,
> Though daintily brought up, with patience more
> Than savages could suffer: thou didst drink
> The stale of horses, and the gilded puddle
> Which beasts would cough at: thy palate then did deign
> The roughest berry on the rudest hedge;
> Yea, like the stag, when snow the pasture sheets,
> The barks of trees thou browsed'st; on the Alps
> It is reported thou didst eat strange flesh,
> Which some did die to look on: and all this—
> It wounds thine honour that I speak it now—
> Was borne so like a soldier, that thy cheek
> So much as lank'd not. (1.4.57–72)[1]

To eat "strange flesh" and drink the "stale of horses" is, in Octavius's estimation, more consistent with Antony's martial identity than the hero's present consumption of delicate fare in Egypt. What marked the hero Antony was that he survived a synaesthetic threat—eating meat that others died merely to *look* on—and that he was able to transform from "daintily" bred noble into savage beast, surpassing in this hybrid form the capacities of both. Octavius intends this account of Antony's multiple transformations to recall the hero to himself, to reawaken the besotted sybarite to his true nature as a "stag" among men, a manly beast whose honor is "wounded" (shades of Adonis) by his present dalliance with Cleopatra and the fruitful, effeminizing world of the Nile. Ironically, in Octavius's perception, Antony was more a "man" when, like a beast, he dined on bark and puddles.

Drinking horses' urine and eating "strange flesh" are not unique to Antony's heroic history; in fact, consuming urine, excrement, and (to us) odd body parts is a commonplace of Renaissance medical texts and husbandry manuals, so Antony's feat of gastronomic hybridity is not especially exceptional, and, as Octavius hints, it might even be therapeutic given the way classical and early modern remedies celebrate the healing powers of bodily wastes. Humans consumed dung and urine, used brains and other internal organs for salves, applied live animals to wounds, ground up both animal and human bones, cooked up messes of snails and worms, and so on in the quest to heal themselves. This process was not one-sided, either: human urine, sweat, and bodily effluvia were fed to animals in a similar attempt to cure. This process of exchange emphasized humans' and animals' common physiology, tending to dissolve theoretical distinctions between the two categories of life.

But the complications of what I am calling in this chapter mutual consumption went far beyond the field of remedies or food. At the most basic level, Renaissance culture understood the process of eating as one that connected the human body to its environment in some surprising ways. Yes, Renaissance humans ate meat, constantly and without apparent ethical qualms; but eating meat was a clear demonstration of the body's essential foulness— meat was inherently corrupt and corrupting, both morally and digestively.[2] In the Renaissance you were what you ate, but you were also all the things that what you ate had consumed in the process of becoming food fit for a human palate. If one ate a pig, for example, one also ate all that pig had ever dined on, which according to many sources could include excrement, foul garbage, even human body parts. "They eat also flesh," notes Edward Topsell, "and herein they differ from most of the ravening creatures, for Dogges will not taste of Dogges' flesh and Beares of Beares, yet will Hogges eat of Swines flesh. . . . And it is found that Swine have not abstained from the flesh of men and children."[3] Having emphasized what thorough omnivores pigs are, Topsell goes on, "To conclude, they love the dung of men."[4] Thus, eating meat could be an act of mutual consumption in a different fashion, putting into the human body at one remove those things that are either ordinarily too devolved to constitute suitable human food or those things that are taboo as human food.

Yet there was one more step in this process: what you ate could also consume you from within. Vermin and parasites dwelt in everything that lived and, once ingested, caused extraordinary suffering, both psychic and physical. Thus, the daily experience of eating was rife with reminders that humans, although putatively the crown of all creation, were embroiled in a multidirectional process that involved eating and being eaten, consuming creation but being invaded, colonized, corrupted, and tortured by it as a result. Antony's consumption of urine and "strange flesh," then, is only one—fairly tame—portion of a complex web of bodily exchanges that rendered early modern "human" identity unstable, inherently degenerative, and emphatically nonsingular. Because the body itself had to violate its own boundaries on a daily basis, especially through acts of consumption, it could not and did not cooperate in policing the supposed distinction of "human" from "animal."

This chapter analyzes several instances of mutual consumption, each connected to the deconstruction of human identity. It considers both the fantasies and the lived somatic experiences of early moderns who engaged in exchanges of sustenance. The cultural consequences of these acts could be positively affirming, as in the case of medical and husbandry literature, which accepted an organic continuum that saw the interpenetration of human and animal bodies as therapeutic; or they could be nightmarish, as in the case of Shakespeare's Hamlet, for whom the idea of providing a dwelling place within the individual body for the most insidious creatures, vermin and parasites, is inimical to the struggle to establish his existence as a unique, individuated human self. Although my subject concerns acts of eating, I exclude those involving wild animals as having more to do with ideologies of domestication versus civilization than with the philosophical issues that face humans who consume and are consumed by familiar creatures of the household and farm. And although the ethical issues attached to meat eating versus vegetarianism are relevant to my argument at many junctures, they are secondary to my investigation of the interpenetration of the flesh, of what it means to share—sometimes willingly, sometimes not—the condition of being embodied.

Strange Remedies

The reason Antony could safely drink the "stale" of horses is that urine is essentially sterile when it emerges from the body; indeed, drinking urine or using it to cleanse wounds is not the worst option when other sources of clean water are lacking. Renaissance medical treatises often use urine as a component in their recipes for various ills. Urine is also warm, which may be significant in a cold climate, and it may, according to Renaissance medical thought, contain important qualities derived from the diet or the nature of the person who passes it. Urine is the product of the "second concoction" of chyle, occurring in the liver, and so achieves a different balance of humors from, for instance, blood, another general remedy in Renaissance treatises.[5] Scholarship is also familiar with the intense scrutiny given to urine as a diagnostic tool, but far less attention has been paid to its use in remedies for both humans and animals—at least, while a great deal of astonished and repetitive attention is paid in the historical and critical literature to the *fact* of its use, as is also true of dung and the variety of strange remedies using body parts, little argument has been offered for *why* excrement and other bodily waste products are a component in such remedies, or what the conceptual consequences might be for the usual distinctions drawn between humans and animals from whom these body substances are taken.

Urine and feces have been used in medicine since ancient times: Galen, Aristotle, and others advise including them for treating everything from acne to fever. According to Dominique Laporte, urine was used to treat headaches and feminine disorders—Pliny, in fact, gives a catalogue of its uses, which resurface in Renaissance folk and professional remedies.[6] Blood from various sources is also a common ingredient: along with semen, milk, and other bodily fluids, blood was, in Piero Camporesi's words, the "juice of life." For one thing, he notes, it was in fact a main sauce in the kitchen, but was also the source of renewal and rejuvenation in medicine.[7] The "blood of a fresh, delicate man, one well-tempered in his humours" could, for instance, slow the aging process, while drinking or bathing in blood restored skin, and eating blood mixed with other herbal ingredients could cure jaundice.[8] Mumia, hair, nails, hooves, mucus, sweat: these and more are regularly included in prescriptions for various ills, sometimes to be ingested, sometimes burned and the smoke inhaled, sometimes applied in salves or possets. Early moderns found therapeutic potential in nearly every part of the body, acting on the premise

that creation was designed for human use, right down to the most unap-
petizing byproducts of animal and human carcasses, living or dead. Galenic
medicine applied cures by a theory of opposites, intended to balance out the
humors; thus, some waste products like urine or dung, which were assumed
to have been transformed humorally by the individual animal's or human's
digestion, could address imbalances efficiently. In the broadest sense, then,
remedies like these effected a disciplining of both body and environment, retaining what was otherwise cast off (waste) to feed the diseased body's need for
humoral regulation. Like the intensely detailed and nuanced humoral regime
itself, which required extensive thought and knowledge to determine the right
balance of hot and cold foods, hot and cold external conditions, and the right
combination of biles, phlegm, and choler for the individual based on native
origin, general temperament, time of year, and so on, cures that included
waste materials or body parts attempted to conserve that waste within the
system rather than allow it to escape exploitation. Excremental material was
thus secured to the service of a rigorous and ordered body within an orderly
universe. Of course the assumption was that in such a tidy scheme as God had
arranged, animals and animal bodies would remain hierarchically subordinate
to human beings. Medical treatises tend to affirm that hierarchy; but books of
home remedies and husbandry manuals do not necessarily do so absolutely.

A sampling of practical recipes for home remedies shows an abundance
of bodily components taken from the household's animal population for
everyday use in healing common afflictions. I include here only a very few,
weighted toward the use of urine, dung, and other body parts because of their
special role in completing a cycle of mutual use that extends to what is definitionally not supposed to be useful. Hannah Woolley's *The Accomplisht Ladys
Delight* (1677) uses urine "from a Man-Child" for an eyewash, and includes
the dung of peacocks in a treatment for the "falling sickness," horse dung for
pleurisy, and goose dung for breast cancer: "Take the Dung of a Goose, and
the juice of Celandine and bray them well in a Mortar together, and lay it to
the sore."[9] Nicholas Culpeper's *Schoole of Physick* recommends rubbing the
brains of a hare or coney on the gums of a child who is teething; using boar's
urine to treat kidney stones, or goat's urine if taken from a goat fed on certain
herbs.[10] According to Culpeper, horse dung in wine cures pleurisy, while dung
from a stallion ("stone-horse") fried in muscatel and applied to the stomach
can cure the flux. Baking the urine of a person sick with the quatrain ague
in a cake and feeding it to a dog will transfer the disease to the unsuspecting
canine host.[11] Gervase Markham's *The English Housewife* suggests wormwood

questioning superiority of humans ⟶
use of animal products for
healing

beaten with the "gall of a bull" for "dim eyes," and a stag's "pizzle" in a recipe to treat the flux.[12] All these examples bring home the fact that such uses of human and animal body wastes and organs were commonplace to nearly every class of reader, whether rural or urban. In Laporte's estimation, waste was "domesticated," or assigned as properly belonging to the home, the domus, where its disposition, use, and eventual disposal became part of the construction of "civilized" subjects.[13]

But the waste-and-body-parts-as-medicine trajectory was not one directional. Human waste was equally salubrious as a treatment for animal ills. The *Widow's Treasure* directs its reader to give cattle swollen with the "taint" a generous helping of "man's urine mingled with salt and Treacle."[14] John Crawshey's *The Compleat Countryman's Instructor* (1636) uses boiled urine with black soap in it to anoint the "warbucks" or "warble," a worm infestation in the animal's skin. He is concerned, rightly, about cattle or horses who ingest blister beetles, which can be deadly: if you find such a case while you are in a field far from your usual sources of treatment, he advises, "piss in your shoe, and take a knife or stick and scrape of the sweatiness, or chafingnesse within your shoe and so mixe with the urine, then give it to the beast to drinke."[15]

Gervase Markham, redacting Conrad Heresbach's regimen for a fighting cock in his *Second Book of the English Husbandman* (1614), implicates the husbandman in a series of exchanges of bodily fluids.[16] To prepare a cock for battle, it must be fed a special diet, warmed in or near an oven, and then: "After foure of the clocke in the Evening, you may take your Cocke out of the stove, and licking his head and eyes all over with your tongue, put him into his Pen, and then taking a good handfull of bread, small cut, put it into his trough, and then pissing into the trough, also give it him to eate, so as he may take his bread out of the warme urine, so this will make his scowring worke, and cleanse both his head and bodie wonderfully."

After the battle,

> the first thing you doe, you shall search his wounds, and as many
> as you can finde you shall with your mouth sucke the bloud out
> of them, then wash them with warme Urine, to keepe them from
> ranckeling, and give him a roule or two of your best scouring, and
> so stove him vp as hot as you can, both with straw and blanketting
> in a close Basket for all that night, then in the morning take him
> forth, and if his head be much sweld, you shall sucke his wounds
> againe, and bathe them with warme Urine, then having in a fine

bagge the powder of the Hearbe Robert, well dryed, and finely
seyrst [sifted or strained], pounce all the sore places therewith,
and then giue the Cocke a handfull of Bread to eate out of warme
Urine, and so put him into the stove againe, and by no meanes
let him feele the ayre till all the swelling bee gone, but twice a day
sucke his wounds, dresse him, and feede him, as is aforesaid.[17]

As Thomas Hamill points out, despite various culturally significant defenses of
cockfighting as a foundational practice of civilization, Markham's version "suggests a system that draws and taxes, a system that demands human excrement
and spit in return for whatever good may come of the blood shed by cocks."[18]
Heresbach and Markham after him are concerned with a regime that imposes
discipline on both human and animal, but in the interests of the ultimate use of
the animal's body to reinforce cultural beliefs about human exceptionalism; yet,
Hamill correctly notes that "the circulation of bodily fluids—the exchange of
sweat, urine, and saliva—disrupts the clear delineation between cocks and men
that the regimental system (even if tenuously) upholds."[19]

What strikes me, however, as much as the exchange of bodily fluids the
fighting cock requires is the strange simulacrum of cooking and eating acted out
in the above passages. Putting the cock into the oven, taking him out, sucking his
wounds, rubbing him with herbs, making him as hot as possible without actually
cooking him: these activities mimic the preparation of a hen for the dinner table,
teasingly bringing both human and cock into a relationship that *performs* cooking and eating, without surrendering the integrity of the cock's valuable flesh. If
so, the passage reimagines meat eating as a process in which humans consume
both self and other, mingled in such a fashion that identity cannot finally be established in one or the other creature. Like the pig that has dined on human flesh
and dung, the cock is an uneasy reminder that dining and physicking are systems
of mutual consumption that transgress the ostensible bodily boundaries between
eater and eaten, beast and caregiver, animal and human.

Hamlet, Parasite

"A man may fish with the worm that hath eat of a king, and eat of the fish that
hath fed of that worm" observes Hamlet, pressed by Claudius to reveal Polonius's whereabouts, tracking a far more unpalatable cyclical process by which all
humans dine regularly on worms, maggots—and other humans: "Not where

he eats, but where 'a is eaten. A certain convocation of politic worms are e'en at him. Your worm is your only emperor for diet. We fat all creatures else to fat us, and we fat ourselves for maggots. Your fat king and your lean beggar is but variable service—two dishes, but to one table. That's the end" (4.3.19–25). In Hamlet's schema, cattle are "fatted" with pasturage that is made rich by worms, who are in turn made healthy and robust by dining on decomposing corpses; when humans rot, they in turn feed the maggots that return flesh to dirt, where good grass may again grow, to feed cattle and so on. All eating is in some degree cannibalism.

Hamlet's observation is, however, simply a commonplace of Renaissance culture, which understood meat eating as invariably a sign of human corruption. John Moore takes up the same theme in his sermon of 1617: "So in our meates (as in a looking-glasse) we may learne our own mortalitie: for let us put our hand into the dish and what doe we take, but the foode of a dead thing, which is either the flesh of beasts, or of birds, or of fishes, with which foode wee so long fill out bodies until they themselves be meate for wormes?"[20] While meat eating affirmed the hierarchical system in which humans were, in Hamlet's language, "served" by lesser creatures, it also subjected human bodies to the indignity of consuming whatever those animals below them on the food chain might in turn consume, a horrifying thought to many early moderns.

Additionally, meat itself was always on the way to putrefaction, a reminder of the body's mortality, and inherently unhealthful. Practices governing the keeping and tenderizing of meat, especially that of game animals, only confirmed its essential rottenness. Hanging meat, or using rich spices to disguise the slightly off flavor of spoiled meats, tended to remind those with some culinary experience that what they consumed was dead and "food for maggots" as much as for humans. Flesh had, in Thomas Tryon's opinion, "more matter for corruption, and nothing so soon turns to putrefaction. Now, 'tis certain, such sorts of food as are subject to putrify before they are eaten, are also liable to the same afterwards. Beside, Flesh is of a soft, moist phlegmy quality; and generates a nourishment of like nature."[21] If you eat what is prone to rot, suggests Tryon, it will cause internal decay; excessive meat eating was blamed by writers on health for the vast majority of ills, despite the sheer demographic fact that most people in the period were starving, not eating vast amounts of meat.

Hamlet's horror at the cyclical nature of food production and consumption is *not* typical of the husbandry manuals that actually gave advice on how to "fat" cattle, care for food animals, and otherwise preserve the health of animals that served, and were served to, early modern humans. And Hamlet's

horror seems reserved for the most verminous interpretation of mutual consumption: he bypasses grass and grain to focus instead on worms and maggots. So perhaps what bothers Hamlet is not so much that humans eat meat,
or that cows graze on grass that may contain worms, but that humans are in
some fashion themselves close kin to parasites, the vermin that they pretend
to fear in their meats.

In this section, I will be revisiting in a highly condensed form an array
of readings of *Hamlet* that cluster around the problem of Hamlet's interiority,
his skeptical relationship to claims about what the body houses, and the connection between both of these and the cultural contexts of human and animal
"nature." Hamlet's world is a universe made up of an almost encyclopedic
procession of persons, animals, objects, processes."[22] In my reading of the play,
Hamlet is fundamentally about parasitism, the kind practiced by animals, and
the kind experienced and practiced by humans—a parasitism that is based on
the confusion of human and animal embodiment, realized in the play mainly
through images of their shared bodily processes. I am not only suggesting that
the play uses metaphors of brute creation to express the material composition of the human body, a frequent element in literary criticism of *Hamlet*—
although that is part of the argument I make. I am going to argue that we
should apprehend its parasites as metaphorical, theoretical, and sometimes
quite literal. I will argue in this section that part of the fear of *Hamlet*, the
character and the play, is that our physical, anatomical selves might *literally*,
physically "house" creation in the form of worms or maggots—or dogs, rats,
mice, and other verminous parasitic entities. Meat eating is implicated in this
system of mutual cannibalization, in which all players become parasites feeding on one another, but it is just one component of a problem that involves
Hamlet's disgust for all things "common," his obsession with death and decay,
and his struggle to assert "that within which passeth show"—a discrete, interior self. *Hamlet* poses a series of questions raised by the experience of shared
corporeality: if our bodies are invaded by and colonized by creatures that
are distinctly other, with their own needs and drives, what kind of "self" can
we claim for human beings? And if humans parasitize other species, feeding
off carcasses like the worms and maggots of Hamlet's imaginary scenario for
Polonius's death, then do we become indistinguishable from the vermin we
house—are we merely "common" vermin as well?

Renaissance human and animal bodies were replete with worms, flukes,
and other internal pests. John Crawshey describes a condition he calls "the
turne," in which a "bladder full of water and little white things like wormes . . .

lieth among the brains" of a horse, "feeding upon them and burning and consuming them."[23] Leonard Mascall's *The Government of Cattel* describes the various kinds of worms that cattle may harbor, those that burrow into the animal's flesh and those that are taken up with feeding.[24] For anyone who has witnessed the excretion of worms in the dung or vomit of a pet or domestic animal, their writhing persistence after expulsion from the body's interior is testimony to their hardiness; worms in cattle or horse dung are merely a reminder of the parasite load that these animals—indeed all animals—must have borne at all times in a premodern world that had no sure ways of killing them off with finality. Humans too lived with worms within: "Men of the pre-industrial age lived—metaphorically and concretely—in a verminous universe unimaginable today,"[25] observes Camporesi as he describes physicians' constant efforts to placate worm colonies within the gut: "Nearly impossible to eliminate, entrenched in their 'sanctuaries', clinging to the narrow cavities of the intestines, master of the entire territory bounded by the throat and sphincter, they could neither be molested nor irritated, under pain of causing the decline of health."[26] William Ramesey's *Helminthologia* (1668) summarizes the misery of intestinal worms "macerating and direfully cruciating" their hosts, mentioning among dozens of examples a man who "evacuated by Urin [*sic*], divers small *worms*," another "macerated by the Head-ache by reason of a *worm*," and yet another who developed a large swelling on the groin from which, when lanced by a surgeon, there "tumbled out two great round *worms*, with much filth."[27] Understood in all these examples is worms' insatiable appetite for human flesh, blood, and other bodily components.

Emetics were dangerous, especially for those with large worm infestations. This perhaps explains more cooperative remedies like that advocated by Nicholas Culpeper, who advises, "If any be troubled with Stomach worms, let him hold a piece of an honey-comb in his mouth and the worms will come out to the Honey."[28] Rather than drink caustics that might annoy the worms within, leading to their rebellion, one should try luring them out with sweets. Hugh Plat, advocating salt as a vermifuge, recalls, "I had six children that died of the worms which I did manifestly perceive as well in the anatomizing of their bodies, as also for that oftentimes they voyded them at their mouths, and when they were drawing to their end, these worms would issue at their nosethrils."[29]

In these descriptions, and the many recipes and treatments included in treatises for human and animal relief from bodily vermin, the creatures who share the human body either in its intestines or burrowed in skin, joints, and other sensitive parts, accrue identity, intentionality, even emotional complex-ity. Mary Fissell has described the way vermin-killing treatises endow their subjects with human qualities.[30] Although she primarily addresses larger mammalian vermin, the same holds true for worms and other internal para-sites. Camporesi's extensive account of Italian medical sources bears out his claims that worms were considered to have definite needs, requirements, that diet and careful support with herbs could assuage. Their cleverness is regis-tered in the number and variety of illnesses that were potentially caused by worms—almost anything, from epilepsy to headache, could be the result of worm activity.[31]

Once the use of microscopes made worms more readily visible, fascina-tion with them increased. In 1690, *Vermiculars Destroyed* by the chemist R. C. appeared in print, with "an Historical Account of Worms Collected from the best Authors":

> *Zacutus Lucitanius*, Tells us of a Patient of his, who voided a Black, Dead Worm, of a pretty length, and thickness, with the Body all over Hairy, a small Head, and a forked Tail.

> *Forestius*, Hath a Patient affected with a Black Worm in the shape of a Weezle, his Cranium being opened and the Worm taken away, which was on the Dura Mater, he Recovered.

> *Jabucius*, Speaks of one that Expelled a Black Worm Five Foot long, Hairy, and of the thicknesse of a Reed.

> *Gesner*, tells us of one that Voided by Stool, a Worm like to a Beetle, Black, long Feet, and Horns.[32]

Worms, that is, had their own history, and now, with this treatise, their own dedicated genre. The author promises to show "what strange and direful En-emies these Depopulating Vermiculars are, not only to Human Bodies, but all Sublunary things," and indeed his portraits, magnified by the "Admirable Invention of the Microscope," establish a cast of fearsome invaders (Figure 22).[33] "Few do imagin [*sic*]," writes the author, "that we carry about with us an Off-Spring of Animals begotten out of our own Blood and Bowels."[34]

Of course, consumed flesh was one source of worms—both in fact (under-cooked meats were and still are one of the most common sources of intestinal parasite infections) and in the Renaissance imagination, which associated the maggots and other wriggling species hatched on and around meat with the meat itself. The practice of hanging meats, especially game meats, before cooking them led to the impression that meat itself could develop in a short space of time a whole colony of tiny creatures; how obvious it must have seemed that meat within the intestines could similarly hatch out into congregations of worms. *Vermiculars Destroyed* suggests taking a piece of flesh and exposing it overnight; in the morning the microscope will reveal that "all the Putrefaction, contracted by the Moon, is degenerated into innumerable Vermiculars."[35] Exposing cheese, milk, vinegar, and similar "Bodies abounding with Putrefaction" will lead to the same results. Too much meat eating could provide too rich an environment in which worms would be encouraged to reproduce and thus lead to misery.[36] Indeed, the overconsumption of meat was associated with sin, for which worms were in turn considered an appropriate punishment. In his *The Hidden Treasures of the Art of Physick* (1659), John Tanner announces his judgment that worms are associated with gluttony, since worms are "bred of such Nourishment as easily putrifieth" and so tend to show up most in "Children and such as are Gluttonous."[37] The potential foulness of the body's interior registered in descriptions of the effects of worms in bad breath, swollen stomach, foul wind, and so on—all reminders not only that worms were eating the body from within or stealing its nourishment, but also that they were themselves voiding into the gut, excrement within excrement. The circular process Hamlet describes, eating meat that has eaten grass that grew in the soil of decomposed flesh produced by worms feeding on corpses, was repeated in miniature inside the human body, where worms went through the entire life cycle over and over again.

For Hamlet, the nature of flesh as food is linked to his obsession with dead, dying, decomposing bodies: from his gleeful grubbing in the bones and dirt of the graveyard scene to his suggestion that the king "nose" Polonius's corpse, which lies "not where he eats but where 'a is eaten" (4.3.19), all his meditations seem to return to the problems of being embodied in flesh— eating, being eaten, passing the matter of the world through the gut: "a king may go a progress through the guts of a beggar" (4.3.32). "Oh that this too, too [solid] flesh would melt,"[38] he soliloquizes, and berates himself, "What is a man, / if his chief good and market of his time / be but to sleep and feed? A beast, no more." His mother's marriage conjures the image of Gertrude "feeding" on both her husbands (1.2.145 and 3.3.67). Hamlet warns Polonius not to allow Ophelia to "walk i' th' sun" lest she conceive by it like the "maggots" it "breeds" in dead dogs.

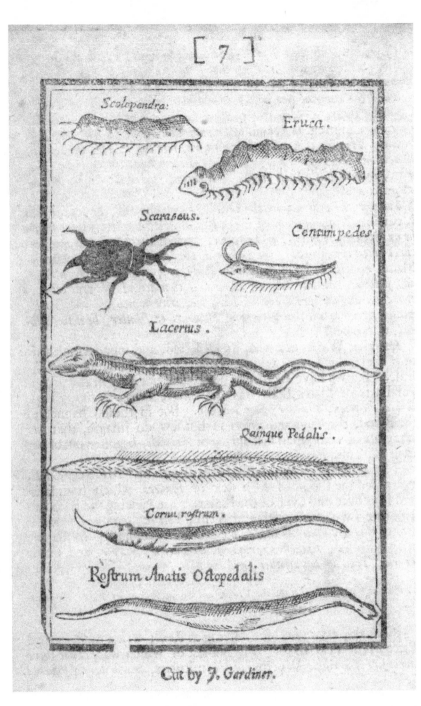

Figure 22. R. C., *Vermiculars Destroyed* (1690) Types of worms. Courtesy of the British Library.

But when Hamlet references worms and maggots, he does so within a network of images that connect these small internal parasites to their larger cousins. It is not merely that we are consumed from within by worms, or that we consume the meat that turns into a verminous mass in our guts. Other, more complex things may dwell within us. David Hillman comments on *Hamlet*'s endless population of mice, rats, weasels, moles, and other mammalian vermin: "These rodential animals," notes Hillman, referring to mice, rats, and others, "share the characteristic of being small and able to gnaw and to burrow into or under a surface with the help of small teeth. . . . They seem to imply . . . an entering of the body."[39] Both rodents and internal parasites thus have the same function in the recycling process. But they also participate in the larger problem of mutual consumption in both material and metaphoric ways that have implications for Hamlet's attempts to establish himself *as* a "self" with some unique interior space—"that within which passeth show." Rina Knoeff has traced early modern medical accounts of "animals within," suggesting that what Hillman wants to characterize as an "implication" (that these rather larger animals might enter and consume the body) was a very concrete, if disconcerting, experience for some. Knoeff recounts several cases of people who claimed to have regurgitated small creatures; worms and flies are not so unusual, but the case of Grietje Willems, who "vomited up a small four-legged creature, which resembled a little dog," seems to stretch belief. Knoeff recounts incidents involving everything from "toads, frogs and lizards" to "a kind of slug with two eyes and an umbilical cord."[40] She argues that these animals were not merely metaphors but were "based on a *real* fear of animals breeding inside people." They show that early moderns "tangibly imagined disease and corruption of the inner body in the form of animals living inside them,"[41] Knoeff's description of small worms within the bone marrow of a human body (Figure 23) makes verminousness structural to human embodiedness.

Two very different Renaissance texts confirm that this experience was widespread. Nicholas Culpeper offers the following remedy:

24. *To expel an Adder being crept into the body.*

If an Adder be crept into a mans body, which is a thing though it happens but seldom, yet it may happen, therefore the cure is not amis; this do. Take a handful of Rue, and bruise it, and boil it in the urine of the party, and let him drink the decoction, and it will make the Beast make more haste out, then it did in.[42]

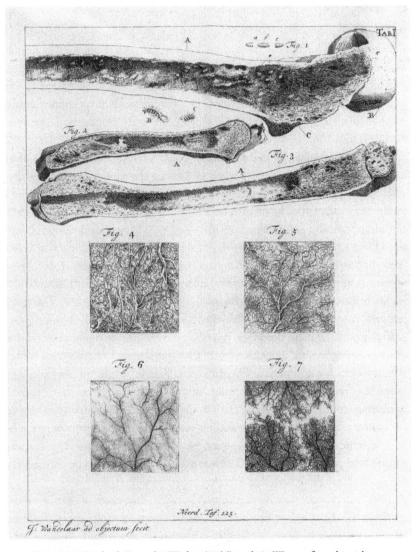

Figure 23. Frederik Ruysch, *Werken* (1744), vol. 3. Worms found inside bones. Courtesy of Groningen University Library.

Here we have a fantasy of invasion and colonization by the quintessential signifier of human sinfulness, the adder, remedied by the ingestion of urine. An English pamphlet of 1655 on prodigies tells of an innkeeper who died after voiding "Twelve Serpents . . . some having heads like Toads and Horses, and others like Newts and Dogs." While it belongs to a genre of monstrous

births, celestial events, and other such phenomena, this report's yoking together of (once again) the serpent, innkeeping, and Gorgon-like hybridity in
the expelled creatures begs us to read this as a cautionary allegory of human
corruption and devolution caused by excessive consumption. The innkeeper's
identity is twice compromised, first by the terrible creatures he has grown
within his guts, and second by their own confused identity, spontaneously
synthesizing mammal with reptile. Grietje Willems, in comparison, seems almost restrained in her mammalian vomitus.

Animals populate Hamlet's language to signify the "common" fate of all
human beings: "all that lives must die / Passing through nature to eternity"
(1.2.73–74), becoming a "quintessence of dust" (2.3.316) in no different a
fashion than any brute beast with no soul.[43] I would argue that the very continuum of creation enforces cannibalism—we eat that which is not stably distinct from what we are, since we share common animal qualities with it (we
"sleep and feed" like beasts). As Thomas Browne puts it, the idea that "*all flesh
is grass*, is not onely metaphorically, but literally, true; for all those creatures
we behold are but the herbs of the field, digested into flesh in them, or more
remotely carnified in our selves. Nay further, we are what we all abhor, *Anthro-
pophagi* and Cannibals, devourers not onely of men, but of our selves; and that
not in an allegory, but a positive truth: for all this mass of flesh which we behold, came in at our mouths."[44] Worms actually living in the gut are merely an
immediate reminder of this. "Parasite" means literally "to eat next to" (*para* =
next, *sitos* = food); Michel Serres clarifies that "the parasite comes from beyond
the border as a contaminant . . . mix[ing] up two things that really ought to be
kept separate."[45] In Hamlet's perplexed imagination, and in the degenerating
world of the play, confusions of identity, overlaps of physical being, are figured
through mammalian as well as invertebrate parasites.

When Francisco asserts at the play's outset that there is "not a mouse
stirring" (1.1.11) in Denmark, he could not be more wrong. There are mice,
rats, moles, weasels, foxes, and other critters skittering about, slinking onto
every page of the play, lurking behind the arras, gnawing on the dead in the
graveyard, thumping beneath the stage. Hamlet's "animals appear at a number
of highly-charged moments," and so I think they deserve a critical space of
their own.[46] The ghost's voice, demanding that Horatio and Marcellus swear
to keep it secret, rises from beneath their feet like some subterranean haunt;
"Well said, old mole," approves Hamlet of its persistence as they move about
to avoid it, "Canst work i'th'earth so fast?" (1.5.171–72).[47] Polonius's extermi-
nation as the rat behind the arras caps Hamlet's wrenching confrontation with

his mother; and Hamlet promises to "catch the conscience of the king" in a play called "The Mousetrap." Moreover, David Hillman connects Hamlet's madness, which is the thing most perplexing to the play's other characters, with accounts of vermin animals' roles in demonic possession.[48]

Mammalian vermin like those listed above are, as Fissell notes, usually represented in early modern texts as trickster figures, endowed with more than animal intelligence, engaged in an eternal battle with humans over real materials essential to human existence—meat, grain, fabrics, wood. Mammalian vermin "poached human food" in which a great deal of time and effort had been invested.[49] Hunting vermin was thus an exceptional challenge. Rat catching, for example, required not merely knowledge of rats and their behaviors, but skills with snares and poisons to be pitted against exponential numbers of quick and clever rodents—talents that could arouse suspicion of the vermin hunter himself (Figure 24). In one series of ballads, "The Famous Ratketcher, with His Travels," and "The Ratketchers Return out of France," the eponymous hero blends ideas of entrapment with social violation. He wanders far and wide throughout England, gleefully seducing women while plying his trade. His unsuspecting prey, "lict" his poisons until they "swell in the waste." The association of travel with the rat catcher's insidious skills with potions makes him the ideal figure for moral transgression that escapes the usual forms of capture and punishment intended to contain bad behavior. He proceeds like an infection throughout the country and even into France, emblazoning his conquests on his banner. But as a traveling source of poison, the rat catcher's nature is indistinguishable from the creatures he hunts. In fact, beast fables, tales of rat catchers, and manuals for the ridding of vermin all seem to come to the same conclusion: that humans and vermin engage in a competition to outtrick, outthink, outsmart one another, but in their constant struggle each becomes more like than unlike the other.

Hamlet's many references to vermin, and Hamlet's self-election to the role of royal rat catcher, thus carry implications for Hamlet's identity; the play's allusions to vermin animals collapse hunter with hunted, or in this case, rat catcher with rat. After all, Hamlet becomes himself a clever, tricksy creature in the course of his pursuit of Claudius. More than simply accepting Hillman's tentative association of Hamlet's madness with vermin animals, I think we should go further, that we should read his madness as the exercise of the very qualities associated with verminous creatures. As a madman, Hamlet moves unpredictably into and out of spaces from which he should be barred—his mother's chamber, for instance, where he stabs "in brainish apprehension"

Figure 24. Rat catcher with tools of his trade: a box of poisons, dead rats. Drawing by Adriaen van de Venne, ca. 1620–26. Trustees of the British Museum.

(4.1.11) the rat Polonius—and glides through social interactions during which he seems to occupy an alternate reality. Conversing with Polonius, Ophelia, or Rosencrantz and Guildenstern, his remarks are at cross-purposes to the apparent topics under discussion; his discourse, we might say, skitters crazily up walls, under foot, and into places others find unnerving. In the clouds he sees camels, weasels, and whales (3.2.385–91), a kaleidoscope of animal images that leave Polonius struggling to respond sensibly. "Hide fox, and all after," Hamlet cries to Rosencrantz and Guildenstern as they hunt Polonius's corpse (4.2.31). Ophelia laments the overthrow of his reason (3.1.151), but Hamlet shares with the pesky vermin of Denmark a "crafty" madness (3.1.8), filled with "method" and acknowledged by Claudius to be dangerous (3.1.165–67).

Then there is "The Mousetrap," the play-trap laid by Hamlet to force Claudius's "occulted gilt" to "unkennel" itself (2.2.612; 3.2.81). While this concoction *should* cast Hamlet as principal rat catcher, it may in fact work to trouble that identity, blurring the boundaries between himself and Claudius, and the division of vermin from vermin hunter. Martha Ann Oberle has suggested that Hamlet's mousetrap is most like an apparatus Leonard Mascall describes in *A Book of Fishing with Hook and Line* (1590), the "square box trap" that is designed to entice the mouse to trap itself.[50] The title of the play Hamlet has commissioned "serves as a warning to his royal audience that Hamlet is on the hunt for truth," concludes Oberle.[51] But, where Oberle attributes to this trap the quality of providence that can impose equal justice on "beast and Man," I think it does something quite different. Indeed, it is entirely possible to argue that it is Hamlet, not Claudius, who is caught by his own trap, like a trickster fox, weasel, or rat ensnared finally by its own exceeding cleverness: he cannot, after all, kill Claudius once the trap is sprung but instead turns his frustrated rage into the murder of Polonius, which then puts him at his uncle's mercy, bound for England on a ship with letters that instruct his execution at journey's end. In the vermin pamphlets and literature analyzed by Fissell, greed is a defining quality of such animals, sometimes leading to comic tales in which they are caught because they can't give up a choice morsel. "Our natures do pursue / Like rats that ravin down their proper bane / A thirsty evil," laments another Shakespeare character, confirming that human and nonhuman animals share this greedy appetite (*Measure for Measure* 1.2.128–30). Hamlet, who has already indirectly aligned himself with his uncle ("My father's brother, but no more like my father / Than I to Hercules," 2.2.152–53), is also like Claudius, a good rat catcher, hard to pin down, facile with language, subtle of purpose—but too greedy about the circumstances under which he determines the king must die. Claudius dispenses poison, false accusations, and a range of trickery to rid himself of Hamlet; Hamlet, using much the same tools, attempts the life of the king. Both simultaneously exhibit qualities of rat and rat catcher—cleverness, facility with language, mastery of traps and poisons, self-destroying greed.

There is, however, another characteristic of mammalian vermin registered in the treatises that is worth considering alongside Hamlet's failure to distinguish himself from his rodential peers. Moles, rats, and mice can be trapped by their affiliation to those of their own kind. Most vermin-killing manuals include at least one version of a trap that relies on either sympathy or lust to catch their targets. Leonard Mascall, for instance, recommends a trap for moles that involves shutting females, or does, into a pot so that their cries attract the males of their species who then also fall into the pots.[52] A *Necessary Family Book* of 1688 includes the following version of such a trap for rats: "Take two or three living Rats or Mice, and put them into an Earthen Pot, the[n] stop the Pot close, that the Rats or Mice may not come forth, then make a fire of Ashen-Tree wood, and place the Pot on the fire, and when it burneth moderately, all the Rats and Mice in the House, hearing the cry of those in the Pot, will run immediately to the place where the Pot standeth on the fire, as if they did intend by force to deliver the Rats and Mice in the Pot."[53] This goes beyond Fissell's list of the attributes of humanized trickster rodents in that it suggests fellow feeling or sympathy on the animals' part, enough to drive them to rescue their trapped brothers. Vermin are not merely human in their worst characteristics; they also match human degrees of compassion and attachment. What incapacitates them in the latter trap is their response to the cry of their own kind. While the author attempts to demonize this, and other moments of rat affiliation (the image of rats and mice congregating like a mob is repeated in a prior recipe, which leads to mice or rats rushing upon a pot of oil "as if it were an Assembly of an Army"[54]), there is no way to deflect the conclusion that mice and rats are perfectly capable of recognizing kinship with their own and privileging it enough to put themselves at risk.

Such a quality lends itself to metaphorization in the human realm, so that discussions of both mammalian and invertebrate vermin are often inextricably woven with fears about humans en masse, especially those who represent an internal threat to social order. Thus Camporesi can draw a strong connection between medical discourse and discourses concerning social vermin of the two-legged variety—vagabonds, drifters, the unwashed masses of the city, the diseased poor.[55] The problem for a play like *Hamlet* is that social distinction, which allows at least a tenuous boundary between rich and poor, high born and low, has gone the way of all flesh: "Alexander died. Alexander was buried. Alexander returneth to dust; the dust is earth; of earth we make loam; and why of that loam whereto he was converted might they not stop a beer barrel" (5.1.209–12). No more than Alexander can be distinguished from the poorest beggar after his dust mingles with the earth can Claudius, King Rat, and Hamlet, rat catcher in chief, be distinguished from one another; even Hamlet's conscience, the faculty that makes him answerable to his father's ghost yet halts him at the moment of crisis from killing Claudius, is little different from a rat's sense of obligation and affiliation to one of his own kind. When he stages "The Murder of Gonzago," Hamlet identifies its killer as "one Lucianus, nephew to the king" (3.2.242). He has unwittingly identified himself as the rat and affirmed his kinship with his uncle.

The play's final scene is appropriately a veritable orgy of entrapment, greed, and trickery fit for such a collection of vermin as are gathered in Denmark's castle halls. Not satisfied with one poison, clever/greedy Claudius puts two in the mix; Gertrude, "carous[ing] to [Hamlet's] fortune" (5.2.291), swipes the cup meant for Hamlet and swills the one, while Laertes falls "as a

woodcock to mine own springe" (5.2.309) to the effects of the other. All are
finally destroyed by their own verminous natures.

Human Host

According to Michel Serres, science would like to deny that large animals and
humans can both be parasites—they must be hosts or predators because "we
do not live in the animals we eat."[56] But in fact we do, in their skins, in their
feathers, in silks, so the bright line science would like to draw disappears into
fable. Philosophical attempts to construct "the human" without parasites are
likewise doomed in Serres' view. The Cartesian experiment in knocking down
edifices of established opinion, for instance, invites his comparison between
Descartes and "a man who sets his house on fire in order to hear the noise the
rats make in the attic at night." He then tries to rebuild it without rats: "But
at night, the rats return to the foundation. I was thinking yesterday, what did
you do in the meantime? You slept, if you please, you ate, dreamt, made love,
and so forth. Well, the rats came back. They are, as the saying goes, always already there. Part of the building."[57] There is no system without parasites; there
is no theory of the human without them. I would add that there are no bodies,
no plays, no theaters, no houses, no cities—and no critics of all these things
without them either. In Serres' work, meaning is made not by the harmonious,
clean, rat-free model of communication, but by the parasite itself. Parasite,
in a fortuitous accident of French, can also signify white noise, the static of
communication, the residue of the message; that noise is the "space of transformation." Without static, the message disappears. Only the vermin-infested
structure, the castle walls teeming with mice and rats, the castle orchard overrun with weasels, the spaces of the human—internal and external—replete
with worms, slugs, even small dogs denote a world in which "the human" is a
concept with any content.

Post-Cartesian humanity tried its level best to constitute the human
without the parasite. Simon Estok has dubbed the drive to eliminate anything
and everything that partakes of "animal" nature, or of the messiness of the
natural world with its dirt, its parasites, its smells and foul things, "ecophobia." He draws a direct line from growing dis-ease with the body's porousness
and openness to the environment in the early modern period to twentieth-
century Western eradication of signs of the body's natural state in everything
from deodorant use to antibacterial cleansers for the home.[58] The modern and

postmodern body is "hygienic," meaning it has eradicated all memory or evidence that it is, in fact, a body and not a machine. Ironically, if we accept this version of history, Descartes triumphed not just in making the human utterly distinct from the animal by naming the latter a machine, but he also inadvertently transformed the human into something else, something that ends up looking far more like a machine than a living organism.

But science is gradually leading us back to a model of the body as an open system, a cooperative venture between human and parasite. In the 1980s, physicians began to offer explanations for the extraordinary rise in allergies and asthma cases among children in industrialized societies; the "hygiene hypothesis," as it became known, sought to explain this phenomena in terms of children's co-development with bacteria, viruses, and parasites in their environment.[59] The more hygienic, that is, free of normal levels of contaminants, the home in which children were raised, the less early exposure children had to these things, which in turn allowed children's immune systems to strengthen, and the fewer targets the immune system had in childhood, the more likely it was to turn against the body itself. The human body is home to a vast array of flora and fauna: the eyebrows, for instance, are occupied by *Demodex follicularum*, the harmless eyebrow mite, while the human gut contains 170 different species of bacteria that help digestion. Even as we feed on the flesh of other animals, we are ourselves a veritable feast for living things.

Recently, more radical cases of human dependence on parasites and vermin have arisen. The relatively benign leech is being used again to reduce swelling in patients with amputations or limb restoration, and even maggots can have benefits in wound treatment where other remedies are unavailable. More dangerous parasites have also proven therapeutic in certain contexts. Western cultures, for instance, have a much higher incidence of intestinal disorders like Crohn's disease, ulcerative colitis, and other inflammatory bowel diseases. Medical hypotheses suggest, and some experiments confirm, that the reason for this is the absence of certain parasites that are common in third world and developing countries. Whipworms (*Trichuris trichiura*, a roundworm that usually infects when its eggs are ingested accidentally), which are widely present in countries as close to the United States as Mexico but absent from American intestines, can actually prevent some bowel disorders by giving the body's immune system a legitimate target for its actions.[60] In the absence of real parasites the immune system apparently turns against its "host" (it is an interesting twist to think of one's own bone marrow and blood as divisible, even hostile to one's own body, but that is how autoimmune diseases work). Hookworms, too, have been used with some success to treat extreme cases of asthma, although this is a controversial use for a dangerous, even life-threatening parasite. The hookworm burrows through the skin, reproducing in the human intestine and then shedding huge numbers of eggs along with human feces. Thus, a sure-fire way to get oneself infected with hookworms is to walk barefoot in feces, or even consume them, something at least one committed allergy sufferer has successfully done: Jasper Lawrence, who has been devastated by asthmatic attacks from his severe allergies for most of his life, found the literature on hookworms as a possible treatment for his condition and traveled to Cameroon to shuffle through a variety of latrines, where he became infected.[61]

Treatments featuring parasites are collectively termed helminthic therapies and are becoming more common, if not fully accepted as medically supervised treatments at present. Their resurgence suggests that when, in the four hundred years since Hannah Woolley, Nicolas Culpeper, Leonard Mascall, and other similar authors wrote their advice and recipes, medicine became "scientific" and rejected those treatments, it may have thrown the baby out with the proverbial bathwater. The colonized, infected body that Hamlet repudiates has returned to haunt postmoderns in the industrialized, hygienic West. We burned down the house; but the rats have returned.

Chapter 4

Animal Architectures: Urban Beasts

The body that *Hamlet* explores, the body that horrifies and perplexes Hamlet, is so thoroughly colonized by vermin that it loses its individuality to the throngs of creatures sharing its internal architectures. But this should not come as much of a surprise: in the ghost's account of Claudius's murderous assault on Hamlet Senior, we learn at the outset that the play's absent core—the body of the old king, Hamlet's father—is already a corpse, thus inhabited by multitudes of worms and other feeders in the earth. Because Hamlet Senior's corpse is also the *corpus politicum*, it further has to be metaphorically understood as a collective, synonymous with the architectural and ideological body that is the state of Denmark:

> Upon my secure hour thy uncle stole
> With juice of cursed hebona in a vial,
> And in the porches of my ears did pour
> The leprous distilment, whose effect
> Holds such an enmity with blood of man
> That swift as quicksilver it courses through
> The natural gates and alleys of the body. [1]

Resting in his orchard, Hamlet Senior occupies a secluded "secure" space within the confines of the castle walls, his seat of rule; the architecture—porches, gates, alleys—of both his body and his nation are defended by the garden and castle walls, until breached by Claudius's poison, which travels like an invading army through a city.

The analogies that link human microcosm (the body) and communal macrocosms (the castle, the city, the abstraction of the state) in this passage are commonplace in early modern writing; their most frequent expression naturalizes social relations by comparing a well-ordered political and social world to the harmonious and temperate body. Renaissance medicine marveled at the elegant plan of the body's internal structures, so like the well-planned castle, estate, or town, appropriating them to describe the balances and attentive regulation necessary to maintain correct relations between the rational leadership and the unruly masses of the commonwealth. Literary works like Spenser's *The Faerie Queene* (in which Guyon is restored in Book 2 by a visit to the House of Alma), and medical self-help treatises like Thomas Elyot's *Castell of Health* (1541), elaborate the analogy's insistence on self-government in the interests of communal prosperity.[2]

The reciprocity of the analogy that compares the body to the state, city, or castle is equally evident in architectural theory from Vitruvius on. In his *Ten Books on Architecture*, Vitruvius establishes the compelling symmetry of the human body as the basis for all edifices: "Without symmetry and proportion there can be no principle in the design of any temple; that is, if there is no precise relation between its members as in the case of those of a well-shaped man."[3] The Renaissance confirmed this relationship in famous instances, such as da Vinci's image of Vitruvian Man, or Alberti's consistent reference to the human body as the paradigm for good building: "We should imitate Nature throughout," Alberti writes regarding vaulting, "that is, bind together bones and interweave the flesh with nerves." The Italians, he notes, through their "inborn thrift," were "the first who made their buildings like animals [that is, bodies]" because "grace of form could never be separated or divorced from suitability for use."[4] In seventeenth-century England, Henry Wotton elaborated: "For what are the most judicious Artisans but the Mimiques of Nature? This led me to contemplate the Fabrique of our owne Bodies, wherein the High Architect of the world, had displayed such skill, as did stupifie, all humane reason. There I found the Hart as the fountain of Life placed about the Middle, for the more equall communication of all the vitall spirits. The Eyes seated aloft, that they might describe the greater Circle within their view. The Armes projected on each side, for ease of reaching."[5] Where Vitruvius analyzes the best symmetry for a temple to the gods, Wotton makes God the ultimate Architect, the human body the temple where his best work is manifest. Indeed, when René Descartes needed a metaphor for his work in the *Discourse on Method*, he turned to the image of houses in a city. The imperfections of a method based on the opinions of many are like buildings designed by committee: "Thus it is observable that the buildings which a single architect has planned and executed, are generally more elegant and commodious than those which several have attempted to improve." Tearing down his own "house" leads to a useful "reformation" of the "body of the sciences" that can advantage the "state."[6]

However, if, as I argued in Chapter 3, the human body is always already inhabited by animal others, then we must, as a logical extension of that discovery, inquire into how the urban and domestic architectures implicated in the body/city, body/state, and body/house analogies might likewise be defined by nonhuman creatures. Up to now, this book has considered the ways animals define the interior spaces of the human body, its anatomy, its pleasures, its morbidity. In this chapter, I turn to the concrete architectures in which human bodies and animal bodies encounter each other—the walls, streets, subterranean spaces, houses, and palaces of the urban and rural environments, as well as the representational partitions and fabrications for which architectures are the medium and the message.

The first chapters of this book have confirmed what others studying animals in the Renaissance have observed, that nonhuman creatures tend to subvert conceptual boundaries between human and nonhuman, but it is worth observing at this point that animals are also transgressive of *physical* environmental boundaries, of both the built edifices of human creation and the conceptual edifices from which built spaces emerge, and which they express. Architecture is at its root a process of codifying the means of enclosing bodies, usually the human body; its linearity is inscribed on the nonlinear paths of nature to establish boundaries of property, of propriety, of purity. Architecture, observes Catherine Ingraham, "attempt[s] to keep things in line, to keep things proper to themselves."[7] Architecture disciplines bodies and the biological process of life, committed as it is, in Ingraham's image, to "standing up" for itself. Animals, if sanctioned domesticated varieties, are sometimes imagined in architectural theory as tamed by the disciplines of architecture; if wild varieties, as the chaotic other without which architecture's linearity would not recognize itself, resisting straight lines, right angles, and regularity of compartmentalization or division of space. Yet animals challenge even the convenience of this wild/tame binary. At the most basic level, for instance, animals cross lines we usually draw imaginatively between wild or rural places and towns or cities—like *Hamlet*'s worms, foxes, rats, and mice, animals creep, skitter, crawl, slink, or fly where they will, nest and feed where they like, and thus resist human struggles to establish the property of the human in specific places; they also, by violating the classifications architecture both arises from and encodes (wild/domesticated, rural/urban, inside/outside), resist conceptual and linguistic boxing in.[8] Animals tend to defeat efforts represented by walls, doors, windows, floors, or fences to demarcate types of space, to contain and restrict identity to a fixed location. The boxes "tame" and "wild," for instance, do not describe the existence of actual animals, which blithely move into and out of places as they are able, shifting from one spot to another at will; a rat, a cat, a bird, a dog, a mouse may be fully wild one day, tame another, or revert to feral and back to tame at random as circumstances dictate. In a counterdevelopment, some few wild species may have been unexpectedly domesticated by human architecture itself: Hans Zinsser speculates that the inexplicable disappearance of the Black Death after its epidemic levels through the seventeenth century may have to do with the "increased domestication" of rats—instead of recurring mass migrations from one place to another, the development of cellars, attics, food storage buildings kept rats "contentedly at home" where they could not spread disease with such efficiency.[9]

Animals are messy, despoiling spaces, places, and categories. There are a number of boundaries that this chapter, in turn, crosses willfully to follow animals' architectural influence: I look at theories of construction and design, at material animal- and human-made structures, at space as social construct, at urban places, interior, exterior, categories of character, urban history—with the hope that I will intentionally implicate all of these in demonstrating that like human bodies, animal bodies are essential to all manifestations of what we call "architecture."

As we have already seen, animals were not absent from early theories of architecture: Vitruvius, Alberti, and Wotton all saw architecture as a natural activity, analogous to the construction of nests by birds, bees, ants, and other animals—the best human architects are but belated and often less perfect imitators of animals, "Mimiques of Nature" as Wotton says.[10] Vitruvius offers this pragmatic role for animals in human building projects:

> Our ancestors, when about to build a town or an army post, sacrificed some of the cattle that were wont to feed on the site proposed and examined their livers. If the livers of the first victims were dark-coloured or abnormal, they sacrificed others, to see whether the fault was due to disease or their food. They never began to build defensive works in a place until after they had made many such trials and satisfied themselves that good water and food had made the liver sound and firm. If they continued to find it abnormal,

they argued from this that the food and water supply found in such
a place would be just as unhealthy for man, and so they moved
away.[11]

Since they shared bodily needs for clean water and uncorrupted food sources,
humans could use animals as prognosticators of healthful sites.

Animal architecture continued to fascinate early moderns who understood
the process of building as an essentially social and cultural activity. Bees and ants
are more traditionally models for morality in Renaissance literature. Their industry inspires envious comparisons to humans, as in the case of Bernard Mandeville's *Fable of the Bees* (1705), or Milton's ironic praise of the devils in hell
building Pandemonium: "As bees in springtime . . . So thick the airy crowd /
Swarmed and were straitened."[12] In the view of Thomas Moffet, "The most high
God did create all other creatures for our use; so especially the Bees, . . . that as
mistresses they might hold forth to us a pattern of Politick and Oeconomick
virtues."[13] As Jonathan Woolfson points out, bees were complexly liminal to
human culture and cultivation: they "formed a part both of untamed nature
and of a human agricultural and economic order. They ruled over themselves
and were self-sufficient and yet could be exploited by humans for honey, with its
alimentary and medicinal properties, and wax, which combined practical and
liturgical uses. Indeed for all these reasons bees were often classified as occupying
an indeterminate position between tame and wild nature."[14] Their hives, like the
webs of spiders, or the conical and spherical nests of birds, likewise functioned
to remind humans that mathematical regularity, symmetry, and harmony in
proportion were natural principals of construction.[15]

Modern or postmodern writers who consider the distinction between animal and human building generally do not credit animals with the capacity to
produce, that is with generating a consciously weighted cultural act. They find
instead in animal labor a "natural" sculpting of bodily material that sidesteps
issues of a stratified and exploitative labor system. The difficulty that current
theories of space have in assimilating the roles of animals reminds us that,
where animals are concerned, we continue to wrestle with a philosophical drag
from an Enlightenment *Weltanschauung*. In *The Production of Space* Henri
Lefebvre announces that "nature does not produce" and meditates on Marx's
initiating question in *Capital* about "whether a spider might be said to *work*:"

Does a spider obey blind instinct? Or does it have (or, perhaps better, *is* it) an intelligence? Is it aware in any sense of what it is doing?

> It produces, it secretes and it occupies a space which it engenders
> according to its own lights. . . . Should we think of this space of the
> spider's as an abstract space occupied by such separate objects as the
> body, its secretory glands and legs, the things to which it attaches
> its web. . . . No, for this would be to set the spider in the space of
> analytic intellection, the space of discourses . . . preparing the way
> for a rejoinder of the type: "Not at all! It is nature (or instinct, or
> providence) which governs the spider's activity."[16]

Lefebvre wishes, as Ingraham describes it, to "unify theories of discourse . . .
with specific analyses of 'real' spaces," that is to redress the overreliance on
discourse alone within some poststructuralist theory, and so he cannot reduce
the spider to an abstraction; it "transcends the realm of 'thingness.'"[17] But
equally he cannot tolerate the idea that the spider has a non-thinglike capacity
for thought, feeling, reflection, and other anthropomorphic characteristics:
"Clearly not: the spider produces, which manifestly calls for 'thought,' but
it does not 'think' in the same way as we do." Where the "gestures, traces,
marks" that create space in human architecture are concerned, the spider may
"perform" gestures but cannot be said to understand the concepts of traces
and marks: "and yet everything happens 'just as though' [it] did."[18] Although
he insists on freeing theories of space from Cartesian reductiveness and poststructuralist abstraction, Lefebvre cannot make the leap to dismantle fully
the human-animal distinction. As a result, his conceptual spider ends up ab-
surdly (unintentionally and rather agonizingly) anthropomorphized—capable
of thought, not a thing, capable of a kind of "performance" of intentional
gestures—yet not anthropomorphic, that is, not *really* capable of any of these.
Ingraham comments: "The spider, without too much exaggeration, gets the
better of Lefebvre": "If the spider secretes a residence, as Lefebvre wants to
argue, it seems to do so only to satisfy a general lack of co-operation of the animal in Lefebvre's bigger project, which is, as is well known, to form a 'science
of space.' In some respects, the theoretical, philosophical and political problems of the spider is [*sic*] that it is all too much like human aliveness—it acts
as if it were thinking, building, designing."[19] The "as if" becomes a point of
extreme pressure; Ingraham notes the proliferation of quotation marks around
terms in Lefebvre's text at this juncture, which discount the value or sidestep
the implications of the animal for the philosophical project to which they are
harnessed. She accounts for a subtractive process that persists in Lefebvre's
work: at the same time that "animals [become] beings that result from the

subtraction of history and self-consciousness from humans," they magnify in importance as philosophical instruments.

Renaissance descriptions of animal builders are more comfortable about anthropomorphizing animal acts of building and about crediting them with the attendant thought processes and cultural context for production, since the mirroring of animal and human allows writers to naturalize divisions and distinctions within the human group. Edward Topsell's account of beavers as builders, for example, constructs a whole castorine economic system, replete with signifiers of class status and a labor strategy involving fellow beavers:

> These beavers use to builde them Caves or Dens neere the waters,
> so as the water may come into them, or else they may quickly
> leape into the water, and their wit or naturall invention in build-
> ing of their caves is most wonderfull. . . . The tree being down and
> prepared, they take one of the oldest of their company, whose teeth
> could not be used for the cutting, (or as other say, they constraine
> some strange Beaver whom they meet withal) to fall flat on his
> backe . . . and upon his belly lade they all their timber, which they
> so ingeniously worke and fasten into the compasse of his legs that it
> may not fall, and so the residue by the taile, drawe him to the water
> side, where these buildings are to be framed, and this the rather
> seemeth to be true, because there have bene some such taken, that
> had no haire on their backs: but were pilled, which being espied by
> the hunters, in pitty of their slavery, or bondage, they have let them
> go away free.[20]

Beavers, as Topsell avers, maintain "roads" to their selected trees, and judge the direction of a gnawed tree's fall, but they also engage in a system of labor that either assigns tasks according to physical capability or suborns labor from way-ward individuals. Beaver and hunter share a world of readable inscriptions, one of which is the bodily sign (hairless backs) of slave labor. Not only do beavers consciously produce their "natural" lairs, but they have a recognizable stratification designed to extract the maximum benefit from the labor of older, toothless members; further, they occupy a clearly demarcated space within the "wild" the boundaries of which, if violated by beaver passers-by, allow those with "property" in the area to demand bondage from "strangers" (a term often applied to out-of-towners in London). The social, economic, cultural, even national systems of architecture, in Topsell's report on beaver-builders, rationalize and justify political, social, and so ideological classifications that undergird human systems. But the price of producing this version of false consciousness is the imagination of a full-blown animal culture.

Beavers and bees create relatively static architectures, however dangerously cultural their work may be. A peculiar and quite different challenge derives from animals' deconstructive movement in space and time, which disrupts the flow of architectural space. Animals in motion—the creeping, digging, wall-vaulting kinds of motion that do not conform to the order of Renaissance architectural theories—overwhelm the generation of categorically defined spaces, spaces meant to have integrity, in much the same way that they overwhelm Hamlet's efforts to distinguish human from animal interiority. Claudius's penetration of Hamlet Senior's secure orchard relies on his own allegorical species and characterological mobility: he is at once serpent, invading the Edenic world of the father's garden, and rat, lurking and hiding to corrupt human space with his leavings, and also rat catcher, bringing the poison to exterminate his enemy. To a cat, a dog, a rat, a mouse, or a snake, a window is a door, and every gap is a window. Architectural classification gives way, if only momentarily, transiently, at the instant of occupation or traversing by the animal invader. The whole ethos of land enclosure, that Renaissance invention, mitigates against random movements and nonlinear, nonhierarchized usages of space, yet the creatures that are enclosed often fail to appreciate their containment, and indeed may be inspired to yet greater efforts at violating the orderliness of their neat boxes.[21]

Perhaps because they can be so hard to pin down, to arrest in time through traditional modes of representation, or perhaps precisely because they deconstruct the entire project of Renaissance architecture, animals' role in creating and defining spatial categories is seldom recognized or studied in depth. However, from the invention of the sentimentalized bourgeois home to the architectures that consecrate interiority and subjectivity, animals are often there first in the flesh and thus either anticipate the arrival of meaning or establish the terms in which people can think a thing, a place—or themselves—into existence.

One important example of animal influence in creating spatial and social definition emerges from the history of pet keeping. Keith Thomas has located an explosion in pet ownership in the late sixteenth century and the early seventeenth: "Pet-keeping had been fashionable among the well-to-do in the Middle Ages. . . . But it was in the sixteenth and seventeenth centuries that pets seemed to have really established themselves as a normal feature of the middle-class household."²² Yet it is the complex *spatial* interaction of animals and humans that may make the very concept of a middle-class household possible in the first place. The *Oxford English Dictionary* defines "pet" as a cade lamb (rejected by its mother) taken into the household to be hand raised. This usage of the word indicates how pets transgress and redefine spatial boundaries—as Ingrid Tague points out, there must be a household whose boundaries are well demarcated and which is free from animals before bringing a lamb inside to nurture it would signify something distinct from normal husbandry.²³ Medieval peasant housing, mingling as it often did farm animals and human beings, does not yet have the conceptual and physical characteristics that allow pets to exist; presumably only aristocratic homes could do so until the Renaissance, when the households of the middle classes, especially in urban settings, regularly excluded, or at least attempted to exclude, the majority of husbandry animals. Richard Fanshawe associates precisely such division with the advent of civilization in his *Progress of Learning* (1647): "The Beasts and they / Promiscuously fed, Promiscuously lay. / As now they are, things were not sorted then."²⁴ For Bruce Boehrer, too, "the evolution of the household pet leads in a desultory way from the rural to the urban; from farmhouse to city dwelling."²⁵ The sixteenth and seventeenth centuries, it has been suggested, mobilized ideologies of space to authorize the concept of "home," a piece of property that signals more than mere ownership²⁶; but it is animals that play a crucial role in the transition from loosely enclosed, public, rural manor household to enclosed, private, bourgeois hearth and home. By the eighteenth century, ownership of a pet would correspond to the image of contented withdrawal from the public world of business, and by the nineteenth, pets would become surrogate vehicles for the bourgeois values that defined the middle classes in England.²⁷

Histories of English barns and stables reveal a different but equally important trajectory in the definitions of household, communal, and animal space. The creation of the category "pet" involved a distinction made between animals that dwelled within the home and those that more properly remained detached from it, outside it, relegated to outbuildings or fields. Barns and stables, however, do not always conform to this narrative. Medieval tithe barns, operated by feudal estates or the Catholic Church, gathered enormous quantities of agricultural products, including animals, into one large repository. So important were tithe barns that they were often constructed before the church they were associated with, so that funds from tithing could support the building of the main edifice. The status of tithe barns as "outbuildings" is thus ambiguous, given their primacy and integral utility to church buildings that accompany them. When the Catholic Church was removed from power in Tudor England, tithe barns naturally disappeared. Yet their symbolic place in the aristocratic estate, at least, might be said to have been replaced by the riding stable for the lord's horses. Giles Worsley and Paula Henderson both note that stables were the only "outbuildings" regularly placed in front of the great houses, despite the fact that other utility buildings of the medieval "base court" had migrated (usually for reasons of health and cleanliness) to the furthest reaches of the estate: "This meant that the outer (no longer a 'base') court could now consist of more salubrious offices or lodgings."[28] The first architectural image a sixteenth- or seventeenth-century visitor to an English noble house appreciated, as a consequence, was that provided by the stables, which were correspondingly created to be both beautiful and grandiose. How large, how efficient, how modern, and how well-appointed were a lord's stables spoke volumes about his status, knowledge of the world, taste, and judgment. Because stables had to house hay and fodder as well as horses, they could not be constructed in the new Renaissance style of the great country estates and so demanded their own vernacular: hay storage and the grooms' lodgings were usually above the stalls, and thus large Palladian windows and high roofs were out of the question, since hay deteriorates in light.

Riding houses (not for keeping horses, but to provide an area for training) went yet a step further toward demonstrating the refinement of a householder's knowledge and practice of the arts of the manège These were fewer in number but were equally important features where they did appear. William Cavendish's riding house of the 1630s at Bolsover Castle suggests that while pet keeping, in Boehrer's words, "leads in a desultory way from the rural to the urban; from farmhouse to city dwelling," horse keeping leads in a less predictable direction. According to Lucy Worsley and Tom Addyman, Cavendish sent his designer, John Smithson, to London to draw some of the new fashions in architecture from urban houses; his riding house has recognizable references in its architecture to "Colonel Cecil's house in the Strand and the pedimented gable from Fulke Greville's house at Holborn."[29] Bolsover's riding house represented an advance on the less coherent design of the riding house at Cavendish's main estate, Welbeck, but its imported urban features suggest Cavendish's desire to include the signs of recent fashion in what is essentially a rural building. The elaborate corniced ceiling at Bolsover has led to assumptions that this structure could not have been intended as part of the riding house range (which included a stables and a smithy), but Worsley and Addyman debunk this error, pointing out that the arts of horsemanship to be demonstrated in the riding house meshed perfectly with such ornamentation, being in themselves an ornamental art.[30] Thus, in Cavendish's riding house we have the importation of urban architecture into rural, and classical interior design into "outbuildings" of the main house. Such a set of cross-fertilizations suggests that while the general history of "pets," as Boehrer has it, moves from the rural to the urban, some aspects of keeping animals work in more complex, unpredictable ways to link urban with rural, house with ideologically inflected "home."

Urban Places and Spaces

Urban spatial organization reflects the lived realities and the ideologies of social organization.[31] "The city," Gail Kern Paster has put it, "is . . . a symbol, expressed in time, of human potentiality and desire in collective form—the *res publica* as central urban monument."[32] The town square, for example, usually built around the central fixtures of life such as wells, churches, and markets, is both a creation of necessity and of opportunity: necessity because these things must be as easily accessed as possible by the greatest number of town-dwellers, and so end up central to the densest parts of human habitation, and opportunity because once established, the town or city square usually becomes a bustling hub of diverse commercial enterprises, or a gathering place for the exchange of information. Its tendency to mingle classes may inspire rigid rules about status and placement or deportment of its inhabitants; or it may be reconstructed to eliminate the threatening disorder of shop stalls at street level and so informal social congress.

But urban *human* society is, of course, in turn dependent in many ways, materially and ideologically, on *animals*. Animals can and do participate in the *res publica* of the city: Chris Philo has even suggested that we might cease looking at plants and animals as an inert backdrop to human habitation, but rather treat them as we do other "outsider" minority groups.[33] Representational opportunities abound in city architecture, which inspires the inclusion of animals as decoration throughout, often used to convey boundaries between "the human" and "the animal" by adorning the parergon that surrounds but is definitionally not the human body, providing ornamentation that often expresses human dominion. Cities invite specific kinds of animal infiltration. Philo points out that people and animals intermingled in urban settings in a variety of ways based on shifting and unstable demarcations of inclusion and

exclusion.[34] At the most intimate level, each human is a veritable colony of
creatures internal and external, from worms and parasites to insects such as
fleas and lice, and these colonies survive especially well on the fruitful crowding of city dwellings. Early modern urban homes, just as much as their rural
counterparts, were also overrun with small pest mammals including rats and
mice that threatened household stores of food, which again was made easier
pickings by close habitation and sheer volume. Cats, dogs, pigs, chickens,
conies, even cattle were kept within city limits. Derek Keene notes that sheep
grazing within urbanized locations often caused damage to walls and other
man-made constructions; in addition, "pigs which had broken out of their
sties were a continuous nuisance," and poultry were guilty of "fouling the
streets and invading neighbors' gardens."[35]

Large markets like Smithfield in London initially occupied convenient
areas outside the city walls where there was ample space for the droving and
penning of cattle but were then quickly absorbed into the city's regular bor-
oughs. According to John Stow, writing in the seventeenth century, "Without
one of the Gates is a plaine field, both in name and deed, where euery fryday,
unlesse it be a solemne bidden holy day, is a notable shew of horses to bee solde,
Earles, Barons, knights, and Citizens repair thither to see, or to buy. . . . In an
other part of that field are to be sold all implements of husbandry, as also fat
swine, milch kine, sheepe and oxen: there stand also mares and horses, fitte for
ploughes and teames with their young coltes by them."[36] Smithfield originated
in the Middle Ages and was paved and drained in 1614 because of its enclosure
within the city. The filth and noise associated with the animals being driven
through city streets to the market pens continued into the nineteenth century,
when it became the motivation for finally moving the giant market entirely
outside London's city limits to what is now the Metropolitan Cattle Market.
Even after its removal, however, Smithfield left its mark on city streets named
Cow Lane, Cocke Lane, Chicken Lane, some of which survive today.[37] Stow
also remarks that Horsepoole, West Smithfield's "great water," where "inhabitants in that part of the city did there water their horses," was, like many other
natural water sources within the city, "stopped up," its "small bottom inclosed
with brick," and was as a result "much decayed"; it was later renamed Smithfield Pond. The grandness of its history, associated with the horses that drank
from it, was overwritten with the more generalized, diminished, man-made
cistern's name. Human urban social space was thus delineated by, delimited
by, occupied by, erected on, and subverted by animals, and by "the animal," in
large and small, abstract and real ways.

A good deal of early modern urban planning relied on animals and
changes in their uses for urban residents. The housing of urban animals was
naturally a constant concern for their owners, given the constraints of space,
limited access to water and pasturage, and the attendant smells and waste
generated. When the Ducal stables at Urbino were designed by Francesco di
Giorgi in the 1480s, these concerns already obtained, leading the architect
to construct a remarkable underground warren for the duke's animals, with
advanced hydraulic and waste disposal systems. Lewis Mumford writes com-
pellingly about advances in the layout and surfacing of Renaissance urban
streets, arguing that the pleasures of fast movement known previously only to
the horseman were extended to other city travelers on foot; this was in part
made possible by more linear city street layouts, which emphasized vistas of
space open to the traveler, and by the architecture of buildings, squares, and
other features that emphasized vanishing points. Like the rider of old who was
elevated above the mire and limitations of a street-level view and whose rapid
negotiation of streets could reduce the city to a rough mental map, the pedestrian in the new Renaissance city could experience the illusion of speed and
freedom of movement. While the horseman himself did not disappear from
the mix—he had, in Mumford's estimation "taken possession of the city," his
ownership inscribed in the widened and straightened avenues—pedestrian
and rider thus could actually claim a more nearly equal degree of ownership of
the city. Of the principles for choosing a building site Wotton notes that some
are optical: "Such I meane as concern the Properties of a well chosen Prospect:
which I will call the Royaltie of sight. For as there is a Lordship (as it were)
of the Feete, wherein the Master doth much joy when he walketh about the
Line of his owne Possessions: So there is a Lordship likewise of the Eye which
being a raunging, and Imperious, and (I might say) and Usurping Sence; can
indure no narrow circumscription, but must be fedde, both with extent and
varietie."[38] This usurping sense of sight, wedded to the "Lordship of the Feete"
characterizes Renaissance city navigation as it is described by Mumford; the
social stratification endorsed by Wotton's text is partially undone by common
access—the Renaissance lower-class everyman on foot now had an imperial
vista to regard and could "ride" the cityscape as if he owned it, or at least as if
he owned a horse to traverse it.

Carriages and stagecoaches also required that routes for travel within and
between cities be transformed. John Taylor, the water poet, called out the
hackney coach especially for its blockage of trade vehicles, but also for its general disruption of life: "Heigh downe, dery, dery downe, / With the Hackney

Coach-men downe, / Their Jumpinges make / The Pavements shake / Their
noyse doth mad the Towne."[39] Montaigne flatly tells his readers, "I loathe all
means of conveyance but the horse, both for town and country. But litters I
can tolerate less than coaches."[40] Although what most appalls Montaigne is
the luxury, vulgarity, and ostentation of the coach, he remarks on its motion,
the "series of broken movements," the more disconcerting when slow as they
are in a coach's jerky progress, which disturbs his "brain and stomach." Both
Taylor and Montaigne, then, react against the coaches of the rich for their
shaking, jumping, and noise—a somatic corollary to the vehicles' disruptive
transformation of the social world of city streets and rural lanes. Of course,
as Andrew McRae points out, it is the coach among other changes in physical traffic systems that merged with changes in trade, monetary circulation,
and exchange to open new prospects in the cultural production of space after
the mid-seventeenth century. Progress eventually drowned out Montaigne's
and Taylor's complaints about cultural upheaval. As cities adjusted to new
animal-powered methods for transport of goods, as architectures reflected
more adequately the needs of this animal mobility, the coach emerged as a
necessary sign of both national trade and individual status. In other words,
rather ironically, in many cases a manufactured box for the human body (a
kind of architectural and engineering marvel) replaced the animal that pulled
it as the primary sign of prosperity and superiority.

For the discussion of *Romeo and Juliet* with which this chapter ends, the
most important city-dwelling creatures to understand are cats and dogs. That
most ubiquitous of pets, the dog, hunted mice and rats in urban and rural
settings, and had a wide set of useful tasks for individual businesses (butchers,
for instance, still used dogs to bait bulls, and the turnspit dog was a fixture
of many kitchens) that brought them into the city in huge numbers. They
figure as pampered pets among some households, but the dogs of the poor
ran loose and presented a problem of urban control. Mark S. Jenner enumer-
ates the thousands of dogs executed in several official orders: The lord mayor
of London established a fine for allowing dogs outside off a lead in 1563 and
called for the killing of loose dogs. Chamber accounts reported by Jenner for
dog massacres associated with plague outbreaks in the late sixteenth century
start at a measly 1,800 or so and rise to numbers above three thousand and
even four. If these were only the masterless or nuisance dogs wandering town
and city streets, then the total number of dogs at large and at home in early
modern urban spaces must have been staggering.[41]

"Harmless, necessary" cats, as Shylock calls them (*The Merchant of Venice*,

4.1.55), were nevertheless, like dogs, culturally positioned as *both* useful *and* dangerous; enemies to household parasites like mice and rats, cats could be valued for their labor on behalf of human society and held in deep suspicion for their alien nature. Associated with witchcraft (as were dogs), cats were famously the targets of massacres as well.[42] In William Baldwin's *Beware the Cat*, the secret convocations and associations of cats are magically revealed to the protagonist, Streamer, who discovers that they have their own language, their own loyalties, their own hierarchy, and that they intervene far more frequently in human affairs than is usually suspected. In Baldwin's allegory, cats and Catholics share more than a syllable: they both creep and sneak about, infiltrating, hiding in walls and priest's holes, suborning good Englishmen and women.[43] The cat's apparent ability to appear and disappear at will, its near invisibility in both public and private places, its very marginality, along with its ability to insinuate itself into human affection, let it stand in for other subtle actors in the social and political landscape.

If every household had need of a cat, then, that did not mean every cat was imagined to be harmless; their very small size, skills, and mobility seemed to render human delimitations irrelevant. Paul de Vos's mid-seventeenth-century painting *Cats in a Pantry* (Figure 25) associates cats' skill at invading domestic spaces meant to be closed to them with their role as mammalian vermin. Five cats compete for the delicacies left unattended within the household's storage area. The largest and fiercest cat is the one launching itself at center, but the cat peering in from outside, clearly poised to join the others in their theft, suggests a possibly endless stream of the animals infiltrating the larder. In this case, the window that leads into the heart of the kitchen and storage areas, easily entered by the cats, reminds the viewer that the threshold that divides public and private, and the measures that protect the house's integrity, are constructs that can be defeated or bypassed. The cat here is thus a vehicle for anxieties about the boundaries of space and place, those that are supposed to divide one room from another, or one household from strangers to it, those that establish property rights, and those that are metaphorically means to distinguish civil, social areas from uncivil, populous, or unregulated ones.

While de Vos's painting might be intended as an allegory for the fragility of civil order via domestication, other examples of cats' ability to enter and leave a residence at will have a more positive twist. A minor tradition of what I will call "carceral cats" exists throughout the Renaissance. These animals are usually figured as saviors of human prisoners: most obvious of these are the Earl of Southampton, who chose to have his liberation from the Tower

Figure 25. Paul de Vos (1595–1678), *Cats in a Pantry*. Museo del Prado, Madrid. Photo: Scala, Art Resource (ART101834).

of London commemorated with a portrait that includes his faithful cat, and Christopher Smart, whose eighteenth-century poem *Jubilate Agno* celebrates his miraculous feline companion Jeffrey. We could add to these at least two other examples of cats important to the incarcerated: the first is an early English story, possibly apocryphal but nonetheless compelling for what it tells us about how cats were seen when associated with imprisonment, concerning Henry Wyatt and his cat "Acater," or "the caterer." Also consigned to the Tower, this time by Richard III, Wyatt was relieved in his misery by a stray Tower cat:

> A cat came one day down into the dungeon unto him, and, as it
> were, offered herself unto him, he was glad of her, laid her in his
> bosome to warm him, and making much of her, won her love. After
> this she would come every day unto him in diverse times, and when
> she could get him one, bring him a pigeon; he complained to the
> keeper of his cold and short fare; the answer was, he durst not better
> it; but said Sir Henry, "If I can provide any, will you promise to
> dress it for me?" "I may well enough" said the Keeper, "are you safe

for that matter" and for him from time to time such pigeons as his
Acater (caterer) the cat, provided for him. Sir Henry in his prosperity would ever make much of a cat, and perhaps you will never find
a picture of him anywhere, but with a cat beside him.[44]

The second example is that of Torquato Tasso, who was occasionally aided
during his self-imposed stay in a madhouse by the cats that hunted mice there.
Two of his sonnets celebrate cats, one for its "orbs of holy sight . . . two stars
as welcome as the northwind dry," the "lanterns of [his] room," the other an-
ticipating Vos's scenario in the larder:

> Good housewife, I admonish you to peel
> Your eyes and watch the pot about to boil:
> Run, look, a cat is carrying off the veal![45]

Dogs overwhelm by sheer numbers, as populous as the urban streets they
roam, but cats "steal" from place to place, violating limits and perimeters
meant to mark the categorical divisions of human culture.

Like *Hamlet*'s worms, moles, and rats, domestic species supposedly tamed
by human society and so made proper to the edifices of the urban landscape
often ran amok, violating both the rules of propriety and the boundaries
that defined property—food, divided rooms, walls, thresholds. This infiltra-
tive, decompositional role could be both literal and figurative. Stow's *Survey
of London*, for instance, records the following description of Houndsditch:
"From Aldgate Northwest to Bishopsgate, lieth the ditch of the Cittie, called
Houndes ditch, for that in olde time when the same lay open, much filth
(conueyed forth of the Citie) especially dead Dogges were there layd or cast:
wherefore of latter time a mudde wall was made inclosing the ditch, to keepe
out the laying of such filth as had beene accustomed."[46] Ben Jonson's "On
the Famous Voyage" travels through the foul passages of London's waters and
records the effluvia of the Fleet, where dogs' hides and the corpses of flayed
cats attest to the questionable practices of the cooks selling pies above; among
"these Tiberts" appears the infamous Banks, "grave tutor to the learned horse,"
whose spirit along with his horse's (both burned abroad as witches) have trans-
migrated into a large grey-eyed cat.[47] The circulation and recirculation of animals as food and waste (the cats here, while rejected by customers when they
are flayed, roasted, toasted, and minced, still "had five lives in future" to come
back as food for the unwary) exemplify the confusion of gullet and anus that

characterizes both the human body and the city that is patterned after it.[48] The arbitrary distinction between cats and dogs, and food animals like sheep and pigs authorizes Jonson's riff on the impossibility of differentiating filth from its opposite; the animal corpses in Houndsditch or the "Famous Voyage" testify to early modern efforts to contain the verminous underbelly of city life and at the same time demonstrate the failure of such containment. Fundamental to the city's business—literally part of its fundament—animals both feed and foul urban architecture.

Romeo and Juliet's Cats and Dogs

In *Romeo and Juliet's* first scene, the language of cats and dogs begins to circulate to implicate the two feuding households in the generation of disorder and incivility:

> Sampson: A dog of the house of Montague moves me.
> Gregory: To move is to stir, and to be valiant is to stand. Therefore
>   if thou art moved, thou run'st away.
> Sampson: A dog of that house shall move me to stand. I will take
>   the wall of any man or maid of Montague's.
> Gregory: That shows thee a weak slave; for the weakest goes to the
>   wall.
> Sampson: 'Tis true; and therefore women, being the weaker ves-
>   sels, are ever thrust to the wall. Therefore I will push Mon-
>   tague's men from the wall and thrust his maids to the wall.
>   (1.1.8–18)[49]

With the entrance of Abram and Balthasar, Sampson and Gregory's violent punning on the "civility" they will show the Montagues' maids turns to uncivil insults and finally swordplay; it takes the entrance of Tybalt, "Prince of Cats," however, to escalate the violence into a full-blown street brawl. Where Sampson challenges the Montagues to "draw if you be men," Prince Escalus implies that such violent outbursts collapse the distinction between men and animals: "You men, you beasts, / That quench the fire of your pernicious rage / With purple fountains issuing from your veins!" (1.1.83–85).

Erica Fudge has charted Shakespeare's use of dogs in *Two Gentlemen of Verona* to define civility as a specifically human trait. In that play, the clown

Launce's unmanageable cur, Crab, pisses on the floor at the feet of a group of
nobles, prompting Launce to quiz him, "When didst thou see me heave up my
leg and make water against a gentlewoman's farthingale?" (4.4.36–38). About
Crab's uncivilized behavior, Fudge writes: "What the civilizing process rein-
forces in humans then is a distinction between reasonable and unreasonable,
self-controlled and uncontrolled, civil and savage. It also underlines a conception of the difference between the private and the public: in one, urination is
allowed, in the other prohibited. Thus, lacking reason, self-control, and civility,
and displaying no concept of the difference between the private and the public,
a pissing dog comes to stand for everything that a human is not, and cannot be"
(Figure 26).[50] Fudge agrees, however, with Prince Escalus that there is always the
potential for slippage from civil human to uncivil beast in such a construction.
So when a human pisses in public, or when servants enter a pissing contest in a
public street, he and they "cannot any longer be counted as human."[51]

The dogs and other beasts that populate *Romeo and Juliet* are not the
well-educated civilized breeds produced by human intervention over time for
useful or noble purposes, the breeds that keep responsible citizens company
in life and work. Rather they are animals with no lineage or status—they
are curs. We find the degenerate human-animal nicely portrayed through a
comparison to curs in Robert Crowley's *One and Thyrtye Epigrammes* (1550):
"A Brawler that loveth / To break the king's peace" is like a "curre dogge, that
setteth upon / Eache mastyfe and hounde / that he may light on."[52] Classes of
men and breeds of dog show their quality by how they fight; human brawlers
show their baseness by attacking their superiors, mastiffs and hounds who
have productive roles in human society. Curs, "mongrels of the rascall sort,"
are given their own descriptive entry in Topsell's *History of Four-Footed Beasts*,
separate from the array of other breeds; these curs are the reason dogs have,
in Topsell's estimation, been reviled by "learned and wise men."[53] Topsell includes "rayling" as a characteristic of the cur: "The voice of a Dogge," he notes,
"is by the learned interpreted as rayling and angry speech," which is why dogs
are sometimes used as "emblems of vile, cursed, rayling, and filthy men."[54]
Montagues and Capulets fight like cats and dogs in order to "be men," to
illustrate, in Sampson and Gregory's terms, macho defiance with mutual insults; in so doing, they break the Prince's peace and become less than human,
degenerate, debased.

The victims of the constant feuding between the two houses are not
merely members of the households, but also those citizens who must "cast by
their grave beseeming ornaments" in order to "Strike!" the combatants, and

Figure 26. Emmanuel de Witte (1617–92), Interior of the Old Church in Delft, 1650–52. Oil on wood, 19 x 13 5/8 in. (48.3 x 34.6 cm). In the foreground, a small dog urinates on a pillar. The Metropolitan Museum of Art. Art Resource (ART337540).

"Beat them down!" (1.1.73), actions that the Prince recognizes do not come as naturally to sober, productive members of the community as they do to the infantile patriarchs of the two houses. The women of each family mock the men's sudden rage to fight: "a crutch! Why call you for a sword" cries Lady Capulet (1.1.76), and Lady Montague manages to hold back her apparently decrepit husband by main force. Like curs and vermin, the brawlers slink away after the fray and the Prince's chastisement, driven from the public scene by their inability to control their violent passions, which disrupt the city's economy and its efforts to achieve "civil" conduct among both masters and men.

Caged again in their palazzos after the first brawl, both families find violence impossible to eradicate from the whelps of their lines. Capulet can't contain the aggression of Tybalt: "You will set cock-a-hoop" (that is, strut with his coxcomb raised to show his masculinity), he upbraids the resistant Tybalt; "You'll be the man!" (1.5.82). But the roving Montague pack who infiltrate the Capulets' party are not exempt from association with beasts—like sneaky pests they come to steal food, fun, love. Romeo himself is marked as beastlike. "That's the dog's name," exclaims the Nurse, prodded by Juliet to speak Romeo's name (2.4. 205).[55] In the Nurse's joke even the "r"s of Romeo's name conjure the vocalizing of curs, linking him to the other railing, brawling young members of both houses.

Nor is Romeo tamed by love or marriage. Rather, love arouses his passions, unmanning him and so dehumanizing him. The language of animal analogy has gender implications in early modern literature and culture: women, like animals, belong to a series of mutually reinforcing binaries that place men at the top of the hierarchy of creation. But Shakespeare typically "toys with the slippages—between woman and beast, for instance, or man and monster—that ground the system of meaning of which he is a part."[56] "Thou art uproused by some distemp'rature" (2.3.40) laments Friar Lawrence over the newly passionate Romeo and later castigates him when he sobs and attempts to stab himself over his banishment for Tybalt's death:

> Art thou a man? Thy form cries out thou art;
> Thy tears are womanish, thy wild acts denote
> The unreasonable fury of a beast.
> Unseemly woman in a seeming man!
> And ill-beseeming beast in seeming both! (3.3.109–13)

From man to woman, from human to beast—Romeo's decline embodies fears about the stability of these ideologically charged categories. If Romeo is only a "seeming" man, that suggests a gap between appearance and reality—Romeo's form "cries out" that he is male, but his actions "denote" him to be something quite different, a woman or an animal, or worse, both. If these terms echo Hamlet's struggle against the charge of "seeming" or the idea that his mourning clothes "denote" him truly, it is because something of the same ideal of unitary selfhood derived from an inner "truth" of being is at stake here for Romeo too. Proper, "beseeming," or fitting, behavior, should body forth the identity within, according to Friar Lawrence; but that unity requires a rational self-consciousness temporarily lacking in Romeo.

The problem for the friar, as for other characters in the play, is that the "true" self of a man turns out to be under constant erasure as passions and wild behavior repeatedly gain the upper hand among Verona's youth. Men descend periodically into the state of animals; the paradox is that they do so, as Sampson and Gregory prove, in the effort of showing themselves precisely to be men—in other words, establishing a distinction between masculine and feminine requires an act of bestial violence that then defeats the human-beast distinction. When violence breaks forth between Romeo, Mercutio, and Tybalt, it arises from this process of category confusion. "Alas poor Romeo . . . is he a man to answer it?" (2.4.16) asks Mercutio when he hears that Tybalt has challenged Romeo to a duel; "Why what is Tybalt?" inquires Benvolio: "More than Prince of Cats" (2.4.18–19). Cats, in early modern literature, are universally understood to be female.[57] Tybalt probably owes his name to the character of Tybert the cat in Caxton's *Reynard the Fox*. Like *Reynard's* Tybert, who is symbolically emasculated in the process of arraigning a rogue, Tybalt's manhood is questionable—he devotes his time to the rapier, with its Continental and vaguely effeminate associations, becoming one of the "antic, lisping, affecting fantasticoes" (2.4.28) who wield such a slender weapon. Even so, Tybalt will turn out to be more "man" than Romeo, who is apparently now a mere fish: he is, scoffs Mercutio, "without his roe, like a dried herring" (2.4.37), suitable food for Tybalt's feline appetite. To salvage the situation in Act 3, Mercutio undertakes to tease the cat:

> Mercutio: Tybalt, you ratcatcher, will you walk?
> Tybalt: What wouldst thou have with me?
> Mercutio: Good King of Cats, nothing but one of your nine lives.
>   (3.1.75–77)

Wounded and dying, Mercutio rails: "Zounds, a dog, a rat, a mouse, a cat, to scratch a man to death!" (3.1.99–100).

Each time the young men of the play enter a public place, they reveal the instability of the human-animal divide that underwrites the civil actions and civilized self-control upon which social interaction in the crowded city environment relies. Their degeneration into bestial behavior thus puts under pressure a series of urban spatial and ideological relationships—public/private, street/house, crowd/individual, master/servant, citizen/brawler. Ian Munro has described early modern fear of street crowds as a reaction to the sense that masses of human beings behave like a beast: "Against a vision of a hier-archical model of urban citizenry stands the idea . . . of the population as a mindless, misconstruing, rebellious beast, ready at any instance to throw off the constraints of order and reason."[58] The organization of the city, including the physical disposition of buildings, thoroughfares, houses, facades, shops, defensive waterways, town squares, and other gathering places can either en-hance or mitigate the crowd's bestial potentiality. Walls and gates, and bridges that divide city center from the suburbs or "Liberties" act as valves that can speed or slow movement in either direction as needed to relieve pressure on or from city-dwellers.[59] Official decrees to remove pushcarts, knock down and rebuild houses and shops, shut down brothels, and close theaters were some of the ways that urban authorities attempted to control civic disorder with adjustments to spatial existence.

Romeo and Juliet divides its action between the public spaces of the street and the square, where people meet and share social and economic life, and which are marked by the infestation of violent creatures, and the private spaces of repose, reason, and retreat, including the Capulets' garden or or-chard, Friar Lawrence's cell, the marital chamber in which Romeo and Juliet consummate their marriage, and the Capulets' tomb. The play's partitioned urban world signals certain assumptions about the relationship between dis-eased street culture and supposedly healing interiorized spaces of love, family, and domesticity. "Nature," in the form of medicinal herbs, for instance, is conveyed by Friar Lawrence from the wild into the social environment; and Juliet's chamber, manufactured on stage by her appearances at her window in 2.2 and 3.5, promises the salvation of union between the families. The very bestial desires that break forth into riot and brawl are meant to be inhibited or policed by the households from which the play's characters issue forth. But the ideological work of private, religious, or familial spaces proves inadequate to cure the sickness that festers within these urban households. Indeed, the brawl inside Juliet's tomb seems to cap a movement of infection that dis-mantles the logic of order through division. Where there should be only the dead, there is Juliet's living corpse; where there should be darkness, quiet, and a sealed tomb, Romeo brings light, the tools of invasion, and a "savage-wild" disposition (5.3.37). Urban spaces, the play thus reminds us, are subject to that certain persistent, subversive, contaminating fluidity we found in Jonson's cloacal passageways in "On the Famous Voyage," or the various dead animal markers of Stow's *Survey*.

Animal references in *Romeo and Juliet* contribute to the construction of both a physical urban geography and a social organization integrally related to that geography. The Capulets' and Montagues' feud moves from the halls and chambers of the family enclaves via a process of contamination that is both social and spatial. "Civil blood" makes "civil hands unclean" in Verona, the chorus tells us at the outset, expressing the problem of contamination, the taint that bleeds forth when its citizens turn bestial. "The quarrel," claims Gregory, "is between our masters and us their men" (1.1.21); having appropriated the family identity by taking on the feud, the servants physically move the fight into the streets, where competing interests—family versus family, kinship loyalties versus legal and political governance, economic interests versus those of honor and status—mingle promiscuously.[60] The city expels Romeo to restore order within its walls, but he returns with poison to invade the Capulets' tomb to "cram" it with more uncivilized "food" (5.3.48). The play suggests that the very constitution of the material structures of the urban world invite irresolvable conflict over goals like civility. In Shakespeare's Verona, humans build to reflect and enforce ideology; animals and animality converge to defeat that project.

Chapter 5

Working Bodies: Laboring Moles and Cannibal Sheep

Among all those creeping, gnawing, devouring pests we encountered in Chapter 3 is Hamlet's mole, the below-stage manifestation of Hamlet's father's ghost, who bumps and knocks and cries out while Hamlet swears Horatio and Marcellus to silence: "Well said, old mole! Canst work i'th'earth so fast? A worthy pioneer!"[1] This fortunate mole has had an unusually rich afterlife, popping up in some unexpected places. For instance, Hegel's conclusion in *Lectures on the Philosophy of History* turns on this "antic" line[2]: "Spirit often seems to have forgotten and lost itself, but inwardly opposed to itself, it is inwardly working ever forward (as when Hamlet says of the ghost of his father, 'Well said, old mole! canst work I' the ground so fast?') until grown strong in itself it bursts asunder the crust of earth which divided it from the sun, its Notion, so that the earth crumbles away. At such a time, when the encircling crust, like a soulless decaying tenement, crumbles away, and spirit displays itself arrayed in new youth, the seven league boots are at length adopted."[3] And in Marx's *Eighteenth Brumaire of Louis Bonaparte*, the mole resurfaces as the proletariat working toward the revolution: "But the revolution is thoroughgoing. It is still journeying through purgatory. It does its work methodically. . . . And when it has done this second half of its preliminary work, Europe will leap from its seat and exultantly proclaim: Well grubbed, old mole!"[4]

Recent critics have appreciated this convergence of philosophers on the role of the mole. Peter Stallybrass seizes on Marx's misquotation to meditate on Shakespeare's proleptic appreciation for the farcical stage of history predicated on the repetition of the tragic: "For Marx, the repetition of the name 'Hamlet' itself covers a double dislocation: the dislocation of the father from palace to cellarage; the dislocation of the father's legacy. . . . Yet unfixing itself depends upon repetition, a repetition which can never be totally detached from both fixity and fixation."[5] Hegel's mole struggles upward to sunlight and air; Marx's mole, transformed through repetition, remains below ground, undermining (pioner, originally the term for a miner) monarchy's regime with its purgative labor.

Margreta de Grazia also finds Hegel's and Marx's borrowed moles significant to a reading of *Hamlet* that returns the play to a lost history, in her case one that concerns the subject of land, not the subject that is Hamlet—rejecting the interpretive paradigm of modernity that he has become. The ruptures of the Reformation and the revolution that influence Hegel and Marx respectively require forward movement, and so each portrays the mole inaccurately, either rising to the surface where it is beset by predators (Hegel's version), or as a creature that moves through "purgatory" like the proletariat, so that one day the revolution might don its "seven-league boots" and match the mole's velocity (à la Marx's "canst work i'th'earth so fast"). Moles, of course, do not burst through the earth's crust as a moment of triumph—they work downward, not upward. As earth-worker, moulewarp, the mole is etymologically descended from the same humus as the human, observes de Grazia: "These semantic overlays between man and clay, human and humus, point toward another history, long predating the nineteenth-century narratives," one in which "land is a form of self-aggrandizement" downsized by death; the play "subscribe[s] to the biblical narrative in which man's life is rounded in dust" (Figure 27).[6] In that narrative, land is the trump, the identifier that supersedes individuation. *Hamlet*, then, is not modern at all; Hegel's and Marx's appropriation of it leave them only with the ghost, the father's burial plot, the hamlet to which Hamlet is reduced when he dies landless, his name extinguished by another son trapped in the cycle of acquisition and loss.

For Hegel, Marx, and Stallybrass, and to a lesser extent for de Grazia, the "moles" of Hamlet are purely metaphoric vehicles that advance their diverse theoretical positions regarding the play, or the play's connections to modern ideologies. However much their rhetoric purports to be "grounded" in the mole, the mole in these examples remains a shell, a convenience, and consequently an absence, hardly discernible as a mole at all, and certainly not as a player in its own right. For early modern audiences attending the first performances of *Hamlet*, however, moles were just the opposite—familiar creatures with a widely known natural history and physiology whose behavior had practical effects on the lives of ordinary farmers. As I noted in my introduction,

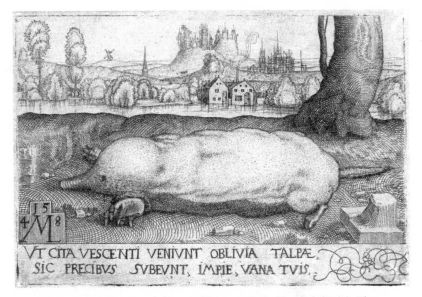

VT CITA VESCENTI VENIVNT OBLIVIA TALPÆ.
SIC PRECIBVS SVBEVNT, IMPIE, VANA TVIS.

Figure 27. Melchior Lorck (ca. 1526/27–ca. 1583), *The Mole* (1548). The mole in the foreground is probably dead, since dead moles are usually depicted splayed like this; however, since a live mole *also* tends to look splayed, its condition is not entirely clear—it might merely be temporarily resting above ground. The Latin couplet translates roughly as "As quickly as forgetfulness comes to a feeding mole, thus—impious man—futility is the response to your prayers." The landscape's human-built structures, especially one on the hill in the distance, either are damaged or under construction, suggesting that what is built on lack of true piety does not last. Trustees of the British Museum.

while I don't discount the metaphoric uses of certain kinds of animals, I am always curious about the way their particular bodily existences and attributes inflect these uses. Hamlet's mole is no exception. If we "re-ground" an analysis of the mole's cultural significance by marking its treatment in sources that are less absolutely committed to metaphorizing it, what complementary or contradictory versions of moleness might we unearth? And because the mole is most often portrayed as a laborer, a worker in the earth, what versions of shared labor and economic activity arise out of early modern stories about moles?

De Grazia rightly points out that the mole's natural behavior discourages it from tunneling upward; she turns to some contemporary nontheatrical accounts of moles, including Edward Topsell's *History of Four-Footed Beasts*, to emphasize the mole's connection to earth, and hence the related human connection to soil, *humus*. But a bit closer examination of the opinions and lore associated with moles advances more complicated perspectives on the mole's links to land, property, and acquisition.[7] Moles in Topsell's account are from the outset defined by terms like "lack" and "want," especially by bodily lacks that connect to their inverted relationship to issues of property. Topsell clarifies that they are not mice as is sometimes mistakenly averred, because they lack the two foreteeth of the mouse, "therefore wanting those as the inseparable propriety of kind."[8] Above all, however, the mole is defined by its blindness, which is the main reason, according to Topsell, it can't survive long above ground.[9] In fact, both Topsell's text and Leonard Mascall's treatise of 1590 on vermin traps note the mole's alternative name of "want," which makes the mole killer a "want-taker," an etymological accident that inadvertently reads both parties in terms of flaws and impoverishment.[10] Ironically, precisely because of its various deficiencies the mole is a powerful competitor to humans for land: "Because by their continual hea[v]ing and laboring for meat, they do much harm to Gardens and other places of their aboad, and therefore in the husband-man's and house-wife's commonwealth, it is acceptable labor to take and destroy them."[11] Rural dwellers occupy a separate commonwealth based on the needs of farm and garden; in that nation, wealth is extracted from the land by both mole and farmer—but their labors work in distinct and opposite realms. The proper labor of the mole is disturbing the soil below the surface; the proper labor of the farmer is disturbing it from above. When these two communities conflict over the use of land, the farmer is justified in killing his competition; but the suggestion in Topsell's repetition of "labor . . . labor" is that both creatures operate rationally to the same end, albeit in contest over the same resource. The domains of humans and moles thus function, in Topsell's formulation, rather like two countries that may at times go to war against each other. Rather than the proletariat undermining the authority of monarchy, as Marx would have it, the moles with which actual laborers in the fields of England were familiar could be imagined as mirror images of the human society above, each group laboring alike in its different "commonwealth."

Erica Fudge categorically dismisses the idea that early moderns might see animals as having property rights over the land on which they labor: "An animal (like most women) does not have the right to own property; animals can only be property. Possession signifies control, and control is willed, and therefore available only to a human. A wild rabbit, for example, does not own its burrow but merely lives in it; the land remains in the hands of the human owner."[12] Fudge's summary grounds her comparison of colonial exploitation of animals with that of some humans, like natives of the New World or some groups within England itself. Because animals lack reason, they lack intentional will; similarly, Europeans perceived native peoples as beasts, living wild upon the lands where they were found, lands that could therefore be appropriated without incurring the charge of theft. While colonists faced a conundrum, it did not emerge out of the idea of competing property rights, but rather, Fudge argues, out of the "missionary zeal" of the colonists that implied future reclamation of the natives' human status through religious conversion.

While it is true that in most cases early moderns did not envision animals having the right to their own labor, or some kind of legal right to the property their labor emended, Topsell's discussion of the mole should give us pause in making this claim an untroubled absolute. In fact, Topsell represents a strain of thought in early modern discussions of actual animals, particularly those that competed directly with humans for space and sustenance, that constantly cedes intention, cleverness, and some form of rational behavior to those animals—as we saw in Chapter 3 above, vermin were especially anthropomorphized in early modern texts. Moles, also usually considered verminous creatures as they are in Topsell's account, exist within their own commonwealth and work on their own behalf in precisely the same way that humans do. Mole labor, however, is envisioned by early moderns as staking a claim to earth and soil that the farmer wants; and since, unlike human beings, moles are no respecters of fences, walls, or other boundaries—indeed, their occupation of the soil beneath the surface makes a mockery of human property markers—the mole-plagued farmer is constantly reminded that legal doctrine is somehow absurd in daily practice, that human efforts to claim property in land happen only belatedly and in competition with the land's other dwellers.[13] Again, the mole's name, "want," also written "wend" or "wand," may be the origin of terms like wending or wandering, a reference to the subterranean passageways of the mole that follow no humanly perceptible rules or order.

Moles, however, were not even uniformly considered pests: like pigs and other animals that dig, they could be useful in small numbers outside the garden, loosening soil for cultivation. Thomas Tusser approves the destruction of moles generally, but advises in one instance that farmers leave moles alone to create oases of drainage:

If pasture by nature is given to be wet
Then bear with the mole-hill, though thick it be set;

> That lamb may sit on it, and so to sit dry,
> Or else to lie by it, the warmer to lie.[14]

Working on their own behalf beneath the soil, moles can function either as pests or as aids in farming—they, of course, are indifferent to the outcome, even if the farmer is not.

Shakespeare uses the mole in *Pericles* to call attention to the futility of protesting the inequities of power:

> The blind mole casts
> Copp'd hills towards heaven, to tell the earth is throng'd
> By man's oppression; and the poor worm doth die for't.
> Kings are earth's gods; in vice their law's their will;
> And if Jove stray, who dares say Jove doth ill? (1.1.101–4)

Pericles' rebuke to Antiochus relies on the repression of a truth both recognize, but which the lesser in status cannot safely reveal: "It is enough you know; and it is fit, / What being more known grows worse, to smother it" (1.1.106–7). And besides, concludes Pericles, he'd like to keep his head on his shoulders. Pericles' "mole" is conversant with human suffering and injustice in a way that humans are not—viscerally and physically through human incursion into his otherwise serene kingdom below ground. He speaks through his manipulation of the earth; the metaphoric use of the mole here levels distinctions between oppressed animal and oppressed human: "man's" oppression of the beasts becomes a figure for human political oppression. Although this appearance of the mole is not supposed to speak about the animal itself but to represent the human conscience rebelling against evidence of injustice, the image nevertheless emphasizes the existence of a quiet, discrete world that is the property of the animals that live within it, violated only by human tillage. Contrary to Topsell's farmers who are at war with their mole competitors, Shakespeare's mole casts humans as the unthinking tyrants of the natural world.

Shakespeare, Hegel, Marx, Stallybrass, and de Grazia: the imaginative genealogy of the mole relies on its physical performance in a dimly grasped environment; the animal mimics human energy and industry while competing with or sometimes aiding the labor of the human farmer above. Not (only) a miner, or a "worker," the mole lays claim to territory that is particularly its "own," in the sense that it navigates skillfully where others do not, and in the sense that the ground it inhabits is transformed by its energies into something more valuable . . . to the mole, not some human overseer. It is a landowner who goes to work with a will. What it wants, it takes. The idea of an underground world, parallel and to some degree analogous in its drives and behaviors to the human world aboveground, links the mole's blind progress to the ghost thumping beneath Shakespeare's stage in the hidden space below. Both are reminders that human dominion is incomplete: the mole, like the ghost, occupies a space into which human agency and perception can only partially extend. Blindness, given this schema, migrates from mole to human observer, who is largely blind to the worlds beyond the material surface of land. After all, in its own commonwealth, the mole "sees" perfectly well; only in comparison to human sight does it lack anything, whereas upright, far-seeing humans, whose verticality is credited by writers such as Helkiah Crooke with conferring godlike vision, have barely any knowledge of what lies right beneath their feet.[15]

Mole catching was a staple for vermin-killing pamphlets, where the preferred method involved the use of a pitfall trap, or a jar filled with water with a trap door that would close behind the animal who dropped into it, buried in the earth along mole paths. It was necessary to have a double means of killing the mole, beyond the mere jar itself, since observers record instances of moles coming to the aid of their trapped comrades by pushing dirt into the jar until the mole inside could avoid drowning and gain exit.[16] Hamlet's "antic" reactions to the ghost's insistence that he swear express an aversion to the "fellow in the cellarage," the emissary from a region that he can't be sure isn't hell. The mole-miner, the "pioneer," is "*hic et ubique*," here and everywhere: Hamlet moves twice to escape it, but can't. His nervous relocations on stage, fleeing the ghost-mole, reflect a species reversal in that the mole entraps him and his companions, who are locked into the pitfall of swearing to uphold the ghost's demands. Blind to the consequences, Hamlet takes the oath, and the community below ground gains the upper hand.

I am arguing, then, that we should be cautious about making moles merely inert examples of either biblical schema or economic philosophy. Early moderns knew them as active laborers in their own right, whose existence and treatment of land, its boundaries, and so property, could disrupt the whole notion of human control, whether the human involved was a simple farmer or a monarch like Antiochus. In the remainder of this chapter, I consider how animals like Hamlet's mole are implicated in protocapitalist (and occasionally modern and postmodern anticapitalist) narratives of land, property, and ownership rights. Specifically, I am interested in how animal bodies become a factor in early modern thought about the establishment of and the limits of legal entitlements to land or labor, the accumulation of material goods, and the preservation and engrossment of economic assets. Apart from this brief analysis of *Hamlet*'s burrowing mole, the chapter reopens the case on Thomas More's Utopian sheep, which invite us to interrogate our own assumptions about how labor and property were represented in the early modern world, and how they have come to be appropriated in subsequent theory.

Property in/of the Body

The association of property in land or physical objects with aspects of embodiment is obvious in most historical accounts of economic and governance systems. In the Middle Ages, discourses of "blood" authorized ownership among the nobility, who held their heritable land rights or tenure from the crown, and whose control in turn extended to the bodies of those who occupied their lands. Vassalage put the body of a fief at the disposal of the manorial lord, usually for carriage of arms; peasants had reciprocal obligations that involved the exchange of their labor for protection from harm. The roots of capitalism in the social upheavals of the sixteenth and seventeenth centuries in England implicated the body as well: as Locke puts it in his *Second Treatise of Government*,

> Though the earth, and all inferior creatures, be common to all men,
> yet every man has a property in his own person: this nobody has
> any right to but himself. The labour of his body, and the work of his
> hands, we may say, are properly his. Whatsoever then he removes out
> of the state that nature hath provided, and left it in, he hath mixed his
> labour with, and joined to it something that is his own, and thereby
> makes it his property. It being by him removed from the common
> state nature hath placed it in, it hath by this labour something an-
> nexed to it, that excludes the common right of other men: for this
> labour being the unquestionable property of the labourer, no man but
> he can have a right to what that is once joined to, at least where there
> is enough, and as good, left in common for others.[17]

The exercise of human bodily faculties creates property in that which is originally common to all. Locke's and Hobbes's theories of property, although arriving at different outcomes (Hobbes finds no guarantee that property will be recognized as such without a greater power who acknowledges it), both rely on what C. B. Macpherson calls "proprietary individualism," which has underwritten much of the debate about institutions and law since the seventeenth and eighteenth centuries.[18] Insofar as individuals have different bodily capacities, inequities in property rights arise; when labor becomes an alienable commodity, further widening of the gap between producers and workers occurs. Trade and expanding economic consumption shifts value from the direct equation of bodily labor to the price of goods, and creates instead exchange value.

All well and good. In Locke's and Hobbes's theories (as in nearly every text addressing land, law, and property before them), "beasts" are unequivocally the property of all mankind, as we are instructed by biblical authority:

> God, who hath given the world to men in common, hath also given them reason to make use of it to the best advantage of life, and convenience. The earth, and all that is therein, is given to men for the support and comfort of their being. And tho' all the fruits it naturally produces, and beasts it feeds, belong to mankind in common, as they are produced by the spontaneous hand of nature; and nobody has originally a private dominion, exclusive of the rest of mankind, in any of them, as they are thus in their natural state: yet being given for the use of men, there must of necessity be a means to appropriate them some way or other, before they can be of any use, or at all beneficial to any particular man.[19]

There is, then, in this system of thought no room for either radical difference among proprietary bodies (such as would be accounted for by the admission of "beasts" to the owning community) or the idea that beastly labor might accrue property rights to anyone other than a directing human influence.

Early modern relationships with actual proprietary individuals, however, and actual laboring beasts did not entirely accommodate these exclusions. The language of ownership, labor, and consumption bleeds across species boundaries in the language of some treatises on animals and in other literary sources. It is hard, just to take a simple example, for some early moderns to claim confidently that bees are not somehow entitled to defend the honey their labors produce; or that bestial humans enjoy full title to the lands and objects they may claim.[20] From Locke to Marx and beyond, economic theories tend to

justify the distinction between natural labor and human labor by granting that
human beings use their imagination to construct an object before creating it,
and that human labor transforms the natural environment, while animal labor
is merely constant repetition without change. Thus, we have Marx's categorization of spiders and bees as nonproducers because they do not imagine their
structures in advance nor exert their will to create them: "At the end of the
labor-process, we get a result that already existed in the imagination of the la-
bourer at its commencement. He not only effects a change of form in the material on which he works. But he also realises a purpose of his own that gives
the law to his modus operandi."[21] An obvious corollary to animal labor, not
coincidentally, is "women's work," the constant grind of housekeeping or the
physiological reproduction that is (arguably) not clearly a product of imaginative creativity. Of course, Marx has no idea whether or not bees and spiders imagine their structures before commencing building, nor does he know
whether they exert will; his assumptions follow from, rather than generate, an
Enlightenment certainty about the distinctions between animal and human
thought—animals *must* be different or there is no category of the human, just
as men *must* be superior to women or there is no sense to the social structures
by which they live. Like women, then, animals are excluded from most labor
theory and most property arguments based on the role of labor because of a
tenuous claim about their internal mental processes that is tied to assumptions
about the implications of their bodily differences from male humans.

Alongside *Hamlet*'s old mole, Thomas More's various beasts work against
early modern and postmodern theories, suggesting that we need to become
more attentive to how animals factor into economic life, whether for early
moderns or their heirs. The facts on the ground, as it were, of animal life
do not always confirm economic theories of labor and property built on the
conceptual distinction of human from animal. On the one hand, if *Hamlet*'s
moles seem to anticipate and underwrite a Marxist reading of the play, More's
sheep, and subsequent Marxist ruminations on them, raise the question of
whether human and animal labor can be qualitatively differentiated—as well
as what is at stake in asserting a difference. On the other hand, unlike Hamlet's mole, More's sheep have been recruited to arguments driven by a desire to
locate in this magisterial Renaissance text the origins of an "ethics" regarding
animals that would be compatible with a truly Utopian version of a Marxist
economy. That pattern of interpretation may miss the more radical use of
More's animals, one that cannot defend the category of *homo economicus* from
contamination and dissolution by its beastly Other.

Cannibal Sheep

It's hard to imagine a creature less like the blind, grubbing mole, which labors mainly to its own ends and needs, than a placid, grazing sheep, dotting the English countryside where it fattens for slaughter or waits for shearing. Leonard Mascall credits sheep as being "no harmful beast, nor hurt at all," cataloguing the many ways the sheep is a benefit to humans:

> These cattel (Sheep) among the rest,
> Is counted for man one of the best,
> No harmful beast, nor hurt at all:
> His fleece of wool doth cloath us all,
> Which keeps us all from extream cold:
> His flesh doth feed both young and old.
> His tallow makes the candles white,
> To burn and serve us day and night;
> His skin doth pleasure divers ways,
> To write, to wear, at all assaies;
> His guts, thereof we make wheel strings;
> They use his bones for other things;
> His horns some shepherds will not loose,
> Because therewith they patch their shooes,
> His dung is chief I understand,
> To help and dung the Plowman's land.
> Therefore the Sheep among the rest,
> He is for man a worthy Beast.[22]

In the imaginative literature of the period sheep represent the purest form of innocent life, destined for service to humanity. Elsewhere in sermons and religious tracts, sheep represent the highest form of meek submission, a paradigm important for Christians aspiring to imitate Jesus in his incarnation as the Lamb of God (John 1:29).

Yet calling out sheep as dangerous animals is exactly what Thomas More does in his *Utopia* through Raphael Hythloday's famous criticism of the effects of enclosure:

> "Your sheep," I replied, "that used to be so meek and eat so little.
> Now they have become so greedy and fierce that they devour

> human beings themselves, as I hear. They devastate and depopulate
> fields, houses, and towns. For in whatever parts of the land the
> sheep yield the softest and most expensive wool, there the nobility
> and gentry, yes, and even some abbots—holy men—are not content
> with the old rents that the land yielded to their predecessors. . . .
> And as if enough of your land were not already wasted on woods
> and game-preserves, these worthy men turn all human habitations
> and cultivated fields back to wilderness. Thus one greedy, insatiable
> glutton, a frightful plague to his native country, may enclose many
> thousands of acres of land within a single hedge."[23]

This is a passage that has justly attracted a lot of critical attention for its as-
tonishing characterization of these greedy, toothy sheep.[24] In general, criticism takes it one of three ways: in one interpretation it is a straightforward
attack on the practice of land enclosure, which diverted common lands away
from yeoman farmers who formerly ploughed and harvested grain crops (as
Hythloday points out, "There is no need for farm labor. . . . One herdsman
or shepherd can look after a flock of beasts large enough to stock an area
that would require many hands if it were plowed and harvested"). In Richard
Halpern's reading of the passage, for instance, Hythloday effects a sly reca-
pitulation of the argument immediately preceding, in which Hythloday also
attacks England's draconian punishments for theft—the sheep are blamed for
the process of enclosure in the same way that thieves are blamed for the system that creates the need to steal. Halpern sees both positions as connected
through the broader fear of vagrancy. He assumes the sheep are mere stand-
ins for those who have been dispossessed of their traditional charitable status
that once made them the deserving poor, and who are being amassed instead
as a potential labor force.[25] While he does note in passing that the passage
endows them with "a malignant *will*," Halpern has to reverse that grant of will
in his full analysis. Otherwise his reading of the sheep as a parodic rebuke to
the lawyer who blames thieves for their own poverty cannot work. Like most
treatments of More's sheep, his otherwise perceptive and influential reading
actually reproduces, if unintentionally, the denial of will to animals Fudge
claims characterized early modern literature's attitude toward property and
animals: again, we might recall her comment that "Possession signifies control, and control is willed, and therefore available only to a human."[26] Erasing
the sheep as sheep, Halpern implicitly accepts the early modern position on
animals' lacks and wants, their essential emptiness as laborers. The only way

sheep have "malignant will" is if they are not sheep at all, but human workers who might ultimately possess something as a result of their labor.

For a critic like Paul Yachnin, the appearance of sheep in the pastoral setting is instead a call to consider the ethics of animal-human relations. *Utopia* (and other texts that use sheep, like Yachnin's primary text, *The Winter's Tale*) "develops a sheepish ideal of human conduct" that instructs the reader in Christian/ovine lessons about life.[27] Likewise, Julian Yates and Christopher Burlinson both see in *Utopia*'s sheep an "ovine summoning" that attempts to enlarge the "table" at which species sit, to include voices and perspectives otherwise marginalized by the humanist project.[28] Yates invites us to imagine what the consequences would be if Hythloday granted sheep the power of speech to join the conversation, and so indicate their own interests in the construction of Utopia, something that he suggests would more fully decenter the human in our reading of More's work.[29] Yet including sheep in a conversation that is already composed of speakers in whose mouths More is placing all the words and arguments seems of questionable value: in a text like that, what "voice" could the sheep have but More's own?

But in all these critical responses to More's passage on cannibal sheep, the sheep are either deemed entirely innocent, transformed into substitutes for (innocent) humans, or given a speculative life as participants in a ventriloquized humanist conversation. If Halpern denies that sheep actually have will, both Yachnin and Yates repeat early modern assumptions about the essentially blameless character of sheep that also erases their willfulness; it would be unthinkable, for instance, in Yates's schema to include sheep at the table and then decide to kill and eat them because they were too dangerous to leave alive. Yates redresses the emptying out of the category of the animal by concluding that it is the human who is "vehicular," merely a vector or bearer of "things, information, phrases—all of us, just like [the sheep], no more than various prosopopoeias, or metaphorical agents engaged in acts of transport."[30] Yet this tit-for-tat reversal does not necessarily reestablish the particularity of sheep, their materiality, their bodily life, needs, and influences. So Yates isn't really conversing with sheep; he is using them as signposts that can point to the conceptual void that is the human.

The appeal of a Marxist or antihumanist stance aside, what is missing then from these readings of More's cannibal sheep is first any consideration of actual "sheep on the ground" (like the moles in the ground that were absent from our earlier critics' discussions) even in the work of the most dedicated materialist critics; and second any willingness to grant to sheep something other than an innocent, unthreatening, positive "nature." Driven by their various ideological agendas, critics generally ignore what would have been as clear as day to some of More's contemporaries: that sheep were indeed toothy, rapacious creatures, and that there was abundant reason to fear them—not merely the humans who bought and sold them or enclosed the lands they grazed, but the sheep themselves. Defanging More's sheep for whatever political purpose seems to me to repeat the very erasure of nature that the metaphorizing of sheep also enacts. And so, in this section I will read More's and others' sheep for what we can learn about their material natures, and for what we can understand about why cannibal sheep are not easily redeemed as poor passive victims, mere instruments of evil human landowners and exploiters of labor. Considering the (early modern) "nature" of sheep will, I further suggest, make it clear to us that current models of labor, alienation, and property are inadequate to account for More's, Marx's, or anyone else's *sheep*, whatever they may accomplish for humans.

Like moles, sheep are competitive participants in a limited ecosystem. Human intervention in traditional agriculture, however, amplifies the destructive effects of sheep on everything from waterways to land availability to labor markets. While the impact of increasing English pastoralism throughout the sixteenth and seventeenth centuries is easy to trace in the displacement of agricultural workers and the intensified policing of vagrants and other transient potential laborers, the ecological impact of sheep may be less obvious. Given England's soil, relatively temperate climate, and careful human manipulation of new practices, including field rotation and the use of root crops as winter fodder, England did not see the effects of widespread overgrazing. The European experience with sheep in its colonies, however, suggests some of what happens when sheep populations explode. "Ungulate irruption," as it is called, occurs when grazing animals reproduce based on available food resources; once the highest level of pasturage is depressed by their grazing, populations that have soared tend to collapse, and then soar and collapse again until an "accommodation" is reached between sheep and the environment. Again, in fertile and herd-adapted countryside like England's, this swelling and failure of herds is less visible (although as we will see, not absent), but in New World environments, where grazing plants are of different varieties with a different ecological history, the process can permanently damage whole regions. Elinor Melville has described the consequences of sheep grazing in Mexico's Valle de Mezquital, where in the first half of the sixteenth century Spanish sheep were imported. From a little under four thousand sheep in the 1550s, herds grew to over two million by 1560. Spanish herders saw the environment not as a fragile ecosystem delicately husbanded by the natives, but as a rich green world that they assumed would support sheep in the same fashion as did their homeland.[31]

Sheep were so numerous in Europe that the annual drives to and from their mountain grasslands could create social and political friction: the Spanish corporation of sheep owners held extensive rights to move their sheep to and from various grazing lands, entitling them to graze in towns and villages as needed, which could inconvenience or enrage locals. The Italian Apennines witnessed similar social effects caused by the pressures of sheepherding: there, shepherds' tents were so numerous they resembled an "invading army."[32] In both countries, the environment suffered terrific degradation but was able to recover. In Mexico, however, "a fertile, densely populated, and complex agricultural mosaic," composed of croplands, woodlands, forests, limestone quarries, and occupied by a thriving population of native Otomí Indians was quickly reduced to a mesquite desert, its topography, botany and society forever transformed.[33] The sheep, local tradition has it, "ate" the Otomí in much the same manner that More's sheep cannibalize England's agricultural laborers.[34] Dispossessed of their ancestral lands, forced into mining or into labor on Spanish farms or government projects, native Indians lost the knowledge that had allowed them to preserve the ecosystem of the Valle for centuries.

So sheep are indeed dangerous, not only to human life as in Hythloday's remarks, but to natural environments that support a variety of human and animal inhabitants. While More's fellow Englishmen might not have known the fate of the Otomí, they certainly knew that sheep were, and are, notorious consumers: they can eat their way through tons of grass or fodder in a short period of time. As grazers, sheep are one of the most damaging because they require so much land and food: by preference, sheep eat as many broad-leafed plants as they can obtain. In comparison to their fellow ruminants (cows, for example), which eat primarily tough grasses, sheep eat such a diverse array of material that they leave little to reseed and grow anew; they also tend to crop close to the ground, which means they can easily overgraze an area if not moved frequently or provided supplementary foods. Melville clarifies that although sheep are often assumed to graze in arid regions, in fact they *create* arid land, especially where human intervention increases herd densities.[35] Rowland Prothero in his history of sheep notes more than once that the maxim "The foot of the sheep turns sand into gold" applied only *after* the sixteenth century, when systems for using sheepfolding to manure ground became a regular part of English husbandry.[36] Without that system, sheep stress and so threaten any environment. So, to follow along with Yates's speculative suggestion, were sheep given a voice at the table, what they would likely demand is more and more and more food.

In addition to having an endless capacity for eating, sheep are consumers of capital and labor: as More's Hythloday makes clear, they create competition for work, displacing the traditional farm labor that is generally used to till the land for grain crops in favor of a more "efficient" (that is, profitable to the landowner) labor economy based on pasturage. Instead of agricultural land's former steady income, early moderns who lived through enclosures saw the amount of labor necessary and available to sustain farm laborers drop precipitously—one shepherd guarding a vast flock substitutes for numerous crop workers digging, planting, and harvesting. Alternatively, however, sheep consume labor in the sense that those few shepherds must work "full time, all day, every day," alone and largely celibate for months of the year as they follow their flocks far from home.[37] To guard against overgrazing, shepherds created the hurdles with which sheep were "folded" or penned, a time-consuming and back-breaking task; these hurdles had to be dismantled and moved manually to new pastures on a regular basis. The practice of cotting sheep leads to another complication for the conscientious shepherd, namely the effects of crowding on individual animals: the author of *The Husbandman's Instructor* advises that any housing for sheep must have "several Partitions of Hurdles, or suchlike, to keep the weaker from the stronger and unruly, lest they be hurt by them," and Conrad Heresbach warns to keep rams away from herds lest the ewes be "lamed with lechery."[38] All is not peaceful in the commonwealth of sheep, where the shepherd has to guard against the usual predators while also protecting the sheep from themselves, from their conflicts with the land and with each other.

Before the invention of sheep dip, sheep also required the application of ointments and tar to treat for flies and scab, a task the shepherd had to perform by hand, taking each individual sheep and anointing its coat segment by segment. And the return on all this investment of time and work could be everything . . . or nothing. Although prices of wool fluctuated throughout the sixteenth and seventeenth centuries, raising sheep was clearly considered a money-making venture—unless the farmer lost an entire herd to disease. Ryder estimates that losses of 30 percent were usual during the Middle Ages and the early Renaissance, and could rise to between 50 and 70 percent, usually from outbreaks of "murrain."[39] Fynes Moryson quotes the proverb "He whose sheepe stand, and wives die (the husbands gaining their dowries) must need be rich," but also cautions that "these rots [murrain] often destroy whole flocks. . . . And the feeding of Sheepe, upon like accident of diseases, often does the owner in his estate."[40] Rose Hentschell points out that although the labor of shepherds is idealized in Renaissance literature, the many troubles and disasters that befell sheep farmers could not be entirely written out of the record—the elegiac, the nostalgic, the sorrowful elements of pastoral are traces of this uncertainty and failure.[41] So while potentially extremely lucrative, sheep farming was a highly risky investment, long on labor for the few employed by it and short on certainties of returns.

Despite the praise that is heaped on sheep in the husbandry manuals for their various body parts and contributions to English trade and wealth, there are often small signs in those texts of sheepy excess. Mascall, who saw in the sheep "no hurt at all," nevertheless writes: "To be short, the shorter and finer the Grasse is, the meter is it for sheepe: and yet is there no pasture so good, or so fine, but with continuall use your sheepe will be wearie of, except the shepheard remedie this fault with giving them salt, which (as a sauce to their foode) bee must set reddie in Sommer when they come from pasture, in little troughes of wood."[42] What Mascall describes is the sheep's need for minerals in its fodder; however, using terminology that has the sheep "wearying" of even the best grass slants the passage, characterizing the sheep as picky, needy consumers to be catered to with "little troughes" to "sauce" their food, as if they were aristocrats at a banquet. Lest the image of sheep as picky (but voracious) eaters seem a stretch, here is Franz Wolfgang on the same subject: "For a sheep loveth green Meadows, and is very delicate; for if she cannot feed in such green Meadows, she will eat nothing at all: and counteth no labour lost if at last she getteth into a field that is green, and then she looketh about for cold, clear water, loving nothing more, not induring to drink of muddy waters."[43] Granted, Wolfgang's incidental purpose is also to illustrate the sheep's proper allegorical use in church discourse; still, there is something provocative in both Mascall's and Wolfgang's characterization of the eating habits of sheep. It may seem a long way from cannibals to epicures, or from destructive grazers to sulky gourmets, but both versions of ovine consumption revolve around extremes of appetite.

The interdependence of humans and sheep could work, then, to the advantage of both, of either, or of neither party, depending on economic and environmental factors often beyond any human or animal control. If, as William Lambarde wrote in his *Perambulations of Kent* (1570), the "whole realme also might rightly be called shepey," then that also meant that the whole realm's fortunes were tied to the vagaries of sheep successes and failures.[44] And if the shift from arable to pasture uses of land increased unemployment for the majority, it intensified the labor of the few until it resembled enslavement to the animal's bodily needs. Sheep care as described in the husbandry manuals thus seems to anticipate the proprietary inversion associated with more recent attitudes about pet ownership: the animal demands so much investment of time, labor, and treasure that its legal designation as property is simply ludicrous, and the question of who "owns" whom is distorted. Beyond observing a certain truth to this cliché even for early moderns, it is worth thinking about how and why the nature, biology, and reputation of animals continue to influence economic thought after More. The next section of this chapter looks at the important role of animals like sheep—even specifically More's cannibal sheep—in Marx's theories of labor and property.

Species at Work

As we saw in Chapter 4, Marx initiates *Capital* by qualifying the labor of animals as distinct in kind from human labor and production with his spiders and bees. But in the final chapters of *Capital* he also acknowledges his debt to More, especially to More's sheep, quoting the cannibal sheep section of *Utopia* at length in a footnote on English agricultural laws.[45] It is fair to say, then, that More literally and theoretically "underwrites" some portion of *Capital*. Certainly animals, More's sheep among them, populate Marx's thought with some density, suggesting that we might profitably consider the relationships between the pre-Enlightenment ideas of More and the post-Enlightenment thought of Marx. By reading "backwards" through Marx, I think we might also arrive at a different perspective on More's use of animals in *Utopia* than has so far obtained in the criticism of that text.

In his *Economic and Philosophical Manuscripts of 1844* Marx describes something he calls "species alienation," the alienation of the worker from his "species being." Species alienation for Marx applies exclusively to human beings:

> Man is a species-being not only in that practically and theoretically
> he makes both his own and other species into his object, but also,
> and this is only another way of putting the same thing, he relates to

himself as to the present, living species, in that he relates to himself
as to a universal and therefore free being.

Both with man and with animals the species-life consists
physically in the fact that man (like animals) lives from inorganic
nature. . . . The universality of man appears in practice precisely in
the universality that makes the whole of nature into his inorganic
body in that it is both (i) his immediate means of subsistence and
also (ii) the material object and tool of his vital activity.[46]

Marx views "nature" as all that is beyond the organic limits of the body but
that is not yet manufactured into commodities; he sees man as "part of nature," but also capable of understanding his "vital activity" (labor that per-
petuates life and adds to life) as a thing separable from himself. "The animal
is immediately one with its vital activity. It is not distinct from it. They are
identical. Man makes his vital activity itself into an object of his will and consciousness."[47] When that process is usurped by capitalism, human labor ceases
to exist for the improvement of the species, and humans labor only for individual life, not species-life: "The animal only fashions things according to the
standards and needs of the species it belongs to, whereas man knows how to
produce according to the measure of every species and knows everywhere how
to apply its inherent standard to the object; thus man also fashions things according to the laws of beauty."[48] For Marx's "man," the essence of his humanity
is realized in his ability to project the end result of his labor, to objectify it and
recognize its significance and historicity.

Clearly, Marx again relies on the Enlightenment distinction between
human and animal (not to mention one that divides male from female, leaving the female entangled in matter, in the body, in "necessity," repeating the
division Locke at least marginally recognized as one created in bad faith).
Only humans (men) can experience labor as this kind of alienation, since
animals cannot understand the product of their labor as an object—they do
not create with intention, let alone reflect on the created object's importance,
consider its value to future generations, appreciate its aesthetics, and so on.
Labor in a capitalist system destroys human species-being, rendering the laborer "like an animal" by making his labor merely individual, and so no longer
fully human. Ironically, this collapse of the species barrier is redressed when
the human rejoins his organic (bodily) self to his "inorganic" self, or nature.
At that point, the transcendent unity and the defeat of alienation promised
by the historical triumph of communism will result in the yet more thorough

division of human from animal through the reinstantiation of a binary that
exempts animals from the "nature" with which humans are reunited.

Where do More's sheep fit into this system? Sheep and humans have
changed places in Hythloday's description of England due to the ravages of
enclosure; cannibal sheep now consume humans, enjoying a new species identity, while human beings, alienated from the land and prior systems of labor,
become bestialized, meat for sheep. More and Marx thus agree that the real
freedom of human beings lies in a clearly maintained dividing line between
species identities. They also agree on the lack of production on the part of
animals—the animal labors only for itself and has no "species-being" of its
own to realize through its labor: "It is true that the animal, too, produces. It
builds itself a nest, a dwelling, like the bee, the beaver, the ant, etc. But it only
produces what it needs immediately for itself or its offspring. It produces one-
sidedly whereas man produces universally; it produces only under the pressure
of immediate physical need, whereas man produces freely from physical need
and only truly produces when he is free."[49] Marx simply can't imagine that
animals might "produce" for the benefit of others, or that animals can enjoy
or see the significance of their production.

In denying so absolutely the connection between human and animal, and
choosing a limited variety of wild creatures as his examples, Marx forecloses
on a number of particularly complex examples of labor and property relations. When humans labor on behalf of sheep, or cows, or conies, or bees,
or any other animal that can generate a product of economic value, they are
not engaging with animals as mere instruments.[50] As Tim Ingold observes,
Marx's formula, because it denies animals will, "relegates animals to the status
of mindless machines. In truth, the domestic animal is no more the physical
conductor of its master's activity than is a slave; both constitute labor itself,
rather than its instruments, and are therefore bound by social relations of
production."[51] As we've seen in the husbandry manuals, sheep do not exist
outside social relations—they have their own herd structure and their own
sexual behaviors, they require specific interventions from specifically trained
individuals, and even their appetites, if excessive, can be expressed in terms
of tribe and class hierarchy. Moreover, the technologies that obtain in sheep
rearing and sheep breeding change the social relations of labor not just among
sheep, but among men—hence the historical shift that leads to More's outcry
against cannibal sheep.

Richard Tapper suggests that a more appropriate rubric for describing the
property and labor relations between sheep and humans in More's day would

be a feudal one—sheep behave more like serfs and peasants on a feudal estate than like workers in a protocapitalist world: "More extensive livestock-rearing by pastoralists involves animals that are not tamed but are herded in communities and following their natural inclinations to move, congregate, graze, and breed. Again, these are subservient to and controlled by human masters, but the relation is like a contract or transaction in which the herders 'protect' the herds in return for a 'rent.' This resembles the Marxian conception of feudal relations between a lord and a serf."[52] Tapper's approach takes into account a natural history of sheep that acknowledges their difference from other animals. Unlike the Marxist version of species, in which sheep are a place holder or empty vessel deployed to construct an ideological category, the human, from which Marx can extrapolate a host of "natural" emotions, conditions and experiences, Tapper's sheep remain sheep. Ironically, though they remain "wild" (if marginally domesticated in some fashion by exploiting herd structures for human ends), early modern sheep in Tapper's description gain attributes of human social organization—community, the capacity to enter into a contract, to pay rent. Again, animals that cannot be extracted from social relations end up inevitably anthropomorphized, a result of the effort to create a system through which their status can be fully represented. In More's account, as well, because sheep are entirely embedded in a system of social relations, they can be (perhaps must be) engaged through an inevitable process of anthropomorphization. But this is not necessarily a negative; anthropomorphization in this instance may recognize a deep sympathy or similarity that requires further exploration in justice to the animals at hand, as is in part the case with More's cannibals.

Erica Fudge remarks that the sixteenth century saw the gradual removal of livestock from the home, simultaneously with a shift in the status of the pet; I have observed elsewhere that the same process rendered livestock a massed collective that could be classified as meat, whereas pets gradually gained something analogous to personhood.[53] The legal ramifications of these changes are confusing: as Fudge points out, the law did not recognize animals kept for pleasure as having value, something with which livestock were clearly endowed, so that theft of a heifer was punishable by law in the sixteenth century, while theft of a beloved pet was not.[54] Indeed, this kind of confusion results in the "separation of the law from our lived relation to our pets," leaving the law of property, ownership, and value detached from a good portion of animal keeping.[55] I would add that theories of property and labor have been and continue to be detached from any real consideration of the diversity of forms of animal labor, with direct consequences for both animals and humans. In this fashion, such theories fail to account fully for the very nature of property and labor, full stop. Tapper's and Ingold's corrections to Marx, and my brief exploration of early modern instances of work and ownership, all indicate that where human-animal relations are concerned, the usual language of labor, production, and property, like the language of Marxist "feudalism" versus "capitalism," may simply not be adequate. Marxism's reliance on Enlightenment definitions of the nature of "the human," its abstraction of "the animal," and its lack of attention to everything from herd structure to individual animals' bodily attributes, impoverishes its accounts of both animal and human labor. Indeed, we can expect that any theory that ignores these aspects of animal embodiment will result in a similarly amputated description.

But what of *Utopia* and its beasts? Like Marx after him, More is invested in a clear distinction between humans and animals: when he invokes "beasts" More generally intends a comparison with humans that violates this distinction. For instance, in discussing pleasure, Hythloday establishes that only human beings experience certain kinds, "for no other living creature doth behold the fairness and the beauty of the world or is moved with any respect of savours, but only for the diversity of meats, neither perceiveth the concordant and discordant distances of sounds and tunes."[56] And later on philosophy, he describes "Man," "whom only he [God] hath made of wit and capacity to consider and understand the excellency of so great a work."[57] Finally, praising Utopians' use of deceit and craftiness to prevent bloodshed in war, Hythloday reiterates the commonplace that many beasts fight more fiercely and with more strength than men, but only men are capable of reason: "For with bodily strength (say they) bears, lions, boars, wolves, dogs, and other wild beasts do fight. And as the most part of them do pass us in strength and fierce courage, so in wit and reason we be much stronger than they all."[58]

Stephen Greenblatt has observed that Utopia is designed "to prevent the existence of a class of laborers reduced to the condition of animals."[59] To accomplish this More has to draw two sets of careful dividing lines, between categories like "man" and "beast," but also between economic systems. It is in its attempt to redraw the second that Utopians run into trouble with the first, as Hythloday's narrative runs into a series of contradictions that raise questions about the links between labor, property, and human exceptionalism.

In Book 2 of the *Utopia,* More establishes immediately that all who live there are defined first and always as agricultural laborers: "Husbandry is a science common to them all in general, both men and women, wherein they be all expert and cunning. In this they be all instructed even from their youth, partly in their schools with traditions and precepts, and partly in the country nigh the city, brought up, as it were in playing, not only beholding the use of it, but by occasion of exercising their bodies practising it also."[60] The common labor of agriculture binds the Utopians to the soil and to each other, and eliminates class distinctions, but it distinguishes them from Europeans whose stratified society renders husbandmen less than beasts:

> For what justice is this, that a rich goldsmith or an usurer, or to be
> short, any of them which either do nothing at all . . . should have
> a pleasant and a wealthy living . . . when in the meantime poor
> labourers, carters, ironsmiths, carpenters, and ploughmen, by so
> great and continual toil, as drawing and bearing beasts be scant able
> to sustain, and against so necessary toil . . . should yet get so hard
> and poor a living and live so wretched and miserable a life, that the
> state and condition of the labouring beasts may seem much better
> and wealthier? For they be not put to so continual labour, nor their
> living is not much worse, yea, to them much pleasanter, taking no
> thought in the mean season for the time to come.[61]

Because all Utopians without exception perform manual labor, Utopia manages its resources exceptionally well: there is enough for everyone, so much indeed that constant and unrelenting work is unnecessary, while a surplus is created that can be traded externally. Instead of being bestialized by such work, the passage above tell us, the ecologically sound foundation of all Utopian society in the common experience of labor guarantees that Utopians can enjoy the limited work, plentiful food, and pleasures in life that outside of Utopia fewer men enjoy less securely than do farm animals.

Yet when Hythloday turns to the actual experiences of Utopians with individual animals, something unusual happens. Take, for instance, this apparently throwaway description of chicken husbandry: "They bring up a great multitude of pullen, and that by a marvellous policy. For the hens do not sit upon the eggs, but by keeping them in a certain equal heat they bring life into them and hatch them. The chickens, as soon as they be come out of the shell, follow men and women instead of the hens."[62] In this instance, agricultural labor *does* lead to a kind of bestialization of the human worker—but one that is clearly being endorsed with a wink, even celebrated. Human caretaking of the animal blurs the distinction between human and animal; even the passage's grammar seems slightly opaque—the "them . . . they" pronouns are indefinite in their referents, although we must surmise from the results of the experiment that the "they" who keep and hatch the eggs are people, not hens. Christopher Burlinson remarks on this strange passage, finding in it evidence that More is rethinking the human-animal binary: while carefully accounting for More's reluctance to overtly elevate animals to quasi-human status, Burlinson sees More's chickens, like his sheep, as an example of the text "rendering the animals that it employs within its own textual figures as rightful objects of our ethical concern."[63] Burlinson remarks that the constant appearance of nonhuman creatures in Utopia appears gratuitous unless we consider it evidence that among the alternatives this world is designed to explore is the world of human-animal hierarchies.

I would not disagree with Burlinson, and I think that the placement of the passage at the very outset of Hythloday's description of *Utopia* signals its importance, since it plays a part in establishing the most fundamental aspects of Utopian life. However, this particular passage may have less to do with some form of ethics than with the effects of dividing Utopia from the rest of its vaguely European neighbors. That is, while elsewhere in the work bestialization is the property of class, labor inequity, and the inefficiencies of a precapitalist mercantilism, here, where Hythloday wants to delve into the morally positive effects of universal agricultural labor, he slips into a fantasy about humans and animals converging in their functions and so trading places. The human-animal divide collapses for a moment precisely because equality of property and labor seems inevitably to extend to the animals that create common wealth, the "multitudes" of chicks that comprise the surplus goods of Utopia.

Perhaps most famously, Hythloday makes another beast comparison while discussing Utopian marriage practices:

> Furthermore, in choosing wives and husbands they observe earnestly and straitly a custom which seemed to us very fond and foolish. For a sad and an honest matron showeth the woman, be she maid or widow, naked to the wooer. And likewise a sage and discreet man exhibiteth the wooer naked to the woman. At this custom we laughed, and disallowed it as foolish. But they, on the other part, do greatly wonder at the folly of all other nations which, in buying a colt, whereas a little money is in hazard, be so chary and circumspect, that though he be almost all bare, yet they will not buy

him unless the saddle and all the harness be taken off, lest under
those coverings be hid some gall or sore, And yet in choosing a wife,
which shall be either pleasure or displeasure to them all their life
after, they be so reckless, that all the residue of the woman's body
being covered with clothes, they esteem her scarcely by one hand-
bredth (for they can see no more but her face).[64]

If, as Greenblatt has argued, the design of Utopian social life is organized to
eliminate "possessive individualism" derived from systems of private property,
then this version of the marriage market seems to cooperate with that process by taking away the romantic and idealized individuation that characterizes marital choice based on a pretty face in England and Europe. "Utopian
marriage, then does not strive for a deep affective union"; Utopians have a
"commitment to human malleability and interchangeability," which not only
prevents any system of inheritance or "bloodline" but extends into the selec-
tion of a mate.[65] The face, that bodily part which makes each human appear
separate and unique, should not be preferred over other, hidden qualities of
those body parts that remain beneath clothing, lest some defect or "foul defor-
mity" render the beloved distasteful to the partner. "And the endowments of
the body cause the virtues of the mind more to be esteemed and regarded, yea,
even in the marriage of wise men," concludes Hythloday.[66]

Paradoxically, however, Utopians achieve the elimination of risk in marital choice by importing elements of the market into their most fundamental
social institution. And, of course, in so doing Utopians bestialize (making
marriageable mates participate in something very like a breed auction, putting
the body at the center of marriage, an institution meant to transcend the material in early modern culture) the very human beings they strive to elevate so
completely over the bestialized laborers of England or Europe. Further, given
More's own marital history, marrying not the young woman he loved, but her
elder sister in order to spare the latter social shame and suffering, we must
wonder whether this passage illustrates some part of More's own willingness
to treat women as substitutable, one for another. We might link this passage,
then, with the result of Utopia chicken raising: in this case, rather than labor
creating a common animality between chicken and human nurturer, the erasure of individuation based on the elimination of private property leads to the
"animalization" of humans.

The danger of animals in Utopia is that they squirm out of neat categories to undermine the apparently easy establishment of equality through

common labor, and the elevation of communal property over private, by then
threatening to subvert the (to More) fundamental distinction between human
and animal. I take Hythloday's description of slaughterhouses as a kind of
imaginative map charting the hazards inherent in Utopia's animals. Because
Utopia's residents are human, a fact that is demonstrated by and confirmed
by their consumption of meat (especially for the Catholic More, given the
religious justification, even necessity of meat eating[67]), they must have a place
for the butchery of their food animals: "But first the filthiness and ordure
thereof is clean washed away in the running river without the city in places
appointed meet for the same purpose . . . Neither they suffer anything that
is filthy, loathsome, or uncleanly to be brought into the city, lest the air, by
the stench thereof infected and corrupt, should cause pestilent diseases."[68] As
Rebecca Totaro argues, this passage and others that concern themselves with
hygiene, reflect More's fear of plague and disease.[69] Appointed in 1514 as the
commissioner of the sewers, More was familiar with the problem of removing
butchers' filth, which so plagued London that its water was known to be too
foul to drink safely; further, given the miasma theory of contagion, the odors
of rotting carcasses were believed to breed disease. Having witnessed the dev-
astation of plague, and knowing a good deal about medicine from his friend,
the royal physician Thomas Linacre, More was aware of how to plan a city
that was less prone to pestilence. That knowledge is reflected in the details of
Utopian infrastructure.

But another reason for the exclusion of the killing fields from the towns is
the problem of moral contamination: "they suffer none of their citizens to kill
their cattle, because they think that pity and good-nature, which are among
the best of those affections that are born with us, are much impaired by the
butchering of animals."[70] If the need to prevent physical contamination gives
rise to good city planning, then the need to prevent moral contamination
leads Utopians to rely on slave labor. Because butchery degrades and coarsens
humans, the Utopians prefer to have other, less "human" workers risk ultimate
and absolute bestialization by it.

What is a bit perplexing about Utopian slavery is the simple fact that
Utopia does not otherwise *need* its slaves. In a land of plenty, where the labor
of all produces a surplus of goods, slavery has no purpose, except, as is the case
with Utopian slavery, as punishment for crimes or a way to handle the con-
demned and poor of neighboring nations. That is, Utopia demonstrates a case
of noncapitalist slavery, which should be a functional dead end, destined for
obsolescence since it has no economic benefit. The fact that Utopian slavery

continues is determined in part by the manufacture of crime and suffering outside Utopia's borders—some proportion of slaves are a result of other nations' errors in economic practice. But Utopia has its own crime as well, and when Utopians descend to bestial ways, there must be a means by which they can be punished: "But their own men they handle hardest, whom they judge more desperate, and to have deserved greater punishment, because they being so godly brought up to virtue in so excellent a commonwealth, could not for all that be refrained from misdoing."[71] Having shown they are not fit to be fully human, slaves may then relieve their more human counterparts in towns and cities of the degrading, brutalizing labor of animal slaughter.

Thus, we must set alongside *Utopia*'s rather heart-warming anecdote on raising chickens this conjunction between animal slaughter and slavery. Both are the direct result of cross-fertilizations between humans and animals (with positive and negative outcomes in More's schema) that are inevitable in an economy that is so deeply invested in common agricultural labor and communal property. To work the fields (like animals), to care for animals, to satisfy a mate sexually, to reproduce children, are all benefits to Utopia's human society. Once many of the markers and circumstances of life like clothing, inherited wealth, bloodlines, or occupations that Europeans assume constitute specifically human identity are eliminated, however, "the animal" then emerges as a threat to deindividuated human identity, whether in a pleasant fantasy of communion with creatures or as a dangerous contaminant, an ugly but ineradicable part of "the human."

More's *Utopia* does, if inadvertently, indicate a way forward for those of us postmoderns seeking a new way to imagine human-animal relations that remedies some of the worst abuses to which both groups have been subjected. Donna Haraway advocates the use of labor to rethink the human-animal relationship: "My suspicion is that we might nurture responsibility with and for other animals better by plumbing the category of labor more than the category of rights with its inevitable preoccupation with similarity, analogy, calculation, and honorary membership in the expanded abstraction of the Human."[72] I too see in labor important potential to point the way to responsive and responsible interaction among species and to answer the distortions created by systems of property and ownership. By showing, entirely against his own clear goals, that the destruction of private property and the related dismantling of possessive individualism have the inevitable consequence of destabilizing the categories of human and animal, More has already laid the groundwork for challenging economic systems that use property relations to distinguish humans from animals. By enforcing a system of global labor that inevitably also challenges distinctions between species on the basis of the work they do, More's work also highlights the flaws in economic systems that create false differences between kinds of labor and/or laboring identities, along with the philosophical, social, and cultural systems that arise from economic practices and provide the structures of thought that continue to enforce them. Although Marx takes More for a fundamental text, I am suggesting that *Utopia* mounts a proleptic, subterranean critique of Marx's theory. Marx's moles, perhaps, knew more about it than he did.

Knowing Animals

In the sixteenth century, Thomas More tried to invent a new society, complete with cultural attributes and values and an economic system that rectified the failures of European societies. To do so, More mobilized examples of embodied human-animal relationships that ultimately demonstrated the impossibility of establishing a bright line between the two categories. While Utopia is "nowhere" in sixteenth-century Europe, it has been this project's goal to insist that the implications of its paradoxical efforts to represent animals are everywhere in early modern culture. The same complex ironies and contradictions that shaped More's efforts also shaped much early modern art, literature, science, and medicine: any human culture that attempts to construct something exclusively human is destined to find that it cannot shed its origins in the experience of embodiment that we share with animals. As I have occasionally indicated, twentieth- and twenty-first-century scientists, ethologists, and zoologists are gradually plumbing the depths and varieties of that experience, and finding that the biology of the mind, among other things, consistently invalidates Cartesian dualism. Darwin's theory of evolution already proposed the common ancestry of humans and animals as evidenced in their related anatomies, making each creature, human or animal, a compendium of past variants of itself and other creatures, as well as of its interactions with environments. Modern medicine is rediscovering the interdependence and benefits for humans of everything from parasites to pets; wild animals are recolonizing our urban spaces with a vengeance—sometimes literally when species come into direct conflict with humans who are unfamiliar with their habits after decades, centuries of alienation and distance. Zoonotic diseases are headline news in the era of AIDS, Ebola, swine and avian flu; the human interventions in the environment that have released these diseases into global populations

are now a familiar storyline in films and novels.[1] Rural "pests" are being reeval-
uated for their role in balanced ecosystems, including those that can include
successful and sustainable agriculture. Investigating the early modern animal
body invites us to consider not only how these "new" discoveries and perspectives should change our relationship to animals and to the environment that
shapes both human and nonhuman creatures, but whether they are even new.
And now, as we will see, even the question of whether animals themselves have
something recognizable as "culture" seems to be on the table.

The introduction to this volume began with Giovanni Battista Gelli's
Circe, and so it is perhaps fitting to end by returning to that text. The sole animal that is transformed by Ulysses' arguments at its conclusion is the elephant,
who, accepting the case for human superiority, is returned to his physical
human form and given back his name, Aglafemos. Unlike the lowly mole,
who asserts that he is "perfecte in thys [his] kynd," the elephant-philosopher
eventually aspires not to the perfection of elephant-kind, but to his former humanity. The elephant's transformation suggests that if form follows function,
then function also follows form—the elephant cannot remain in that body
once his mind has begun to desire what Ulysses promises. Bodies and minds
must conform to one another. After his transformation, Aglafemos celebrates
his new condition: "Oh, what a fayre thynge, Oh what a marveylous thing it is
to be a man! Oh how well I nowe knowe it better then I did before, for I have
proved the one and the other: oh, howe fayre the lyghte seemeth to be unto
him, who is alwaies wont to be in darkenes, and howe muche the good semeth
better unto him, that is accustomed to prove the evill!"[2]

Gelli's elephant is the pinnacle of animal creation because only he is sensible of the advantages of being human, and so he is rewarded with a human
appreciation for God, the transcendental despot who ensures meaning in
Ulysses' system of reason. Following his restoration to human form, Aglafemos sings a hymn in praise of the "first mover":

Ye woodes kepe scilence, and ye windes, repose your selves in fine:
Whiles of this order of the hole, so marvailous and so fayre,
Of the first mover I do sing, cause of earth and ayre
Of all incorruptible thinges.[3]

The elephant, who fortuitously saves Ulysses from the shame of failing utterly
to convince even a single of Circe's enchanted creatures that being human is
better than being an animal, has become a fit worshipper of the deity that

other creatures cannot recognize in their benighted, animal condition. Gelli's elephant is thus a guarantor that the hierarchy of being is valid, and that there are some animals, superior to their fellows, who can perceive the justice of such a hierarchy, if dimly. We might say, then, that it is the elephant, not God, who ensures the "order of the [w]hole" for the local logics of Gelli's work.

The natural philosopher Edward Topsell would have agreed with Gelli's schema insofar as he too finds the elephant displaying qualities that mimic human empathy and reason, and attributes religion to the animal. Like so many early modern natural philosophers, Topsell had no qualms about either anthropomorphism or scientific accuracy when he described elephants—alongside stories about how their cold blood is irresistible to dragons, he includes accounts of their love of and extreme loyalty to humans, their ability to tell weights and measures, and their sexual chastity.[4] He also details their grieving rituals:

> I cannot omit their care, to bury and cover the dead carkasses of their companions, or any other of their kinde; for finding them dead, they pass not by them until they have lamented their common misery, by casting dust and earth on them, and also green boughs, in token of sacrifice, holding it execrable to do otherwise; and they know by a natural instinct some assured fore-tokens of their own death. Besides when they wax old and unfit to gather their own meat, or fight for themselves, the younger of them feed, nourish and defend them, yea they raise them out of Ditches and Trenches into which they are fallen, exempting them from all labour and perill, and interposing their own bodies for their protection: neither do they forsake them in sickness, or in their wounds, but stand to them, pulling out Darts of their bodies, and helping both like skilful Chirurgions to cure wounds, and also like faithful friends to supply their wants.[5]

Topsell's language here emphasizes analogy, not identity: elephants are "like" chirugeons, and "like" faithful friends, but thus by linguistic sleight of hand, not those things. The passage thus manages to capture the implicit elevation of elephants to quasi-human status we see in Gelli's location of his elephant at the top of a chain of being without actually confirming that the abyss between species can be crossed.

When Gelli's elephant is rewarded for his human recognition of reason, he is transformed physically into a human, discarding his elephant body as he gains a human name. Both the posited mirroring of elephant and human mind and the erasure of the animal that Gelli's text portrays are being repeated, materially and rhetorically, in the late twentieth and early twenty-first centuries. Elephants, say zoologists, neuroscientists, and ethologists, are undergoing cultural collapse brought on by environmental damage, constant poaching, and other forms of human intervention. In a 2006 article for the *New York Times*, Charles Siebert reported on the phenomenon, describing first the centrality of elephant grief rituals to herd culture:

> When an elephant dies, its family members engage in intense mourning and burial rituals, conducting weeklong vigils over the body, carefully covering it with earth and brush, revisiting the bones for years afterward, caressing the bones with their trunks, often taking turns rubbing their trunks along the teeth of a skull's lower jaw, the way living elephants do in greeting. If harm comes to a member of an elephant group, all the other elephants are aware of it. This sense of cohesion is further enforced by the elaborate communication system that elephants use. In close proximity they employ a range of vocalizations, from low-frequency rumbles to higher-pitched screams and trumpets, along with a variety of visual signals, from the waving of their trunks to subtle anglings of the head, body, feet and tail. When communicating over long distances—in order to pass along, for example, news about imminent threats, a sudden change of plans or, of the utmost importance to elephants, the death of a community member—they use patterns of subsonic vibrations that are felt as far as several miles away by exquisitely tuned sensors in the padding of their feet.[6]

What might seem extraordinary in this description (apart from how much it echoes Topsell) is first that it asserts for elephants command of everything from language to complex social organization to collective memory of the herd—and second, that most readers of the article probably did not take exception to any of these claims. We seem to be witnessing a moment in postmodernity when the idea that animals might possess something called "culture" is once again popularly palatable.

Siebert goes on to describe how elephant grief rituals become impossible when an entire family is massacred for tusks and other body parts. Already

suffering the consequences of social disruption due to herd management (cull-
ing, moving herds away from traditional grounds to parks or enclosures) and
habitat destruction, human predation shatters the herds' remaining cultural
anchors: "As a result of such social upheaval, calves are now being born to
and raised by ever younger and inexperienced mothers. Young orphaned elephants, meanwhile, that have witnessed the death of a parent at the hands of
poachers are coming of age in the absence of the support system that defines
traditional elephant life." The result is what we might call elephant sociopaths,
who attack humans without provocation, deliberately uproot fields of crops,
turn on their own, and commit other "crimes" irreconcilable with patterns
of elephant behavior in the past. Siebert's article is careful to parry the possible accusation of anthropomorphism; the factual evidence, he points out,
for trauma-induced behavioral changes is overwhelming—elephant outbursts
have become so common, in fact, they have earned an acronym: HECs, or
Human-Elephant Conflicts.

Cognitive function in mammals is not qualitatively different; the fact that
elephants' brains receive and interpret information in much the same way
that humans do should not therefore be surprising, nor by extension should
their susceptibility to psychological breaks from trauma. Elephants in particular have an enlarged hippocampus, the brain's memory-storage unit, and
structures in the limbic system that are associated with emotions. Elephants
are one of the few species to respond as do humans in mirror self-recognition
tests, which identify self-consciousness.[7] With their complex herd structures,
reliance on matriarchs for the transmission of knowledge, practices of communal parenting, and well-developed communication within and between
herds, elephants may thus seem to resemble humans even more than Gelli
and Topsell could appreciate. But the idea that what counts about elephants
is their resemblance to humans reinstantiates the very anthropocentrism that
critical animal studies and posthumanist theory are hard at work trying to dis-
lodge. We might compare for a moment More's cannibal sheep with Siebert's
elephants: critics seem uncomfortable comprehending the former *as sheep* at
all (in all their real, sometimes violent or destructive complexity) and rather
cast them as place holders for some other literary, historical, or ideological
"thing," while the latter appear to exist in scientific and popular literature *as*
themselves, replete with psychological complexity and self-consciousness, even
though (or possibly because?) they are being recorded for displaying all the
horrifying violence that is so impossible to associate with early modern sheep.
Where we assume the fictionality of More's animals, then, we accept the reality

of Siebert's. Our imposition of limits on our interpretive work where these animals are concerned suggests how difficult it is, as Erica Fudge puts it, to "perceive" animals through the confusion of social, cultural, historical, and disciplinary constructions that attach to them.[8] We can and should admire those, including Siebert, who struggle mightily to salvage what damage we have wrought on elephant culture by informing the public and perhaps changing its views, but we need not become uncritical in how we read their efforts.

The idea that elephants can resemble or mirror the human and so deserve special attention from specialists or laymen conveys an ethical problem already evident in Gelli's and Topsell's texts: setting the elephant apart confirms a hierarchy based in humanist anthropocentrism that confers superior status on the human and all species that resemble it. Cary Wolfe points out that this kind of discrimination continues in postmodern attempts to protect endangered and abused animals. Citing the efforts of the Great Ape Project, he argues that its flaw lies in the fact that "the model of rights being invoked here for extension to those who are (symptomatically) 'most like us' only ends up reinforcing the very humanism that seems to be the problem in the first place."[9] Following a lengthy interrogation of postmodern ethics in the work of Zygmunt Bauman, Niklas Luhmann, and Jacques Derrida, Wolfe arrives at the following reformulations of the Cartesian proposition: "I am *human* before I think," and "I *can* be *inhuman* only *after* I think."[10] This authorizes what Wolfe calls elsewhere a "humanist posthumanism," the ethics of which are grounded in reason; but through reason those engaging in the study of or defense of animals must then rigorously and continuously deconstruct their own premises.

To return to Topsell's and Gelli's accounts of elephants, both historical texts raise in different ways the question of how we read representations of animals—from what set of criteria, with what expectations, and with what blindnesses we construct our relationships with animals. Gelli is recognizably solving a textual and ideological problem: how to end his work, after so many creatures have rejected the superiority of humankind, with a convert for Ulysses that can prove humans are the epitome of creation. Topsell's account belongs to a long list of early modern works that are expected to summarize or incorporate stories from prior, particularly classical texts. Topsell delivers the goods: Zoroaster's assertion that the sight of a ram will "tameth and dismayeth" an elephant is repeated, as is Aristotle's claim that elephants can distinguish human royalty from commoners, and tales from Arianus of elephants avenging a master's betrayal by an adulterous wife or exposing a servant shortchanging their feed.[11] In each case, we might consider how such diverse, even contradictory, and in some cases manifestly fictional narratives constitute a genre, or how these tales instructed readers in the qualities that were valued most in humans as in the higher mammals; or we might relate Topsell's digest of classical sources to early modern strategies of authorship, or appreciate the text's sense of a rich and copious God-created nature. Written before the advent of academic disciplines, however, these texts resist the kind of sorting and prioritizing that is often enforced by modern divisions of knowledge into specific fields, with their attendant shaping imperatives.

G. A. Bradshaw, upon whose work Siebert's article is largely dependent, has highlighted the role of disciplinarity in current attitudes toward animals, accounting in her book *Elephants on the Edge: What Animals Teach Us about Humanity* for the resistance of scientists to recognizing patterns of elephant culture and psychology, which stems from science's disciplinary conditioning and a lingering Cartesian influence on how observation is interpreted.[12] As I pointed out in the introduction to this volume, opposition in the sciences to what is assumed to be anthropomorphizing can, as happened in the case of Clever Hans, radically skew conclusions about what is happening when an animal's behavior is in question. Ethologists and zoologists continue to fight a battle that is the legacy of Cartesian dualism, a battle against the belief that animals and humans simply cannot share those attributes of the mind—reason, emotion, moral judgment—that define the category "human" (and by extension inevitably justify human supremacy). Despite the degree to which the "mind" has been identified as a set of biological processes, the experience of thought and reason have not yet been fully resituated in the body, while the emotions and the meanings that are assumed to be attached to emotions remain suspects in the fight over what constitutes proof or accurate observation. When we see what looks like "human" behavior, that line of thinking goes, we are deluding ourselves into fallacies, failing to achieve true objectivity, as if the same behaviors in humans, as opposed to animals, originated in some completely different place outside the structures and chemistry of the brain. Cartesian doubt maintains its death grip on "evidence" in such a scenario. Many theorists and some scientists are increasingly aware that antianthropomorphism in this environment can become a kind of speciesism in disguise for its insistence that we do not, cannot, and should not imagine that we share much of anything with animals. Bradshaw notes that the assumed barriers that condition science to reject what it sees before it in animals is slowly falling to new, often interdisciplinary scientific ventures. Indeed, many in the field of critical animal studies share this straddling of disciplines, some of which are entirely outside academia. Donna Haraway, for instance, combines a background in biology and her expertise in feminist theory with extensive knowledge from her work training and competing her dogs; Vicky Hearne, perhaps most famously, combined interests in horse and dog training with a background in literary criticism and linguistics. In addition to their background in literature, both Donna Landry and Richard Nash, who study the eighteenth century, work extensively with horses, Nash in racing and Haraway with hunters. Bradshaw herself combines fields, using her background in both psychology and ecology to make a compelling case for changing the way we perceive and treat elephants. She borrows from neuroscience and therapeutic records, from philosophy and native knowledge to create her portrait of suffering elephants.

Interdisciplinarity, however, has its limits, and Bradshaw, along with most who work in multiple fields but wish to convince the majority, must in the end concede to the requirement for "evidence," thus legitimizing science's claim to authority over judgments about what is real and what is fictional. In presenting Bradshaw's position to a general public, for instance, Siebert feels compelled to defend it: "What Bradshaw and her colleagues describe would seem to be an extreme form of anthropocentric conjecture if the evidence that they've compiled from various elephant researchers, even on the strictly observational level, weren't so compelling."[13] Evidence, particularly statistical evidence wedded to advances in neurological science, is king here, condescending to affirm what African villagers and gamekeepers have been seeing and recounting for some time. But academic, theoretical animal studies often also suffer from disciplinary blindnesses: "interdisciplinary" in such work often excludes expertise that originates extra-institutionally, excludes knowledge derived from disciplines that have no place in our post-Enlightenment order of things. Carlo Ruini did not see his equestrian skills and his medical education as divisible; Philip Sidney could write nothing that did not contain at least traces of his talents in the manège. If writers did not themselves claim such expertise with animals, they inevitably knew well those who did—unlike our own general Western distance from the everyday experience of most animals except pets, early moderns could not escape the need to know.

A rigorous, reasoned deconstruction of reason's role in dividing human from animal, and humans from animals, thus requires its own historical narrative. Taken as literature, Gelli's and Topsell's works represent an imaginative engagement with animals that should be suggestive to postmoderns precisely because it is not bounded or prevented by the same post-Enlightenment disciplinary structures that we continue to engage. As literature, both texts offer moments when the grit of shared embodiment in the world hinders the smooth operation of division. Simply attending to those hesitations, those seizures of the epistemological machine, makes its pressures visible, hints at its artificiality, and beyond that, points to the desires that built it and keep it running. As history, early modern texts that include representations of animals can obviously suggest that the beliefs, conditions, and relationships governing human interaction with animals have recognizable origins and so endings—as Foucault has made clear, there is nothing inevitable, natural, or inviolable about the ways we categorize, organize, or explain objects and events.[14] The compelling thing about both Gelli's and Topsell's works, like so much of their contemporaries', is that they nevertheless described something *real* for both authors and readers. That fact might lead us to question upon what fictions our own version of the real is built. Reading Gelli's and Topsell's works before turning to Siebert's or Bradshaw's writings on elephants makes it less easy to gloss over the disciplinary obeisances of Siebert's article, or the anthropocentrism that Bradshaw mobilizes to "save" elephants (even while we appreciate and condone the positive interventions both seek to make). The fact that all these effects of reading past texts have become clichés in academic defenses of the study of history or literature does not diminish their importance.

Philosophers and critics interested in the "question of the animal," and the related, but not more pressing, question of the human, invite us to attend with "greater specificity, greater attention to [their] embodiment, embeddedness, and materiality, and how these in turn shape and are shaped by consciousness, mind, and so on."[15] But to do so, we should also be creating historical and literary traditions that privilege such attention. Continued study of the history and literature of animal bodies, therefore, should always be part of that invitation, and part of the response to it. This book only begins what I hope will be an ongoing effort to provide a wider, more complete narrative of the historical traces of animal embodiment in the early modern canon.

Notes

INTRODUCTION

1. Giovanni Battista Gelli, *Circes of John Baptista Gello, Florentine*, trans. Henry Iden (London, 1557), sig. c5v–r, m1r. A sort of lineage of the story of Ulysses and Gryllus can be found in Merritt Y. Hughes, "Spenser's Acrasia and the Renaissance Circe," *Journal of the History of Ideas* 4:4 (October 1943): 381–99; Hughes also describes the arguments by humanists for and against the theriophilic position Gelli and other similar dialogists seem to adopt, as well as the *Circe*'s influence on authors from Montaigne to Spenser. All references to Gelli's text are to this edition.

2. Most of the animals also cite social distortions that produce misery among humans, but the body seems the starting point for almost all the eventual points of happiness—particularly the notion repeated often that each animal is perfect in itself as nature made it, and therefore is happier than any human who can never be so perfect.

3. Erica Fudge, *Brutal Reasoning: Animals, Rationality and Humanity in Early Modern England* (Ithaca, NY: Cornell University Press, 2006), 88–93. Fudge's discussion of Plutarch's *Gryllus* sets it against the Homeric and Ovidian versions, in which Gryllus is thrilled to be restored to humanity; Gelli's text, unlike Plutarch's, does obviously embrace an Aristotelian system, which clearly provides the structure to Ulysses' arguments, dividing rational from sensitive and even vegetative soul.

4. Helkiah Crooke, *Microcosmographia* (London, 1615), 9. All references to this text are by page number to this edition.

5. Thomas Browne, *"Religio Medici," "Letter to a Friend," and "Christian Morals,"* ed. W. A. Greenhill (London: Macmillan, 1926), 341.

6. Fudge's works include *Brutal Reasoning*; and *Perceiving Animals: Humans and Beasts in Early Modern English Culture* (New York: St. Martin's Press, 2000). Bruce Boehrer, *Shakespeare among the Animals: Nature and Society in the Drama of Early Modern England* (New York: Palgrave, 2002), and *Animal Characters: Nonhuman Beings in Early Modern Literature* (Philadelphia: University of Pennsylvania Press, 2010); Laurie Shannon, "The Eight Animals in Shakespeare, or Before the Human," *PMLA* 124:2 (2009): 472–79: Simon C. Estok, "Theory from the Fringes: Animals, Ecocriticism, Shakespeare," *Mosaic* 40:1 (March 2007): 61–78; Virginia DeJohn Anderson, *Creatures of Empire: How Domestic Animals Transformed Early America* (Oxford and New York: Oxford University Press, 2004);

and Juliana Schiesari, *Beasts and Beauties: Animals, Gender and Domestication in the Italian Renaissance* (Toronto: University of Toronto Press, 2010). Shannon's *The Accommodated Animal: Cosmopolity in Shakespearean Locales* (Chicago: University of Chicago Press, 2012) belongs in this category, although it appeared too late to be fully considered for this project.

7. Cary Wolfe, *Animal Rites: American Culture, the Discourse of Species, and Posthumanist Theory* (Chicago: University of Chicago Press, 2003), 6.

8. René Descartes, *"Discourse on Method" and "Meditations,"* trans. John Veitch (New York: Prometheus Books, 1989), 45.

9. Ibid., 84.

10. Fudge, *Brutal Reasoning*, 48.

11. Boehrer, *Animal Characters*, 8–9.

12. Fudge, *Brutal Reasoning*, 179. Fudge includes Stephen Greenblatt and Francis Barker in this group.

13. Jacques Derrida, *The Animal That Therefore I Am*, ed. Marie-Louise Mallet, trans. David Wills (New York: Fordham University Press, 2008).

14. See Gilles Deleuze and Felix Guattari, *A Thousand Plateaus: Capitalism and Schizophrenia* (Minneapolis: University of Minnesota Press, 1987): the Tenth Plateau addresses "Becoming-Intense, Becoming-Animal, Becoming-Imperceptible" (232–309).

15. Donna J. Haraway, *When Species Meet (Posthumanities)* (Minneapolis: University of Minnesota Press, 2008), 20.

16. Steve Baker, *The Postmodern Animal* (London: Reaktion Books, 2000), 95.

17. See Donna Landry, Cary Wolfe, et al., "Speciesism, Identity Politics, and Ecocriticism: A Conversation with Humanists and Post-Humanists," *The Eighteenth Century* 52:1 (2011): 87–106. Yet this forum does not include any extended consideration of animal bodies, despite the participants' apparent sympathy to that approach.

18. Boehrer (*Shakespeare among the Animals*) and Schiesari (*Beasts and Beauties*), for example, treat issues of bestiality; on dogs and national identity, see Ian MacInnes, "Mastiffs and Spaniels: Gender and Nation in the English Dog," *Textual Practice* 17 (2003): 21–40; on vermin, see Mary E. Fissell, "Imaging Vermin in Early Modern England," in *The Animal-Human Boundary: Historical Perspectives*, ed. Angela Creager and William Chester Jordan (Rochester, NY: University of Rochester Press, 2002), 77–114.

19. Foucault's work has broad implications for animal studies, but his treatment of madness specifically references the use of images of animality in representations from the Renaissance and after; see Michel Foucault, *Madness and Civilization: Insanity in the Age of Reason* (New York: Vintage Books, 1988), "The Insane," 65–84.

20. See Gail Kern Paster, *The Body Embarrassed: Drama and the Disciplines of Shame in Early Modern England* (Ithaca, NY: Cornell University Press, 1993); Jonathan Sawday, *The Body Emblazoned: Dissection and the Human Body in Renaissance Culture* (New York: Routledge, 1995); Michael Schoenfeldt, *Bodies and Selves in Early Modern England* (Cambridge and New York: Cambridge University Press, 1999); and see also David Hillman, *Shakespeare's Entrails: Belief, Skepticism and the Interior of the Body* (New York: Palgrave Macmillan, 2007); Jonathan Gil Harris, *Foreign Bodies and the Body Politic: Discourses of*

Social Pathology in Early Modern England (New York: Cambridge University Press, 1998).

21. To anyone familiar with Merleau-Ponty, it will be clear that this project clearly owes a great deal to his work, especially *The Visible and the Invisible*, trans. Alphonso Lingis (Evanston, IL: Northwestern University Press, 1968). Generally, the insistence on embodiment as the basis for any phenomenological venture has important repercussions for the status of animals; for a fuller exploration of the intersection of Merleau-Ponty's work with animal ethics, see David B. Dillard-Wright, *The Ark of the Possible: The Animal World in Merleau-Ponty* (New York: Lexington Books, 2009). Michel Serres too explores the role of sensory being in *The Five Senses: A Philosophy of Mingled Bodies*, trans. Margaret Cowley and Peter Sankey (London: Continuum, 2009).

22. James Gibson, *The Ecological Approach to Visual Perception* (Boston: Houghton Mifflin, 1979).

23. Edwin Hutchins, *Cognition in the Wild* (Cambridge, MA: MIT Press, 1995).

24. Andy Clark and David Chalmers's paper "The Extended Mind" was first published in *Analysis* 58 (1998): 10–23; it is also included in David Menary's collection, *The Extended Mind* (Cambridge, MA: MIT Press, 2010), 27–42. An early and important figure in questioning the limits of mind/body dualism is Gregory Bateson, whose work on systems theory and ecology is collected in *Steps to an Ecology of Mind: Collected Essays in Anthropology, Psychiatry, Evolution and Epistemology* (Northvale, NJ: Jason Aronson, Inc., 1972, 1987). Bateson offers the famous example of a blind man's cane, "Suppose I am a blind man, and I use a stick. It go tap, tap, tap. Where do *I* start? Is my mental system bounded at the handle of the stick? Is it bounded by my skin? Does it start halfway up the stick?" (465). These are, Bateson says, "nonsense" questions.

25. Tuan's work, *Dominance and Affection: The Making of Pets* (New Haven, CT: Yale University Press, 2004), while powerful, limits itself to the most reductive, negative versions of pet ownership.

26. Marc Shell, "The Family Pet," *Representations* 15 (Summer 1986): 121–53; Donna Haraway, *The Companion Species Manifesto* (Chicago: Prickly Paradigm Press, 2003) and *When Species Meet (Posthumanities)*; and James Serpell, *In the Company of Animals: A Study of Human-Animal Relationships* (New York: Cambridge University Press, 1996; rev. 2nd ed. 2008).

27. Shell, "The Family Pet," 142.

28. Serpell argues that animals provide a specific kind of social interaction that humans do not, and this has beneficial effects on health and well-being since sociability is a biological human need (*In the Company of Animals*, 108–43). In her chapter "Training in the Contact Zone: Power, Play, and Invention in the Sport of Agility," Haraway explores the interanimal experience that is work or training, or rather work as play, taking seriously that training influences animal, as well as human, happiness (*When Species Meet*, 204–46).

29. Julia K. Parrish and William M. Hamner, *Animal Groups in Three Dimensions* (Cambridge: Cambridge University Press, 1977), 165, from John Steinbeck and E. F. Ricketts, *The Sea of Cortez* (London: Penguin Books, 1951).

30. We should, Merleau-Ponty advises, recognize the gestural as language that is pred-

icated on shared corporeality and perception; thus, reading a dog's bodily movements as communication is not anthropomorphic, but is an acknowledgment of the shared embodiment that makes all languages possible. See Merleau-Ponty, *The Visible and the Invisible*; Dillard-Wright, *The Ark of the Possible*, 45, 83, 98–99.

31. Nicholas Morgan, *The Horseman's Honour* (London, 1620), 171–72.

32. Horses, like dogs, are particularly adapted to creating this mutual, novel language. Proops, Walton, and McComb observe that in part because horses can appropriate the signals of other species into their own repertoire of predator-warning signs (including, for example, other species' warning calls), they are primed to respond to *human* cues; see their "The Use of Human-Given Cues by Domestic Horses (*Equus caballus*) during an Object Choice Task," *Animal Behaviour* 79 (2010): 1205–9.

33. Parrish and Hamner remark on human fascination with animal aggregates in their introduction to their *Animal Groups in Three Dimensions*, 1.

34. Wayne K. Potts, "The Chorus-Line Hypothesis of Coordination in Avian Flocks," *Nature* 24 (1984): 344–45.

35. Parrish and Hamner, *Animal Groups in Three Dimensions*, 165, from John Steinbeck and E. F. Ricketts's *The Sea of Cortez*.

36. Grandin's designs, which have generated controversy as well as transformed the meat industry where they are implemented, rely on her own extreme sensitivity to stimuli, a product of her Asperger's syndrome. See Temple Grandin and Catherine Johnson, *Animals in Translation: Using the Mysteries of Autism to Decode Animal Behavior* (New York: Scribner, 2005) for an account of how her theories work.

37. *The Works of Mr. Abraham Cowley* (London, 1668), 19–20.

38. Gail Kern Paster, "Melancholy Cats, Lugged Bears, and Early Modern Cosmology: Reading Shakespeare's Psychological Materialism across the Species Barrier," in *Reading the Early Modern Passions: Essays in the Cultural History of Emotions*, ed. Gail Kern Paster, Katherine Rowe, and Mary Floyd-Wilson (Philadelphia: University of Pennsylvania Press, 2004), 113–29; Laurie Shannon, "Invisible Parts: Animals and the Renaissance Anatomies of Human Exceptionalism," in *Animal Encounters*, ed. Tom Tyler and Manuela Rossini (Leiden: Brill, 2009), 137–58.

39. E. P. Evans, *The Criminal Prosecution and Capital Punishment of Animals* (London: William Heinemann, 1906); Boehrer, *Shakespeare among the Animals*, 41–70; Dympna Callaghan, "(Un)Natural Loving: Swine, Pets and Flowers in *Venus and Adonis*," in *Textures of Renaissance Knowledge*, ed. Philippa Berry and Margaret Trudeau-Clayton (Manchester: Manchester University Press, 2003), 58–78.

40. See Marc Bekoff, *Minding Animals: Awareness, Emotions, and Heart* (Oxford: Oxford University Press, 2003), and *The Emotional Lives of Animals: A Leading Scientist Explores Animal Joy, Sorrow, and Empathy and Why They Matter* (Novato, CA: New World Library, 2007) for examples of Bekoff's extensive work studying animal emotions and morality.

41. Just the tiniest smattering of examples, limited to the few animals I mention in this section, gives a sense of how enormous and diverse this new investigative path is: see,

for instance, Lori Marino, "Dolphin Cognition," *Current Biology* 14 (2004): R910–11; D. Reiss and L. Marino, "Mirror Self-recognition in the Bottlenose Dolphin: A Case of Cognitive Convergence," *Proceedings of the National Academy of Sciences* (2001): 98, 5937–42; K. Guo, K. Meints, C. Hall, S. Hall, and D. Mills, "Left Gaze Bias in Humans, Rhesus Monkeys and Domestic Dogs," *Animal Cognition* 12 (2009): 409–18; Proops, Walton, and McComb, "The Use of Human-Given Cues by Domestic Horses," 1205–9; K. McComb, A. M. Taylor, C. Wilson, and B. Charlton, "Manipulation by Domestic Cats: The Cry Embedded within the Purr," *Current Biology* 19 (2009): R507–8; Irene Pepperberg, *The Alex Studies: Cognitive and Communicative Abilities of Grey Parrots* (Cambridge, MA: Harvard University Press, 2000). Elephant cognition is the subject of a report released in the *Chronicle of Higher Education* while this manuscript was being prepared: "The Intelligence of Beasts" reports on the move away from a "chimpcentric" idea of intelligence; elephants in one study were found to easily plan and execute cooperative strategies for food gathering (*Chronicle Review Online*, http://chronicle.com/article/The-Intelligence-of-Beasts/127969/, accessed June 28, 2011). The results of such studies challenging human cognitive exceptionalism emerge almost daily.

42. Bankes's first name is never mentioned; see Fudge, *Brutal Reasoning*, 123–46.

43. Ibid., 145.

44. Vinciane Despret, "The Body We Care For: Figures of Anthropo-zoo-genesis," *Body and Society* 10:2–3 (2004): 111–34, quotation on 115.

45. Studies sensitive to animal morality, intelligence, and behavior frequently attract accusations of anthropomorphism on the assumption that anything an animal does that seems to resemble human behavior must, as in the case of Clever Hans and Morocco, be the result of human wishful thinking and projection. However, the social anthropologist Tim Ingold argues vigorously against the trend, especially in the sciences, to resist anthropomorphism at all costs (namely, any rational understanding of animals and humans) in "The Animal in the Study of Humanity," *What Is an Animal?*, ed. Tim Ingold (London: Unwin Hyman, 1988, 1994), 84–99. Ingold's position is that denying animals any capacity that is usually deemed "human" is bad science, and speciesist; there has been a general movement in most disciplines to accept such a charge and try to move beyond it.

46. William Baldwin, *Beware the Cat: The First English Novel*, ed. William A. Ringler Jr. and Michael Flachmann (San Marino, CA: Huntington Library Press, 1988).

47. Edward Topsell, *The History of Four-Footed Beasts* (London, 1607), 104.

48. Franz Wolfgang, *The History of Brutes; Or a Description of Living Creatures* (London, 1672), 151–52. Wolfgang's description of cats as "hot" is at odds with Paster's analysis of cats' usual humoral nature in "Melancholy Cats."

49. Topsell, *History of Four-Footed Beasts*, 104–5.

50. Constance Classen, David Howes, and Anthony Synnott, *Aroma: The Cultural History of Smell* (New York: Routledge, 1994), 3.

51. Ibid.; Alain Corbin, *The Foul and Fragrant: Odor and the French Social Imagination* (Cambridge, MA: Harvard University Press, 1986).

52. Classen, Howes, and Synnott, *Aroma*, 165–69; the smell-marking of immigrants

and others Classen describes seems directly descended from the odors of sin perceived by early moderns in the poor, vagrants, criminals, and also reviled religious groups (e.g., the foul scents of the Catholic priest in the nose of the Protestant; the foul smell of women in the noses of men).

53. See Stefano Zuffi, *The Cat in Art*, trans. Simon Jones (New York: Abrams, 2005), 192–93.

54. Human resistance to diseases contracted through the process of domestication of other species is one of the central subjects of popular books like Jared Diamond's *Guns, Germs, and Steel: The Fates of Human Societies* (New York: W. W. Norton, 1999), which, whatever one thinks of its claims, has generated wider interest in a more complex ecological explanation of the "rise and fall" of civilizations.

55. See G. Fornaciari, V. Giuffra, S. Marinozzi, MS.Picchi, and Masetti, "'Royal' Pediculosis in Renaissance Italy: Lice in the Mummy of the King of Naples Ferdinand II of Aragon (1467–1496)," *Mem Inst. Oswaldo Cruz* (Rio de Janeiro) 104:4 (July 2009): 671–72. Fleas and lice were not seen as completely different in many Renaissance texts, although it appears quite clear that the black creature Donne laments is definitely an actual flea.

56. Hans Zinsser, *Rats, Lice, and History* (Boston: Little, Brown and Co., 1934, 1935), 137–38. "MacArthur" is unidentified.

57. Brendan Lehane's *The Compleat Flea*, although it eschews footnotes or a bibliography, is a useful source of such flea lore (New York: Viking Press, 1969), 12.

58. Linda Woodbridge, *Vagrancy, Homelessness and English Renaissance Literature* (Urbana: University of Illinois Press, 2001), 180.

59. Piero Camporesi, *Bread of Dreams: Food and Fantasy in Early Modern Europe*, trans. David Gentilcore (Chicago: University of Chicago Press, 1989).

60. Robert N. Watson, "The Ecology of Self in *Midsummer Night's Dream*," in *Ecocritical Shakespeare*, ed. Lynne Bruckner and Dan Brayton (Burlington, VT: Ashgate, 2011), 33–56, quotation on 33.

61. Ibid., 55.

62. Raymond Williams, *Marxism and Literature* (Oxford and New York: Oxford University Press, 1977), 11. As Williams also points out, while society and economy had evolved new definitions by the late seventeenth century, "culture" was "still a noun of process: the culture *of* something—crops, animals, minds," well into the eighteenth century (13).

63. Schoenfeldt's *Bodies and Selves* works counter to the version of the humoral body proposed by Gail Kern Paster in *The Body Embarrassed* by arguing that the porous humoral body was not merely a site of anxiety, but also a source of the pleasures of self-regulation, examination, balance, and so on that contribute to the establishment of selfhood in early modern literature.

64. The idea of interanimality is incompletely explored in Merleau-Ponty's later work, but I use the term here in a literal sense to suggest that there is no discrete boundary between concepts like "animal" or "human," or between their lived physical realities.

65. John Locke, *Two Treatises of Government*, ed. Mark Goldie (London: J. M. Dent, 1993), 128 (my italics).

66. Readers may notice that I avoid the use of the term "nonhuman animal" for instance, a choice that departs from most recent posthumanist or animal-rights-oriented discussions of animals. What started as a well-intentioned way to remind us that we cannot divide ourselves from the spectrum of species has in many cases become paradoxically, I think, a continued reminder of difference—after all, of all animals only *we* feel we need to signal our *lack* of distinction. If we never refer to a human as a "non-canine" animal, then we have only created a new taxonomy that relies on our unique status.

CHAPTER 1

1. Jonathan Sawday, *The Body Emblazoned: Dissection and the Human Body in Renaissance Culture* (New York: Routledge, 1995), 23. Sawday contrasts this with the post-Cartesian idea of the body as a clockwork machine.

2. The language of partition versus unity belongs both to Sawday's work (*The Body Emblazoned*, 2–3) and to the introduction of David Hillman and Carla Mazzio's *The Body in Parts: Fantasies of Corporeality in Early Modern Europe* (New York: Routledge, 1997), xiv, xv, and xiii.

3. So Sawday notes with regard to the "Harveian or Cartesian" body (*The Body Emblazoned*, 23), and Hillman and Mazzio note with regard to Burckhardt's version of the Renaissance individual (*The Body in Parts*, xiv).

4. See, for example, Erica Fudge's *Perceiving Animals: Humans and Beasts in Early Modern English Culture* (Champaign: University of Illinois Press, 2000) and her *Brutal Reasoning: Animals, Rationality and Humanity in Early Modern England* (Ithaca, NY: Cornell University Press, 2006); Bruce Boehrer's *Shakespeare among the Animals: Nature and Society in the Drama of Early Modern England* (New York: Palgrave, 2002); Laurie Shannon's *The Accommodated Animal: Cosmopolity in Shakespearean Locales* (Chicago: University of Chicago Press, 2012), deserves mention, although it appeared too late for inclusion in this study.

5. In *Bodies and Selves in Early Modern England: Physiology and Inwardness in Spenser, Shakespeare, Herbert, and Milton* (Cambridge: Cambridge University Press, 1991), Schoenfeldt argues that humoral theory encouraged regimes of self-discipline that "produced the parameters of individual subjectivity" (15); however, the medical literature of the period could not help but be influenced also by progress in anatomy, which, in tandem with humoralism, gave new relevance to the body's interior organs and their functions.

6. René Descartes, *"Discourse on Method" and "Meditations,"* trans. John Veitch (New York: Prometheus Books, 1989), 39.

7. Ibid., 39.

8. Fudge's work in *Brutal Reasoning* puts extreme pressure on the Cartesian model of animal unreason, yet in my opinion by focusing on that single aspect of animal life it does not fully extricate itself from a lingering mind-body dualism; in contrast, Laurie Shannon's essay "Invisible Parts: Animals and the Renaissance Anatomies of Human Exceptionalism,"

in *Animal Encounters*, ed. Tom Tyler and Manuela Rossini (Leiden: Brill Publishing, 2009), 137–58, takes up issues of animal embodiment and begins some of the groundwork for this project. Boehrer has recently turned to the analysis of animal "character" in his *Animal Characters: Nonhuman Beings in Early Modern Literature* (Philadelphia: University of Pennsylvania Press, 2010), but his earlier book, *Shakespeare among the Animals*, does pay attention to the way embodied being plays into metaphors of animality, especially in his treatment of gender.

9. Another Renaissance horse anatomy of note is Laurentius Rusius's *Hippiatria* (1532); I limit my discussion to Ruini and Snape only because of the nature of their images and the overlap in their illustrative plates. A brilliant online exhibit of early modern human and horse anatomies was developed by the National Library of Medicine while this monograph was being written; see http://www.nlm.nih.gov/exhibition/horse/introduction.html.

10. Shannon's essay "Invisible Parts" focuses on Vesalius's text and its relationship to its Galenic precursor, on Harvey's work, which took as its object a specific organ, rather than a species, and Burton's *Anatomy of Melancholy*, which makes the organ of human distinction (the seat of the soul) unlocatable, invisible, and so "not proven" (154).

11. Andreas Vesalius, *On the Fabric of the Human Body, a Translation of "De Humani Corporis Fabrica Libri Septem" by Andreas Vesalius*, trans. William Frank Richardson and John Burd Carman (San Francisco: Norman Publishing, 1999), 1: iv. Further references to the *Fabrica* are to this edition by volume number and page number.

12. See also Martin Kemp, "Temples of the Body and Temples of the Cosmos: Vision and Visualization in the Vesalian and Copernican Revolutions," in *Picturing Knowledge: Historical and Philosophical Problems Concerning the Use of Art in Science*, ed. Brian S. Baigrie (Toronto: University of Toronto Press, 1996), 40–85.

13. Fudge, *Perceiving Animals*, 105.

14. Iolanda Ventura, in "On the Representation of the Animal World in the Collections of Natural Questions between Late Middle Ages and Early Modern Times," *Reinardus* 21 (2008): 182–200, gives an overview of how animals are used comparatively in medieval question books, not for knowledge of animals themselves, but for knowledge of humans as greater and more perfect examples of creation. The certainty that comparisons will inevitably result in evidence of human exceptionalism is under extreme pressure in the medical and scientific literature of the sixteenth and seventeenth centuries, as the remainder of this chapter demonstrates.

15. Fudge, *Perceiving Animals*, 114.

16. Harald Moe, *The Art of Anatomical Illustration in the Renaissance and Baroque Periods* (Copenhagen, Denmark: Rhodos, 1995), 21.

17. Andrea Carlino, *Books of the Body: Anatomical Ritual and Renaissance Learning*, trans. John Tedeschi and Anne C. Tedeschi (Chicago: University of Chicago Press, 1999), 8.

18. Ibid., 43.

19. Ibid., 51.

20. Moe names the former in his *The Art of Anatomical Illustration*, 24, Carlino the latter in his *Books of the Body*, 48.

21. Luke Wilson, in his "William Harvey's *Prelectiones*: The Performance of the Body in the Renaissance Theater of Anatomy," *Representations* 17 (Winter 1987): 62–95, reads the title page illustration of the *Fabrica* slightly differently, and in a way that cooperates with my own general view here: for Wilson, the dog and monkey "behave like men" and contrast with the fighting men under the anatomist's table, who behave like animals; "the distinction between observers and cadavers, between men as spectators and men as animals, bodies, potential subjects for dissection, loosens" (71).

22. Moe, *The Art of Anatomical Illustration*, 23.

23. Felix Plater, *De Corporis Humani Structura et Usu* (Badle: Ambrosius Froben, 1583). Moe gives a full description of the frontispiece, ibid., 94, including a judgment that the object the monkey holds is indeed an apple, despite its rather ambiguous shape.

24. Vesalius, *On the Fabric of the Human Body*, 2: 89.

25. On the point of the image, see J. B. Saunders and C. D. O'Malley, *The Illustrations from the Works of Andreas Vesalius of Brussels* (Cleveland: World Publishing Co., 1950), 58.

26. Vesalius, *On the Fabric of the Human Body*, 2: 10, 107.

27. Shannon, "Invisible Parts," 147–48.

28. In fact, Vesalius himself comments that he could not obtain enough human jaw bones to finally be sure that there is no suture in the lower jaw; Vesalius, *On the Fabric of the Human Body*, 2: 107.

29. Aristotle, *The Works of Aristotle*, trans. Darcy Wentworth Thompson (Oxford: Oxford University Press, 1949), 4: 1848.

30. F. J. Cole, *A History of Comparative Anatomy from Aristotle to the Eighteenth Century* (New York: Dover Publishing, 1975, repr. of 1945 edition), 128.

31. Thomas Willis (1621–75) made significant discoveries on nerves. That Snape was familiar with his work was unremarkable—an educated, curious, or aspiring natural philosopher would naturally be informed about the most interesting current discoveries. As farrier to Charles II, Snape operated in an era before the professionalization of veterinary medicine, when "farriers" included men of widely varying classes and educational backgrounds.

32. For a specific comparison of Harvey and Severino, see C. B. Schmitt and C. Webster, "Harvey and M. A. Severino, a Neglected Medical Relationship," *Bulletin of the History of Medicine* 45 (1971): 49–75.

33. Charles Singer, *A Short History of Anatomy and Physiology from the Greeks to Harvey* (New York: Dover Publications, 1957), 153. See Robert Dunlop, *Medicine, an Illustrated History* (New York: Mosby, 1996), 242–43, for a contrary opinion.

34. Dunlop, *Medicine*, 244.

35. Singer, *A Short History*, 153.

36. Cole, *A History of Comparative Anatomy*, 85.

37. ". . . gli altri & divini misterii, & profuni degreti della sagace, & provida Natura commune s'auolge. Effendo, che per questa via sola, si venga, non solamente alla diletteuole cognitione di tutte le cose naturali; ma ancora al perfetto conoscimento (per quant è lecito all'huuomo) del primo principio, & prima causa di tutte le cose geneate, insieme con

l'eterne; oltra l'incompresnibile grandezza di quello dal saper dell quali cose dell'anima nostra, come di proprio cibo, si pasce, & sinutrice; & acquista per quanto n'è conceduto, l'inteiera sua perfectione; per la quale fassi in parte l'huomo simile a Dio, più che per qualunque altro mezo, che in esso sia; del che sopra ogn'altro oggetto deue ragioneuolamente l'huomo esser desideroso, & acceso." Carlo Ruini, *Anatomia del Cavallo, Infermità e Suoi Rimedii* (Venezia, 1558), preface, 1–2. All references to the Italian are translated by me, with the kind assistance of Isabella Watt; all mistakes in translation are mine.

38. Cole, *A History of Comparative Anatomy*, 88.

39. Anatomy texts are full of images conveying examples of animals in such slings and rigs, although in most cases the rigs are, of course, smaller.

40. Indeed, Vesalius dissected at least six dogs while demonstrating his human anatomy for students according to the records of his first demonstrations; horse anatomy is radically different in many respects from humans,' something that makes many of Snape's claims false.

41. Edward Topsell, *The History of Four-Footed Beasts* (1607), 281.

42. "Oltra l'esse dotato di tante, & sì lodeuoli, & rare qualità; che perauenture a non sistroua verun' altro privuo di ragione." Ruini, *Anatomia del Cavallo*, preface.

43. Andrew Snape, *The Anatomy of an Horse* (New York: Howell Book House, 1997), poem accompanying plate facing title page.

44. "Un' amor grande verso l'huomo," "cagionali grandissimo contento, & aiuto." Ruini, *Anatomia del Cavallo*, preface.

45. "Ma che dirò poi del suo valore? Del'quale sapiena sede la continue & lunga esperienza, & l'ampia testimonianza, che ne rendono gli illustri fatti di molti cavalli, per li quali Re più saggi & gli emperatoi più grandi gli hanno in sommo pregio hauuti." Ibid.

46. Snape, *The Anatomy of an Horse*, frontispiece.

47. "Per la qual cosa essendomi ciò caduto nell'animo, & per quanto è stato da me conosciuto, & imparato, & per la dolcezza, & diletto, che dal cercar di sapere suolnascere; fra me stesso hò pensato, come potessi in qualche parte par acquisito di quello, ch'io guidicaua douere ogni ben nato huomo, con ogni diligenza procurare di compitamente conseguire; e dopo lungo riuolgiment di pensierie nell' animo, finalment venni in opinione di poter mandar ad effetto questo da me giudicato honesto desiderio, qual volta mi volgessi alla consideratione dell'artificioso magistero nel corpo del cavallo, & dell'historia dell sua compositione. . . . ." ". . . che sempre hò hauuto di giouare à cosi nobile animale, del quale sin di teneri anni mi son dilettat, & servito; & in questo proponimento tanto più mi confirmai, quanto che nessun'altro sin ad hora (ch'io sappia) hà scritto in tal materia, con'io disederaua. Stimando silmilmente douer questo mio discorso esser grto à molti, no nmeo che profitteuole, scoprendo loro il modo di conoscer le parti & di socorrere all'infirmità d'un sì necessario, & generoso animale, & tanto utile al monno, & di giouamento sì viuo alla salute loro, il qual modo fino à questio tempo in buona parte (per quanto si vede) è stato à gli huomini nascosto." Ruini, *Anatomia del Cavallo*, preface.

48. See Pia Cuneo, "(Un)Stable Identities: Hippology and the Professionalization of Scholarship and Horsemanship in Early Modern Germany," in *Early Modern Zoology: The*

Construction of Animals in Science, Literature, and the Visual Arts, ed. Karl A. E. Enenkel and Paul J. Smith (Boston and Leiden: Brill, 2007), 2: 339–59; and Wendy Wall, "Renaissance National Husbandry: Gervase Markham and the Publication of England," *Sixteenth Century Journal* 27:30 (Fall 1996): 767–85.

49. Cuneo, "(Un)Stable Identities," 348.

50. The Neapolitan breed was the ancestor of today's Lipizzaners (the horses of the Spanish Riding School in Vienna), bred in Italy for the "manège," or dressage.

51. Kemp, "Temples of Knowledge," 42.

52. Andrew Cunningham, *The Anatomical Renaissance: The Resurrection of the Anatomical Projects of the Ancients* (New York: Ashgate, 1997), 111.

53. Baldesar Heselar, *Andreas Vesalius' First Public Anatomy at Bologna 1540: An Eyewitness Report*, trans. Ruben Eriksson (Uppsala, Stockholm: Almqvist and Witsells, 1959), 71.

54. The relationship of the visual to the tactile as a historical and ideological factor in representation of science and medicine is too complex and well argued by critics to summarize here. Lucien Febvre, for example, situates a shift from multisensory engagement with the world to visual engagement at the change of century: "the sixteenth century did not see first: it heard and smelled, it sniffed the air and caught sounds. It was only later, as the seventeenth century was approaching, that it seriously and actively became engaged in geometry. . . . It was then that vision was unleashed in the world of science." Febvre, *The Problem of Unbelief in the Sixteenth Century: The Religion of Rabelais*, trans. Beatrice Gottlieb (Cambridge, MA: Harvard University Press, 1982), 432. However, this argument for a radical transition flies in the face of much criticism that targets the visual nature of Western art, philosophy, and science from the Greeks forward. It is safe to claim for the Renaissance a different emphasis on visual experience, which is associated with the "geometry" of perspective; and certainly Vesalius is at the inception of a tradition in medicine and science that privileges sight as a means to knowledge. Martin Kemp and Marina Wallace discuss the visual nature of Vesalian illustrations for the *Fabrica* in *Spectacular Bodies: The Art and Science of the Human Body from Leonardo to Now* (Berkeley: University of California Press, 2000), esp. 13, 23, 96; Kemp write in *The Science of Art: Optical Themes in Western Art from Brunelleschi to Seurat* (New Haven, CT: Yale University Press, 1990) that physiognomics (like Della Porta's, for instance) arose as a "tool through which we could both rationalize and refine our seeing of faces in terms of birds and beasts" (6), connecting the visual/tactile nature of science illustration to the need to explain human bodily animality. An excellent overview of the problem of the visual regime can be found in Martin Jay's *Downcast Eyes: The Denigration of Vision in Twentieth-Century French Thought* (Berkeley: University of California Press, 1994), 21–82. For my purposes, the ability of the visual to render to the viewer a substitute or analog of touch, or the collapse of the tactile into the visual, is only important insofar as it eventually makes connections between illustrations, hands, horses, and the massive, excessive body under dissection in Ruini's treatise.

55. Cunningham, *The Anatomical Renaissance*, 14. See Heselar, *Andreas Vesalius' First Public Anatomy*, 107.

56. Cunningham, *The Anatomical Renaissance*, 114 (my italics).

57. Luke Wilson points out that in illustrations of pre-Vesalian anatomies (mainly a most famous one represented in a thirteenth-century woodcut of Luzio Mondino performing an anatomy), in which the dissector is the barber-surgeon while the lecturer remains above the process on a raised dais, the surgeon's gaze is directed not at the lecturer/anatomist, but at a text (likely of Galen) laid out nearby, thereby referring all action to the text as the primary source of knowledge; see Wilson, "William Harvey's *Prelectiones*," 68ff.

58. Martin Kemp, *The Science of Art*, 1.

59. Helkiah Crooke, *Microcosmographia* (1615), 729.

60. John Bulwer, *Chirologia, or the Natural Language of the Hand* (London, 1644), preface.

61. Carlino, *Books of the Body*, 49.

62. Bulwer, *Chirologia*, 164.

63. Katherine Rowe, "'God's Handy Worke': Divine Complicity and the Anatomist's Touch," in *The Body in Parts: Fantasies of Corporeality in Early Modern Europe*, ed. David Hillman and Carla Mazzio (New York: Routledge, 1997), 285–309.

64. Bernard F. Scholz, "Ownerless Legs or Arms Stretching from the Sky: Notes on an Emblematic Motif," in *Andrea Alciato and the Emblem Tradition: Essays in Honor of Virginia Woods Callahan*, ed. Peter M. Daly (New York: AMS Press, 1989), 249–83.

65. Sawday, *The Body Emblazoned*, 102.

66. Ibid., 112, 113.

67. Kemp notes that the "military fighting men in the Battle of Anghieri were locked into a physiognomic and pathognomic unity with their military horses." Kemp, *The Science of Art*, 43.

68. Heselar, *Andreas Vesalius' First Public Anatomy*, 107.

69. Ibid., 55; see also Glenn Harcourt, "Vesalius and the Anatomy of Antique Sculpture," *Representations* 17 (Winter 1987): 28–61.

70. Ozias Humphrey, *A Memoir of George Stubbs and Joseph Mayer* (London: Pallas Athene Press, 2005), 203.

71. Sawday, *The Body Emblazoned*, 101.

72. Dante, *The Divine Comedy:* vol. I, *Inferno*, trans. Mark Musa (London: Penguin Classics, 1984), 178 (my italics); the Italian reads "ci sproni," or "we spur ourselves" or "we are spurred."

73. Niccolo Machiavelli, *The Prince*, trans. Daniel Donno (New York: Bantam Books, 1966, 1981), 62.

74. Ibid., 63.

75. Douglas J. Stewart, "Falstaff the Centaur," *Shakespeare Quarterly* 28:1 (Winter 1977): 5–21, esp. 6–8.

76. Tricking or trapping a centaur could enable a human to gain information from it; Chiron's death scene with Achilles in Ovid makes explicit the paternal connection.

77. Sir Philip Sidney, *The Countess of Pembroke's Arcadia*, ed. Maurice Evans (London: Penguin Books, 1977), 248.

78. For more on centaurs, see Eric C. Brown, "Many a Civil Monster: Shakespeare's Idea of the Centaur," *Shakespeare Survey* 51 (1998): 175–91; Elizabeth Porges Watson, "(Un) Bridled Passion: Chivalric Metaphor and Practice in Sidney's *Astrophil and Stella*," *Reinardus* 15:1 (2002): 117–29.

79. Crooke, *Microcosmographia*, 4.

80. Ibid., 5.

81. Suzanne J. Walker, "Making and Breaking the Stag: The Construction of the Animal in the Early Modern Hunting Treatise," in *Early Modern Zoology: The Construction of Animals in Science, Literature, and the Visual Arts*, ed. Karl A. E. Enenkel and Paul J. Smith (Boston and Leiden: Brill, 2007), 2: 317–37, quotation on 317.

82. Erasmus links the hunt's dismemberment of the deer to dissection and anatomy in *The Praise of Folly*, trans. Clarence Miller (New Haven, CT: Yale University Press, 1979): "This class of madness also includes those who look down on everything except hunting wild animals and whose spirits are incredibly exhilarated whenever they hear the nerve-shattering blasts on the horns or the baying of the hounds. I imagine that even the dung of the dogs smells like cinnamon to them. And then what exquisite pleasure they feel when the quarry is to be butchered! Lowly peasants may butcher bulls and rams, but only a nobleman may cut up wild animals. Baring his head and kneeling down he takes a special blade set aside for that purpose (for it would hardly do to use just any knife) and exercises the most devout precision in cutting up just these parts, with just these movements, in just this order. Meanwhile, the surrounding crowd stands in silent wonder, as if they were seeing some new religious ceremony, although they have beheld the same spectacle a thousand times before. Then, whoever gets a chance to taste some of the beast is quite convinced that he has gained no small share of added nobility. Thus, though these men have accomplished nothing more by constantly chasing and eating wild animals than to lower themselves almost to the level of the animals they hunt, still in the meantime they think they are living like kings" (61).

CHAPTER 2

1. See, for instance, Dante, *Inferno*, trans. Mark Musa (Bloomington, IN: Indiana University Press, 1995): "That one there is Nessus, / Who dies from loving lovely Dejanira, / And made of himself, of his blood, his own revenge" (12.67–69).

2. Describing orgasm, Alphonse Lingis writes: "Our sense of ourselves, our self-respect shaped in fulfilling a function in the machinic and social environment, our dignity maintained in multiple confrontations, collaborations and demands, dissolve; the ego loses its focus as center of evaluations, decisions, and initiatives. Our impulses, our passions are returned to animal irresponsibility." Lingis, "Animal Body, Inhuman Face," in *Zoontologies: The Question of the Animal*, ed. Cary Wolfe (Minneapolis: University of Minnesota Press, 2003), 172. Lingis details at length the bodily changes that accompany orgasm, from the distorted face, the collapse of posture, to the production of fluids, all of which he calls "transubstantiation."

3. *Sir Philip Sidney: "An Apology for Poetry" and "Astrophil and Stella": Texts and Contexts*, ed. Peter C. Herman (Glen Allen, VA: College Publishing, 2001), 155.

4. William Shakespeare, *The Complete Works of Shakespeare*, ed. David Bevington, 5th ed. (New York: Longman, 2004). All subsequent citations to Shakespeare's plays and poetry are from this edition, with the plays being cited by act, verse, and line, and the poems by line.

5. These lines refer to contemporary bawdy language and wordplay between *whores* and *horse*.

6. John Donne, *The Complete English Poems*, ed. A. J. Smith (New York: Penguin Books, 1986), 103.

7. This is true of Boehrer's very thorough and subtle readings of bestiality in Shakespeare's plays in *Shakespeare among the Animals: Nature and Society in the Drama of Early Modern England* (New York: Palgrave, 2002); Erica Fudge has briefly analyzed the rise in the sixteenth century of legal and religious concern over bestiality in "Monstrous Acts: Bestiality in Early Modern England," *History Today* 50 (2000): 20–25. Dympna Callaghan's essay "(Un)Natural Loving: Swine, Pets and Flowers in *Venus and Adonis*," in *Textures of Renaissance Knowledge*, ed. Philippa Berry and Margaret Trudeau-Clayton (Manchester: Manchester University Press, 2003), 58–78, discusses the role of pet love in threatening the divisions that supposedly separate human and animal, making the idea of a clear choice between love or bestiality impossible. Most works on animals and erotics cite the important work of E. P. Evans, *The Criminal Prosecution and Capital Punishment of Animals* (London: William Heinemann, 1906), which includes extended descriptions of several important criminal cases involving bestiality.

8. Boehrer, *Shakespeare among the Animals*; Callaghan, "(Un)Natural Loving"; and Jeanne Addison Roberts, "Horses and Hermaphrodites: Metamorphoses in *Taming of the Shrew*," *Shakespeare Quarterly* 43:2 (Summer 1983): 159–71.

9. Roberts, "Horses and Hermaphrodites," 170.

10. Callaghan, "(Un)Natural Loving," 59.

11. Ibid., 64.

12. Ibid., 75.

13. Edmund Spenser, *The Faerie Queene*, ed. Thomas P. Roche Jr. (London and New York: Penguin Books, 1987), 2.3.48–54.

14. Roberts, "Horses and Hermaphrodites," 164.

15. Boehrer, *Shakespeare among the Animals*, 44; see also on yoking, Sid Ray's essay, "'Those Whom God Hath Joined Together': Bondage Metaphors and Marital Advice in Early Modern England," in *Domestic Arrangements in Early Modern England*, ed. Kari Boyd McBride (Pittsburgh: Duquesne University Press, 2002), 15–47, in which the connection between women and beasts extends to link men to them as yoke-fellows. It is likely no accident that, as Boehrer's chart of bestiality indictments shows, by far more cases of buggery with mares occurred (followed closely by cows; sheep are actually barely present) (51).

16. Indeed, while Boehrer's excellent reading of the Bottom episode in *A Midsummer Night Dream* redresses critical blindness to its bestial content, nowhere does he suggest

that an "ass" might actively love a woman—that there might be some form of pleasure involved for the animal as well as the human—although he does point out that it is as the lover Pyramus that Bottom is cast in the mechanicals' production. It is possible to argue that Bottom is a complete patsy in Oberon's plot, and left no scope of will in Titania's suffocating attentions, yet it seems at least worth asking the question. Bestiality cases appear to allow for some role for the animal "victim" when they provide for the animal's execution alongside its defiler.

17. Although it does not precisely address the question of animal-human relations, Carla Freccero's *Queer/Early/Modern* (Durham, NC: Duke University Press, 2006) is a valuable articulation of the potential in queering Renaissance narratives, methodological and otherwise; Freccero has also analyzed the specific encounter between Derrida and his cat, analyzing *The Animal That Therefore I Am* for its situation of issues of queer animality, touching on issues of bestiality and sexuality.

18. Elisabeth Le Guin, "Man and Horse in Harmony," in *The Culture of the Horse: Status, Discipline and Identity in the Early Modern World*, ed. Karen Raber and Treva J. Tucker (New York: Palgrave Macmillan, 2005), 175–96.

19. John Astley, *The Art of Riding* (London, 1580), 5.

20. Ibid., 3.

21. Le Guin, "Man and Horse," 183.

22. The excesses of Grisone's *Gli Ordine di Cavalcare* (1550) are largely omitted from Blundeville's redaction and translation of his work for an English audience (see the following note), although subsequent authors were clearly aware of some of the more bizarre methods.

23. Both of Thomas Blundeville's horsemanship manuals relied heavily on Grisone: *A New Booke Containing the Arte of Horsmanshippe* (London, 1560) contains mainly direct translations; *The Four Chiefest Offices Belonginge to Horsemanhippe* (London, 1566) follows in this tradition.

24. Gervase Markham, *A Discource [sic] of Horsemanshippe* (London, 1593), sig. B3r.

25. Antoine Pluvinel, *Le Maneige Royal*, trans. Hilda Nelson (London: J. A. Allen, 1989), 26.

26. Astley, *The Art of Riding*, 4; William Cavendish, *A General System of Horsemanship: A Facsimile Reproduction of the Edition of 1743* (London: Trafalgar Square Books, 2000), 3.

27. Raymond Gibbs Jr., *Embodiment and Cognitive Science* (Cambridge: Cambridge University Press, 2005, 2007), 19–21.

28. Keri Brandt, "A Language of Their Own: An Interactionist Approach to Human-Horse Communication," *Society and Animals* 12:4 (2004): 199–316.

29. Kenneth Shapiro, "Understanding Dogs through Kinesthetic Empathy, Social Construction,and History," *Anthrozoös* 3 (1990): 184–95; Thomas J. Csordas, "Somatic Modes of Attention," *Cultural Anthropology* 8:2 (May 1993): 135–56. See also Keri Brandt, "A Language of Their Own."

30. The great horse ballets of the later seventeenth century, massive coordinated drills of riders on highly trained animals performed to music, are examples of this, as is the current role of music in competitive dressage "freestyle" classes.

31. Barrey's comments appear in Vinciane Despret's "The Body We Care For: Figures of Anthropo-zoo-genesis," *Body and Society* 10:2–3 (2004): 111–34, quotation on 115. "Isopraxism" describes deep-seated neurologically based mimicry. In Despret's work, and in Barrey's approach to riding, the horse and rider "share a mind" through this neurological responsiveness.

32. Paul Patton, "Language, Power and the Training of Horses," in *Zoontologies: The Question of the Animal*, ed. Cary Wolfe (Minneapolis: University of Minnesota Press, 2003), 83–99, quotation on 95.

33. Ibid., 97.

34. Astley, *The Art of Riding*, 7, 5.

35. Ibid., 18.

36. Ibid., 32–33, 38, 39.

37. Ibid., 14.

38. Ibid., 33.

39. Pluvinel, *Le Maneige Royal*, 2, retrained this bay Barb, which was believed to be too sensitive in mouth and flanks to ever be ridden properly, by using a bit of satin (21); the dance he executes, to which le Grande refers as a sarabande, is a complicated series of the airs above the ground.

40. Juliana Schiesari, *Beasts and Beauties: Animals, Gender, and Domestication in the Italian Renaissance* (Toronto: University of Toronto Press, 2010), 46.

41. Ibid., 51.

42. Kenneth Clark, *Animals and Man: Their Relationship as Reflected in Western Art from Prehistory to the Present Day* (New York: William Morrow and Co., 1977), 36.

43. In the *Oxford English Dictionary*, the first listed definition is haptic; simultaneously the term acquired the meaning of using the mouth to register flavor roughly 1200–1300. "Tasting" also means to make a trial of, or put to the test.

44. For Boehrer this passage and all of Hotspur's bestial associations speak to the character's childishness: he is associated with "women, fools, and children" and so Hal rightly "suppressed the bestial and childish impulses of a rebellious subject" when he killed Hotspur. Boehrer attaches the problem of "erotic transference" to Hotspur's discussion with his wife, not with this moment, although he does note its poetic "amalgamation" of horse and rider, as well as rider and rider (*Shakespeare among the Animals*, 24). I am amplifying Boehrer's reading by emphasizing the hints about consumption in the passage, which serve also as a segue from this chapter to the next.

45. In *Hamlet*, the Norman's reported name means death (or that he is death personified, an interpretation made possible by the fact that he is actually named "Lamord," a form of "la morte"—in the second quarto the text is "Upon my life, Lamord" [4.7.92]).

CHAPTER 3

1. William Shakespeare, *The Complete Works of Shakespeare*, ed. David Bevington, 5th ed. (New York: Longman, 2004). All subsequent quotations are from this edition.

2. For this argument, see Erica Fudge, "Saying Nothing but Concerning the Same: On Dominion, Purity, and Meat in Early Modern England," in *Renaissance Beasts: Of Animals, Humans and Other Wonderful Creatures*, ed. Erica Fudge (Urbana: University of Illinois Press, 2004), 70–86.

3. Edward Topsell, *The History of Four-Footed Beasts* (London, 1607), 667.

4. Ibid., 669.

5. Work on Renaissance digestion and remedies includes David Hillman's "Visceral Knowledge: Shakespeare, Skepticism, and the Interior of the Early Modern Body," in *The Body in Parts: Fantasies of Corporeality in Early Modern Europe*, ed. David Hillman and Carla Mazzio (New York: Routledge, 1997), 81–105; Andrew Wear, *Knowledge and Practice in English Medicine, 1550–1680* (Cambridge: Cambridge University Press, 2000); Mary Lindeman, *Medicine and Society in Early Modern Europe* (Cambridge: Cambridge University Press, 1997); Roy Porter, *The Greatest Benefit to All Mankind: A Medical History of Humanity* (New York: W. W. Norton and Company, 1997).

6. Dominique Laporte, *The History of Shit*, trans. Nadia Benabid and Rodophe El-Khoury (Cambridge, MA: MIT Press, 2000), 98.

7. Piero Camporesi, *The Juice of Life: The Symbolic and Magic Significance of Blood*, trans. Robert R. Barr (New York: Continuum, 1995), 18.

8. Ibid., 17.

9. Hannah Woolley, *The Accomplisht Ladys Delight* (London, 1677), 146, 143.

10. Nicholas Culpeper, *Culpeper's Schoole of Physick* (London, 1678), 110, 134, 136–37.

11. Ibid., 133, 111. Culpeper notes that the stallion must be one that is kept in a stable.

12. Gervase Markham, *The English Housewife Containing the Inward and Outward Virtues That Ought to Be in a Complete Woman* (London, 1615), 17, 32.

13. Laporte, *The History of Shit*, 28.

14. Anon., *The Widow's Treasure* (London, 1639), 53.

15. John Crawshey, *The Countryman's Instructor* (London, 1636), 5.

16. Conrad Heresbach's *Whole Art of Husbandry Contained in Four Books* (1631) is published with Markham's name attached, although the work is in print from the 1580s on; this suggests that Markham's account of care for fighting cocks may be derived from Heresbach's, something omitted from Hamill's work: Thomas A. Hamill, "Cockfighting as Cultural Allegory in Early Modern England," *Journal of Medieval and Early Modern Studies* 39:2 (Spring 2009): 375–406.

17. Gervase Markham, *Second Book of the English Husbandman* (London, 1614), 50.

18. Hamill, "Cockfighting," 389.

19. Ibid., 390.

20. John Moore, *A Mappe of Mans Mortalitie* (London, 1617), 40; cited also in Fudge, "Saying Nothing," 74.

21. Thomas Tryon, *The Way to Health, Long Life, and Happiness* (London, 1683), 376.

22. Bert O. States, *Hamlet and the Concept of Character* (Baltimore: Johns Hopkins University Press, 1992), 174. In his chapter on "The Melancholy Dane," which States deems his most "synoptic view of Hamlet's character and his unique relationship to the world in which Shakespeare has put him" (xxiii), States imagines in "the mind's eye" the mouse who indeed stirs in the play's first scene on the battlements "scurrying along a dank wall of the imagination and disappearing into such darkness as might shroud a ghost . . . So the mouse—like the glow worm, the woodcock, the mole, the porpentine, the weasel, the kite, the crab, and the serpent—is a creature of some brief influence in the creation of the unique space in which Hamlet's story unfolds" (173). Where States issues this observation in the service of a turn toward aesthetics and character-formation, his terms (the list of animals, the mention of "space") strike me as begging to have their material referents considered more closely.

23. *Countreymans Instructor C,* 2. Crawshey may be referring to some version of either a nematode that infects the brain of an animal, or a fluke; flukes were likely to have once been much more common parasites of horses than they currently are, since they are the cause of sheep "rot" and are associated with wet manured fields. Crawshey's name for this condition may derive from the common consequence of any brain parasite in a horse, that is a tendency to turn in one direction and be unstable on its feet.

24. Leonard Mascall, *The Government of Cattel* (London, 1662), 16, 41–42.

25. Piero Camporesi, *Bread of Dreams: Food and Fantasy in Early Modern Europe*, trans. David Gentilcore (Chicago: University of Chicago Press, 1989), 152.

26. Ibid., 152.

27. William Ramesey, *Helminthologia* (London, 1668), 41, 43. Ramesey's work, like many of the texts cited by Camporesi, is later than Shakespeare's time; the revelations of the microscope encouraged physicians and eventually laymen to investigate and recognize more readily these tiny organisms. The work, however, does offer insights into the ubiquity of parasites and the suffering they caused.

28. Culpeper, *Schoole of Physick,* 105.

29. Hugh Plat, *The Jewel House of Art and Nature* (London, 1653), 105.

30. Mary E. Fissell, "Imaging Vermin in Early Modern England," in *The Animal-Human Boundary: Historical Perspectives*, ed. Angela Creager and William Chester Jordan (New York: University of Rochester Press, 2002), 77–114.

31. Camporesi, *Bread of Dreams,* 154–55.

32. R. C., *Vermiculars Destroyed* (London, 1690), 5–7.

33. Ibid., 3–4.

34. Ibid., 9.

35. Ibid., 11.

36. Camporesi, *Bread of Dreams,* 152–53.

37. John Tanner, *The Hidden Treasures of the Art of Physick* (London, 1659), 247.

38. Bevington uses "sullied" in this first soliloquy. I'm substituting "solid," an equally available, and in some ways more sensible editorial choice, since it supports the images of thawing and melting.

39. David Hillman, *Shakespeare's Entrails: Belief, Skepticism and the Interior of the Body* (New York: Palgrave, 2007), 107–8.

40. Rina Knoeff, "Animals Inside: Anatomy, Interiority and Virtue in the Early Modern Dutch Republic," *Medizinhistoriches Journal* 43 (2008): 1–19, quotations on 5.

41. Knoeff, "Animals Inside," 5, 2.

42. Culpeper, *Schoole of Physick*, 156.

43. As Hillman points out, Hamlet locates human identity in the physical flesh of the body, unable to establish the existence of the soul or spirit that would make him more than a beast. Human anatomy ultimately demonstrates that identity, "that within which passes show" (1.2.85), is blood, guts, organs—food for worms, offal for vermin.

44. Thomas Browne, *"Religio Medici," "Letter to a Friend," and "Christian Morals,"* ed. W. A. Greenhill (London: Macmillan, 1926). 60.

45. Isabella Winkler, "Love, Death and Parasites," in *Mapping Michel Serres*, ed. Niran Abbas (Ann Arbor: University of Michigan Press, 2005), 226–42, quotation on 228. While Serres' work is usually read as a critique of media, its constant emphasis on meals, banquets, and those who join to consume them invites its use in my reading here. See also n. 56 below.

46. Hillman, *Shakespeare's Entrails*, 107. Building on links made in recent criticism between public anatomy displays and the interior bodily location of subjectivity, Hillman discovers in Hamlet the disintegration of boundaries that demonstrate the problems with moving from a regime of bodily porousness to one of bodily enclosure; Hillman's argument about the location of Hamlet's identity in the physical flesh of the body offers a provocative version of early modern subjectivity. He positions the play at the "border" of the premodern and the modern; for Hillman, Hamlet dies "of internal fracture" from trying to bridge the "faultlines" of a historical shift in the construction of identity (116). I intend my argument to cooperate with Hillman's materialist reading of the body, but as I've noted I prefer to treat animals as primary, rather than subordinating them to other elements in the play. See below for Serres' comments on regimes of purity and enclosure.

47. Margreta De Grazia in *Hamlet without Hamlet* (New York: Cambridge, 2007) argues for a reconsideration of Hegel's use of *Hamlet*'s mole to convey the dialectic of history; in her analysis, the mole more appropriately signifies the end of history in the return to dust. Her reading of the mole—whether a skin blemish, or an animal that tunnels to find food—suggests associations between flesh, dust, dirt, and land that resonate with Hillman's reading and mine.

48. Hillman, *Shakespeare's Entrails*, 108.

49. Fissell, "Imaging Vermin," 77–114.

50. Martha Ann Oberle, "Hamlet's Mousetrap and Trapping Mice in Shakespeare's England," *Discoveries* (Fall 1998): 5–6. The trap in Mascall's work is essentially a precursor of the current humane trap, in which food entices an animal until the trap shuts behind it, leaving it alive "yet in the control of . . . another," (5). The box structure of the trap, its enclosure of "many mice," and its ability to shift power and authority inspire Oberle to read it as a possible image of the space of the stage per se. See Mascall, *A Book of Fishing With Hook and Line* (London, 1590), 73.

51. Ibid., 6.

52. Mascall, *The Government of Cattel*, 290.

53. R. W. gent[leman]., *A Necessary Family Book* (London, 1688), 37.

54. Ibid., 36.

55. Camporesi, *Bread of Dreams*, 163–71.

56. Michel Serres, *The Parasite* (Minneapolis: University of Minnesota Press, 2007), 9–10. Serres finds that science and the beast fable share an essentially fictional status.

57. Ibid., 12.

58. See Simon C. Estok's introduction to his *Ecocriticism and Shakespeare: Reading Ecophobia* (New York: Palgrave Macmillan, 2011), for the fullest articulation of this idea to date.

59. The first to publish on the topic was David Strachan, "Hay Fever, Hygiene, and Household Size," *British Medical Journal* 299:6710 (November 1989): 1259–60.

60. R. W. Summers et al., "Trichuris Suis Seems to Be Safe and Possibly Effective in the Treatment of Inflammatory Bowel Disease," *American Journal of Gastroenterology* 98:9 (2003): 2034–41. Pig whipworms have also been used to treat food allergies.

61. Lawrence's case is notable not just because he went very public with his story (see his website, http://www.asthmahookworm.com/ and his blog site, http://www.jasper-lawrence.com/), but also because he began a business selling hookworm eggs to other allergy sufferers; the worm eggs, however, were banned by the FDA, and although Lawrence still sells them, he does so from Mexico and the United Kingdom without medical or governmental sanction.

CHAPTER 4

1. *Hamlet*, 1.5.62–68. This and all further references to Shakespeare's plays are to *The Complete Works of Shakespeare*, ed. David Bevington (New York: Longman, 2004).

2. Possibly the better-known Shakespearean version of the body/state analogy is Menenius's fable of the belly in *Coriolanus*, although it bypasses the architectural aspects that interest me in Hamlet Senior's version. The importance of the analogy underwrites a number of recent critical works that inform my thinking, including Jonathan Gil Harris, *Sick Economies: Drama, Mercantilism and Disease in Shakespeare's England* (Philadelphia: University of Pennsylvania Press, 2004), and *Foreign Bodies and the Body Politic: Discourses of Social Pathology in Early Modern England* (Cambridge: Cambridge University Press, 1998); and Margaret Healy, *Fictions of Disease in Early Modern England: Bodies, Plagues and Politics* (Basingstoke: Palgrave, 2001).

3. Vitruvius, *The Ten Books on Architecture*, trans. Morris Hicky Morgan (New York: Dover Publications, 1960) 72.

4. Leon Battista Alberti, *On the Art of Building in Ten Books*, trans. Joseph Rykwerts, Neil Leach, and Robert Tavernor (Cambridge, MA: MIT Press, 1988).

5. Henry Wotton, *The Elements of Architecture: A Facsimile Reprint of the 1624 Edition* (Charlottesville: University of Virginia Press for the Folger Shakespeare Library, 1968), 7.

6. René Descartes, *"Discourse on Method" and "The Meditations,"* trans. John Veitch (New York: Prometheus Books, 1989), 17–19.

7. Catherine Ingraham, *Architecture and the Burdens of Linearity* (New Haven, CT: Yale University Press, 1998), 44.

8. Chris Philo speculates on whether it would be appropriate to ascribe to animals as a "social group . . . some potential for what might be termed 'transgression' or even 'resistance' when wriggling out of the cages, fields, and wildernesses allotted to them by their human neighbors": "Animals, Geography, and the City: Notes on Inclusions and Exclusions," in *Animal Geographies: Place, Politics, and Identity in the Nature-Culture Borderlands,* ed. Jennifer Wolch and Jody Emel (New York: Verso, 1998), 52.

9. Hans Zinsser, *Rats, Lice, and History* (Boston: Little, Brown and Co., 1934, 1935), 68–69.

10. Wotton, *Elements,* 7.

11. Vitruvius, *Ten Books,* 20.

12. *Paradise Lost,* 1.768–76, in John Milton, *A Critical Edition of the Major Works,* ed. Stephen Orgel and Jonathan Goldberg (New York: Oxford University Press, 1991), 374–75.

13. Appended to a later edition of Topsell's *History of Four-Footed Beasts* (London, 1658).

14. Jonathan Woolfson, "The Renaissance of Bees," *Renaissance Studies* 24:2 (2009): 281–300, quotation on 286.

15. Henry Wotton notes that the circle has "the approbation of Nature, when she worketh by Instinct . . ." and is exemplified by the spherical nests of most birds, *Elements,* 17.

16. Henri Lefebvre, *The Production of Space,* trans. Donald Nicholson-Smith (Malden, MA: Blackwell, 1991), 174. Marx's original comment is as follows: "A spider conducts operations that resemble those of a weaver, and a bee puts to shame many an architect in the construction of her cells. But what distinguishes the worst architect from the best of bees is this, that the architect raises his structure in imagination before he erects it in reality. Karl Marx, *Capital,* trans. Samuel Moore and Edward Aveling (New York: Modern Library, 1906), 198.

17. Catherine Ingraham, *Architecture, Animal, Human: The Asymmetrical Condition* (New York: Routledge, 2006), 190; Lefebvre thus wants to take theory beyond what is available either in Foucault or in the writings of someone like Bachelet (whose treatment of poetics is "naturally" full of animals) by addressing the materiality of spaces. Bodies produce space; they are themselves also space, and have space—the distinctions between container and contained disappear in the immediacy of Lefebvre's formulation. In analyzing Lefebvre's theory of space, however, Ingraham insists that we recognize that symmetries such as that between the body and space are themselves ideological; symmetry is an inherited ideal from the Renaissance, one that definitionally excludes the animal (202).

18. Lefebvre, *The Production of Space,* 173, 174.

19. Ingraham, *Architecture, Animal, Human,* 191.

20. Topsell, *History* (1607), 46.

21. Thomas More's description of how enclosure creates beggars and vagrancy figures

in Chapter 5; William C. Carroll recounts arguments in the period for and against enclosure, with a focus on the same problem of whether enclosure was the source or the cure for vagrancy in "'The Nursery of Beggary': Enclosure, Vagrancy, and Sedition in the Tudor-Stuart Period," in *Enclosure Acts: Sexuality, Property and Culture in Early Modern England*, ed. Richard Burt and John Archer (Ithaca, NY: Cornell University Press, 1994), 34–47. Both More's Utopian version and those covered by Carroll rely on the counterpoint of proprietary barriers and the violation of them through mobility; underlying all extrapolations on the meaning of enclosure or its consequences, then, is the fact on the ground of animal mobility, which is the object of enclosure in the first place.

22. Keith Thomas, *Man and the Natural World: Changing Attitudes in England 1500–1800* (London: Penguin, 1983), 110.

23. Ingrid H. Tague, "Dead Pets: Satire and Sentiment in British Elegies and Epitaphs for Animals," *Eighteenth-Century Studies* 41:3 (2008): 289–306. Although Tague covers a much later period, her brief insights into the interdependence of space, location, and definitions of the pet are useful to this study.

24. Richard Fanshawe, *Shorter Poems and Translations*, ed. N. W. Bawcutt (Liverpool: Liverpool University Press, 1964).

25. Boehrer, "Shylock and the Rise of the Household Pet: Thinking Social Exclusion in The Merchant of Venice," *Shakespeare Quarterly* 50:2 (Summer 1999): 152–70, 154. Both Boehrer and Tague ("Dead Pets") find relevant the fact that the term defines humans as well: when used to describe a person, "pet" is a term that denotes privilege, someone who comes first in the affections of a powerful figure (like a teacher's pet), simultaneously diminishing the person so named by aligning her or him with a favored animal. This usage actually predates most modern uses of the word to refer to privileged animals.

26. Don E. Wayne's *Penshurst: The Semiotics of Place and the Poetics of History* (London: Methuen, 1984) gives an extended reading of Jonson's poem that revolves around exactly this process.

27. See, for instance, Kathleen Kete, *The Beast in the Boudoir: Petkeeping in Nineteenth-Century Paris* (Berkeley: University of California Press, 1994, 1995).

28. Giles Worsley, *The British Stable* (New Haven, CT: Yale University Press, 2004), 31; and Paula Henderson, *The Tudor House and Garden: Architecture and Landscape in the Sixteenth and Early Seventeenth Centuries* (New Haven, CT: Yale University Press, 2005), 13.

29. Lucy Worsley and Tom Addyman, "Riding Houses and Horses: William Cavendish's Architecture for the Art of Horsemanship," *Architectural History* 45 (2002): 194–229, quotation on 197.

30. The Bolsover riding house has been revived by English Heritage with performances for the visiting public of dressage and airs above the ground, which should dispel any notion that it was not used for the purpose; having ridden in it myself, however, I can attest that the horses must have been smaller and the training more compactly accomplished in Cavendish's day than in ours, which might have had some effect on previous observers' opinions about its utility.

31. Henri Lefebvre's work is important to my understanding of space in this project. Lefebvre argues for the agency of space, rather than its passive function as a container, dividing space into three (sometimes indistinguishable and unstable) categories: spatial practices of everyday life, representations of space (in designs, maps, and so forth), and representational space, or the ideation of space through symbols, stories, and so on. Space is thus at once ideological and physical. See Henri Lefebvre, *The Production of Space*). In this chapter if I oscillate between versions of space, I do so in the interest of deconstructing the assumption that different registers of space can be extracted one from the other.

32. Gail Kern Paster, *The Idea of the City in the Age of Shakespeare* (Athens: University of Georgia Press, 1985), 220.

33. Philo, "Animals," 51–71, esp. 54 and 66.

34. Ibid., 66–67.

35. Derek Keene, "The Medieval Urban Landscape, AD 900–1540," in *The English Urban Landscape*, ed. Philip Waller (Oxford: Oxford University Press, 2000), 94.

36. John Stow, *A Survey of London* (1603), 79–91.

37. On Smithfield as a location of particular interest to animal geography, see Philo, "Animals," 58–65, which remarks on it as a locus of "volatile mixing of beasts and people" (61).

38. Wotton, *Elements*, 4.

39. "The Coaches Overthrow," attributed to John Taylor, London, 1643.

40. Michel de Montaigne, *The Complete Essays*, trans. M. A. Screech (London and New York: Penguin Books, 1987, 1991, 2003), 2019–20.

41. Mark. S. Jenner, "The Great Dog Massacre," in *Fear in Early Modern Society*, ed. William G. Naphy and Penny Roberts (Manchester: Manchester University Press, 1997), 44–61.

42. The classic account of a cat massacre is Robert Darnton's *The Great Cat Massacre and Other Episodes in French Cultural History* (New York: Basic Books, 1999). The French apprentices who initiate the massacre do so partly as an act of social revenge against the privileged pet cats of their masters; Darnton comments on the growth in the number of pet cats owned by French bourgeois (76), which seems to make them almost as great a nuisance as London's dogs. And, incidentally, it is their squalling across the city that seems partly to blame for setting off the apprentices.

43. See William Baldwin, *Beware the Cat: The First English Novel*, ed. William A. Ringler Jr. and Michael Flachmann (San Marino: Huntington Library Press, 1988), xvi–xviii.

44. The story of Wyatt and "Acater" can be found at http://www.xmission .com/~emailbox/acater.htm (accessed July 2011). The Web site contains information and sources that are not otherwise available in print.

45. John Hollander, ed., *Sonnets* (New York: Alfred A. Knopf, 2001), 49 and 50.

46. Stow, *Survey*, 128. Houndsditch was originally part of the city's system of defense, dug to enhance the wall around the city; later after it became impossible to keep it clear of refuse such as dead dogs it was filled in and paved over.

47. Ben Jonson, *The Complete Poems*, ed. George Parfitt (New Haven, CT: Yale University Press, 1975), 86–92, lines 140–71.

48. "Jonson audaciously juxtaposes putrefaction and sustenance, death and sexuality, in a manner which typifies his purpose in the poem" writes Andrew Macrae; "while confusion involves the 'filth, stench, noyse' of disorder and decay, it also fosters a distinctive creativity, evident as much in the tumultuous character of Jonson's distended epigram as it is in the grotesque environment of the London underworld. The Fleet Ditch is thus figured as a kind of heterotopia." Andrew Macrae, "'On the Famous Voyage': Ben Jonson and Civic Space," *Early Modern Literary Studies*, 1st ser., 3 (September 1998): 26, 9. David L. Pike analyzes the role of subterranean spaces like the sewer (or London's ditches and channels) in "Sewage Treatments: Vertical Space and Waste in Nineteenth-Century Paris and London," in *Filth: Dirt, Disgust and Modern Life*, ed. William A. Cohen and Ryan Jonson (Minneapolis: University of Minnesota Press, 2005), 51–77.

49. This and all further references to Shakespeare's plays are to *The Complete Works of Shakespeare*, ed. David Bevington (New York: Longman, 2004).

50. Erica Fudge, "The Dog Is Himself: Humans, Animals, and Self-Control in *The Two Gentlemen of Verona*," in *How To Do Things with Shakespeare: New Approaches, New Essays*, ed. Laurie Maguire (Malden, MA: Blackwell, 2008), 185–209, quotation on 198.

51. Ibid., 198.

52. Robert Crowley, *One and Thurtye Epigrammes* (London, 1550), sig. Bv.

53. Edward Topsell, *The History of Four Footed Beasts* (London, 1607), 175, 143.

54. Ibid., 139, 143. Darlene Ciraulo has argued in an unpublished paper presented at a meeting of the Shakespeare Association of America (Philadelphia, April 13–17, 2006) that the cat and dog imagery in the play is related to an opposition between the comic verbal dueling and name calling, associated with the trivializing effect of animal references, and the tragic brutality of the play's second half, in which bestial behavior becomes not a label, but a quality of action ("Cats and Dogs in *Romeo and Juliet*"). Cats also have notably awful voices: "At the time of their lust . . . they have a peculiar direfull voice" (Topsell, *History*, 105).

55. Later when banished, Romeo laments the fact that "every cat and dog / And little mouse" may look on Juliet, although he will not (once they are both dead and decomposing) (3.3.30–31), as if he would choose to become exactly a species of vermin to remain in Juliet's presence.

56. Bruce Boehrer, *Shakespeare among the Animals: Nature and Society in the Drama of Early Modern England* (New York: Palgrave, 2002), 70.

57. Topsell's *History* refers to the cat as a "she" throughout, except when discussing mating, which is typical of most texts' use of the female pronoun for all cats.

58. Ian Munro, *The Figure of the Crowd in Early Modern London: The City and Its Double* (New York: Palgrave, 2005), 34. Chris Fitter actually argues that *Romeo and Juliet* "is manifestly concerned to address street violence directly," in his view the food riots and urban chaos of the late 1590s. Fitter, "'The Quarrel Is between Our Masters and Us Their Men': *Romeo and Juliet*, Dearth and the London Riots," *English Literary Renaissance* 30:2 (Spring 2000): 154–83, quotation on 164. The play's scenes of "careless patrician feasting" (159) would have been especially meaningful to hungry audiences; the food/death imagery Fitter sees in the play intersects with my discussion of *Hamlet*, below.

59. Stephen Mullaney's *The Place of the Stage: License, Play and Power in Renaissance England* (Chicago: University of Chicago Press, 1988) argues that the theater, situated in the suburbs, participated in such a process; see esp. 26–59.

60. Christopher F. Black observes that the actual families of early modern Italy often developed enclaves through the transformation of architecture; in contrast, famous Italian piazzas were celebrated as "great meeting places" of the populace. Black, *Early Modern Italy: A Social History* (New York: Routledge, 2001), 64. The contradictions and tensions inherent in these two concurrent developments seem to influence the action in Shakespeare's Verona, even though the play may be more about London than any Italian city.

CHAPTER 5

1. William Shakespeare, *The Complete Works of Shakespeare*, ed. David Bevington, 5th ed. (New York: Longman, 2004), 1.4.162.

2. Peter Stallybrass emphasizes the "antic" nature of this moment in the play as part of his argument that tragedy degenerates into farce; see his "'Well Grubbed, Old Mole': Marx, Hamlet, and the (Un)Fixing of Representation," *Cultural Studies* 12:1 (1998): 3–14, reprinted in *Marxist Shakespeares*, ed. Jean Howard and Scott Cutler Shershow (New York: Routledge, 2001), 16–30. References to the essay are to the latter version.

3. G. W. F. Hegel, *Lectures on the Philosophy of History*, trans. Hugh Barr Nesbit (Cambridge: Cambridge University Press, 1975).

4. Karl Marx, *Selected Writings*, ed. David McLellan (New York: Oxford University Press, 1977), 316.

5. Stallybrass, "'Well Grubbed,'" 28.

6. Margreta de Grazia, *Hamlet without Hamlet* (New York: Cambridge University Press, 2007), 31, 43.

7. Karen Edwards gives an extensive account of the mole, including an analysis of the name's etymology and several cases of the mole's appearance in contemporary texts, in her "A Milton Bestiary: Mole," *Milton Quarterly* 42:2 (May 2008): 117–19. However, perhaps because of the origins of her interest in Milton, she emphasizes the mole's association with hell and destruction over any other aspect of the creature's history.

8. Edward Topsell, *History of Four-Footed Beasts* (London, 1607), 388.

9. Ibid., 389.

10. According to the *Oxford English Dictionary*, "want" (mole) is derived from Old English, and before that Old Norse or Middle Swedish ("vanta," or "vand," meaning to throw, as the mole does dirt); "wont," "wond"; "molewarp" and its variants are found in Dutch and Old Saxon. The molewarp, or "mouldwarp" is literally a thrower of earth. Topsell's comment on the mole "wanting" teeth for "propriety" with the mouse seems a half-conscious play on these intersections of property, soil, and lack. See also Leonard Mascall, *A Booke of Engines and Trappes* (London, 1590), sig. 55.

11. Topsell, *History*, 390. Topsell writes "hearing," which I translate as "heaving" on

the assumption that he is marking the effect of the mole in gardens and farmlands. However, given the subject of the entry, "hearing" one's food is indeed what the mole does, using its sensitivity to sound and vibration to track insects in the dirt, so Topsell may have intended "hearing."

12. Erica Fudge, *Brutal Reasoning: Animals, Rationality and Humanity in Early Modern England* (Ithaca, NY: Cornell University Press, 2006), 56.

13. In *Upon Littleton* (London, 1628), Edward Coke described the legal concept of land ownership thus: "And lastly the earth has, in law, a great extent upwards, not only of water, as hath been said, but of air, and of all other things, even up to heaven; for *cujus ets solum just est usque ad coelum*" (4a). The idea of "to the heavens" was matched in some case law by the assumption that ownership extended *ad centrum*, or to the center of the earth, as *Blackstone's Commentaries* noted in the eighteenth century. Mole competition for rights over the realm beneath the surface of the soil inevitably represents a challenge to these legal premises, indirectly registered in the texts I am covering here.

14. Thomas Tusser, *Five Hundred Points of Good Husbandry* (London, 1580), 111.

15. How widespread is this sentiment attached to the mole is demonstrated by the same animal's comments in Gelli's *Circe*, discussed in this book's Introduction. Helkiah Crooke's *Microcosmographia* (London, 1615): "The frame and composition which is upright and mounting toward heaven, the moderate temper, the equal and just proportion of the parts. . . . Man onely is of an upright frame and proportion" (4–5).

16. For more on the widespread use of the pitfall trap, see Blaise Vyner, "Mole Trapping in South Wales," *Folk Life* 17 (1979): 14–19. R. W., in *A Necessary Family-Book* (London, 1688), notes the use of a live mole roasted to catch others who come to rescue it (23).

17. John Locke, *Two Treatises of Government*, ed. Mark Goldie (London: J. M. Dent, 1993), 128.

18. C. B. Macpherson, *The Political Theory of Possessive Individualism* (Oxford: Clarendon Press, 1962).

19. Locke, *Two Treatises*, 127–28.

20. Samuel Hartlib, for instance, emphasizes the idea of mutual defense and shared revenue, rather than a model of exploitation that defeats bee productivity; human and bee are engaged in a kind of corporate venture, so to speak, and so the title of his work references the idea of a "commonwealth" not only to suggest the social structure of beehives, but to propose genuinely sharing the wealth of honey. See his *The Reformed Commonwealth of Bees, Presented in Several Letters* (London, 1655), esp. 12–14.

21. Karl Marx, *Capital*, trans. Samuel Moore and Edward Aveling, ed. Fredrick Engels (New York: Modern Library, 1906), 198.

22. Leonard Mascall, *The Government of Cattel* (London, 1662), 196.

23. Thomas More, "*Utopia*," in *Three Early Modern Utopias*, ed. Susan Bruce (Oxford: Oxford University Press, 1999, 2008); this text uses the 1556 revision of Ralph Robinson's 1551 translation of the Latin.

24. More's use of the image of cannibal sheep is not exclusive, however: Thomas Bastard's *Chrestoleros* (1598) also remarks that "sheepe have eate up our medows an dour

doones," cited in Rowland E. Prothero, *English Farming Past and Present* (New York: Longmans Green, 1912), 62.

25. Richard Halpern, *The Poetics of Primitive Accumulation: English Renaissance Culture and the Genealogy of Capital* (Ithaca, NY: Cornell University Press, 1991), 154.

26. Fudge, *Brutal Reasoning*, 56.

27. Paul A. Yachnin, "Sheepishness in *The Winter's Tale*," in *How to Do Things with Shakespeare*, ed. Laurie Maguire (Oxford, UK and Malden, MA: Blackwell Publishing, 2008), 210–29, quotation on 217. Yachnin's citation of primary sources on sheep is a tour of sheepish innocence and passivity; I have tried to locate opposite views in some of the same sources to balance the apparent uniformity of thought on sheep.

28. Julian Yates has written two pieces on More's sheep: "Humanist Habitats, or 'Eating Well' with Thomas More's *Utopia*," in *Environment and Embodiment in Early Modern England*, ed. Mary Floyd Wilson and Garrett A. Sullivan Jr. (New York: Palgrave, 2007), 187–209; and "Counting Sheep: Dolly Does Utopia (Again)," *Rhizomes* 8 (Spring 2004), http://www.rhizomes.net/issue8/yates2.htm. Christopher Burlinson has also written on More's sheep in "Humans and Animals in Thomas More's *Utopia*," in *Utopian Studies* 19:1 (2008): 25–47. The quotation is from Yates's "Humanist Habitats," 205.

29. Responding to Yates, Ivo Kamps and Melissa Smith point out, however, that such a gesture might merely "replac[e] one common human trait, say . . . feel[ing] superior to animals, with another human trait, which is to feel alienated from one's surroundings." Ivo Kamps and Melissa Smith, "Utopian Ecocriticism: Naturalizing Nature in Thomas More's *Utopia*," in *Early Modern Ecostudies: From the Florentine Codex to Shakespeare*, ed. Thomas Hallock, Ivo Kamps, and Karen Raber (New York: Palgrave Press, 2008), 115–30, esp. 127.

30. Yates, "Counting Sheep," 3.

31. Elinor G. L. Melville, *A Plague of Sheep: Environmental Consequences of the Conquest of Mexico* (Cambridge: Cambridge University Press, 1994).

32. See Elizabeth Starr Cohen and Thomas Vance Cohen, *Daily Life in Renaissance Italy* (Westport, CT: Greenwood Press, 2001), 149.

33. Melville, *A Plague of Sheep*, 31.

34. Ibid., 39.

35. Ibid., 114.

36. Prothero, *English Farming*, 59.

37. Michael L. Ryder, *Sheep and Man* (London: Duckworth, 1983), 655.

38. A. S. Gent, *The Husbandman, Farmer and Grazier's Instructor* (London, 1697), 60; Conrad Heresbach, *Four Books of Husbandrie* (London, 1596), 138.

39. Ryder, *Sheep and Man*, 448. Sheep "murrain" during the period is a catch-all term for a number of wasting diseases. The first outbreak of foot-and-mouth disease occurred in Italy in the sixteenth century, but it quickly spread through Europe. Murrains were the terror of the later Middle Ages, resulting in huge herd die-offs. See C. A. Spinage, *Cattle Plague, a History* (New York: Plenum Publishers, 2003).

40. Fynes Moryson, *The Itinerary of Fynes Moryson* (Glasgow: James Maclehose and Sons, 1908), 4: 168.

41. Roze Hentschell, *The Culture of Cloth in Early Modern England: Textual Constructions of a National Identity* (New York: Ashgate, 2008), 220ff.

42. Mascall, *The Government of Cattel*, 140.

43. Franz Wolfgang, *The History of Brutes; Or a Description of Living Creatures* (London, 1672), 185.

44. Quoted in Hentschell, *The Culture of Cloth*, 225–26.

45. Marx, *Capital*, 808, n. 1. In addition to the entire passage in which Hythloday describes enclosure's effects, Marx cites Holinshed's *Chronicles* for the huge number of thieves executed under Henry VIII; he also quotes from Strype's *Annals of the Reformation*: "there was not one year commonly wherein three or four hundred were not devoured and eaten up by the gallowes," suggesting that Marx was not only investigating the history of enclosures, but that he was attuned to the language of alimentary consumption that frames discussions about sheep and the law.

46. Marx, *Selected Writings*, 81.

47. Ibid., 82.

48. Ibid., 90–91.

49. Ibid., 90.

50. Each of these examples requires, as I will indicate below, a different understanding of labor and product. Conies, for example, were established as fully wild creatures on estates by the simple expedient of encouraging colonies; with minimal human intervention, they constructed an exploitable resource. Even the concept of domestication requires more nuanced thought than is usually afforded it, since the degree to which a sheep or cow is "domesticated" differs hugely from the degree to which bees or conies are.

51. Tim Ingold, Introduction to *What Is an Animal?* (London: Routledge, 1994), 8.

52. Richard L. Tapper, "Animality, Humanity, Morality, Society," in *What Is an Animal?*, ed. Tim Ingold (London: Routledge, 1994), 47–58, quotation on 53.

53. Erica Fudge, *Animal* (London: Reaktion Books, 2002), 28; see also Karen Raber, "From Sheep to Meat, from Pets to People: Animal Domestication 1600–1800," in *A Cultural History of Animals*, vol. 4: *1600–1800*, ed. Matthew Senior (London: Berg, 2007), 73–99.

54. Fudge, *Animal*, 29.

55. Ibid., 30.

56. More, "*Utopia*," 84.

57. Ibid., 87.

58. Ibid., 99.

59. Stephen Greenblatt, *Renaissance Self-Fashioning: From More to Shakespeare* (Chicago: University of Chicago Press, 1980), 39.

60. More, "*Utopia*," 57.

61. Ibid., 120.

62. Ibid., 51.

63. Burlinson, "Humans and Animals," 25.

64. More, "*Utopia*," 90.

65. Greenblatt, *Renaissance Self-Fashioning*, 43.

66. More, "*Utopia*," 90–91.

67. See Erica Fudge's discussion of meat eating's justification in Christian thought in "Saying Nothing but Concerning the Same: On Dominion, Purity, and Meat in Early Modern England," in *Renaissance Beasts: Of Animals, Humans and Other Wonderful Creatures*, ed. Erica Fudge (Urbana: University of Illinois Press, 2004), 70–86.

68. More, "*Utopia*," 64.

69. Rebecca Totaro, "English Plague and New World Promise," *Utopian Studies* 10:1 (1999): 1–12.

70. More, "*Utopia*," 64.

71. Ibid., 88–89.

72. Donna Haraway, *When Species Meet* (Minneapolis: University of Minnesota Press, 2008), 73.

CONCLUSION

1. During the year in which this project evolved (2011), Steven Soderbergh's film *Contagion* was released, with its ultimate attribution of a disastrous flu epidemic, reminiscent of the influenza outbreak of 1918, to the clearing of forested land for development.

2. Giovanni Battista Gelli, *Circes of John Baptista Gello, Florentine*, trans. Henry Iden (London, 1557), sig. t2v.

3. Ibid., sig t2r.

4. Of Topsell's passage on elephant chastity, Bruce Boehrer has written that it stands as an example of how early modern anthropomorphic writing can cooperate with what appears to be its opposite, anthropocentrism, by establishing the standard against which human excellence, and so human distinction from animals, will be measured; Bruce Boehrer, *Shakespeare among the Animals: Nature and Society in the Drama of Early Modern England* (New York: Palgrave, 2002), 33. However, it is worth pointing out that Topsell's clear intention is not always supported by the text: for instance, in the quote below the bodily vulnerabilities that require elephants to act "like chirurgeons" are clearly shared with humans, and the use of boughs and plants in mourning rituals evokes their use in human analogues. Moreover, the ability of the elephant to extrapolate from its own bodily suffering to another's is clearly evoked in Topsell's accounts of elephants coming to their fellows' aid. So alternative positions are available to the text's apparent anthropomorphism and anthropocentrism.

5. Edward Topsell, *The History of Four-Footed Beasts* (London, 1607), 163.

6. Charles Siebert, "An Elephant Crackup?" *New York Times* (October 8, 2006), http://www.nytimes.com/2006/10/08/magazine/08elephant.html?pagewanted=all.

7. G. A. Bradshaw, *Elephants on the Edge: What Animals Teach Us about Humanity* (New Haven, CT: Yale University Press, 2009), 2–3.

8. Fudge uses Stephen Greenblatt's famous "desire to speak with the dead" to introduce

animals as "absent-presences" in historical and literary evidence from the past; "they do not speak my language, and they do not write," and so there is no way to access "the animal" without going through the distortions of human perception. Erica Fudge, *Perceiving Animals: Humans and Bests in Early Modern English Culture* (New York: St. Martin's Press, 2000), 2–3.

9. Cary Wolfe, *Animal Rites: American Culture, the Discourse of Species, and Posthumanist Theory* (Chicago: University of Chicago Press, 2003), 192.

10. Ibid., 206.

11. Topsell, *History*, 156, 162, 163.

12. Bradshaw, *Elephants*, 221–47.

13. Siebert, "An Elephant Crackup?"

14. Foucault's denaturalizing interrogation of epistemological paradigms appears in *The Order of Things: An Archaeology of the Human Sciences* (New York: Pantheon, 1971) and *The Archaeology of Knowledge* (New York: Harper and Row, 1972).

15. Cary Wolfe, *What Is Posthumanism?* (Minneapolis: University of Minnesota Press, 2010), 120.

Bibliography

A. S. Gent[leman]. *The Husbandman, Farmer and Grazier's Instructor*. London, 1697.

Alberti, Leon Battista. *On the Art of Building in Ten Books*. Trans. Joseph Rykwerts, Neil Leach, and Robert Tavernor. Cambridge, MA: MIT Press, 1988.

Anderson, Virginia DeJohn. *Creatures of Empire: How Domestic Animals Transformed Early America*. Oxford and New York: Oxford University Press, 2004.

Anon. *The Widow's Treasure*. London, 1639.

Aristotle. *The Works of Aristotle*. Vol. 4. Trans. Darcy Wentworth Thompson. Oxford: Oxford University Press, 1949.

Astley, John. *The Art of Riding*. London, 1580.

Baker, Steve. *The Postmodern Animal*. London: Reaktion Books, 2000.

Baldwin, William. *Beware the Cat: The First English Novel*. Ed. William A. Ringler Jr. and Michael Flachmann. San Marino: Huntington Library Press, 1988.

Bateson, Gregory. *Steps to an Ecology of Mind: Collected Essays in Anthropology, Psychiatry, Evolution and Epistemology*. Northvale, NJ: Jason Aronson, 1972, 1987.

Bekoff, Marc. *The Emotional Lives of Animals: A Leading Scientist Explores Animal Joy, Sorrow, and Empathy and Why They Matter*. Novato, CA: New World Library, 2007.

———. *Minding Animals: Awareness, Emotions, and Heart*. Oxford: Oxford University Press, 2003.

Black, Christopher F. *Early Modern Italy: A Social History*. New York: Routledge, 2001.

Blundeville, Thomas. *The Four Chiefest Offices Belonginge to Horsemanshippe*. London, 1566.

———. *A New Booke Containing the Arte of Horsmanshippe*. London, 1560.

Boehrer, Bruce. *Animal Characters: Nonhuman Beings in Early Modern Literature*. Philadelphia: University of Pennsylvania Press, 2010.

———. *Shakespeare among the Animals: Nature and Society in the Drama of Early Modern England*. New York: Palgrave, 2002.

———. "Shylock and the Rise of the Household Pet: Thinking Social Exclusion in the *Merchant of Venice*." *Shakespeare Quarterly* 50:2 (Summer 1999): 152–70.

Bradshaw, G. A. *Elephants on the Edge: What Animals Teach Us about Humanity*. New Haven, CT: Yale University Press, 2009.

Brandt, Keri. "A Language of Their Own: An Interactionist Approach to Human-Horse Communication." *Society and Animals* 12:4 (2004): 199–316.

Brown, Eric C. "Many a Civil Monster: Shakespeare's Idea of the Centaur." *Shakespeare Survey* 51 (1998): 175–91.

Browne, Thomas. *"Religio Medici," "Letter to a Friend," and "Christian Morals."* Ed. W. A. Greenhill. London: Macmillan, 1926.

Bulwer, John. *Chirologia, or the Natural Language of the Hand.* London, 1644.

Burlinson, Christopher. "Humans and Animals in Thomas More's *Utopia.*" *Utopian Studies* 19:1 (2008): 25–47.

Callaghan, Dympna. "(Un)Natural Loving: Swine, Pets and Flowers in *Venus and Adonis.*" In *Textures of Renaissance Knowledge*, ed. Philippa Berry and Margaret Trudeau-Clayton. Manchester: Manchester University Press, 2003: 58–78.

Camporesi, Piero. *Bread of Dreams: Food and Fantasy in Early Modern Europe.* Trans. David Gentilcore. Chicago: University of Chicago Press, 1989.

———. *The Juice of Life: The Symbolic and Magic Significance of Blood.* Trans. Robert R. Barr. New York: Continuum, 1995.

Carlino, Andrea. *Books of the Body: Anatomical Ritual and Renaissance Learning.* Trans. John Tedeschi and Anne C. Tedeschi. Chicago: University of Chicago Press, 1999.

Carroll, William C. "'The Nursery of Beggary': Enclosure, Vagrancy, and Sedition in the Tudor-Stuart Period." In *Enclosure Acts: Sexuality, Property and Culture in Early Modern England*, ed. Richard Burt and John Archer. Ithaca, NY: Cornell University Press, 1994: 34–47.

Casserio, Giulio. *Pentaesthesion.* Venice, 1609.

Cavendish, William. *A General System of Horsemanship: A Facsimile Reproduction of the Edition of 1743.* London: Trafalgar Square Books, 2000.

Ciraulo, Darlene. "Cats and Dogs in *Romeo and Juliet.*" Paper presented at the meeting of the Shakespeare Association of America, Philadelphia, April 13–17, 2006.

Clark, Andy, and David Chalmers. "The Extended Mind." *Analysis* 58 (1998): 10–23.

———. "The Extended Mind." In *The Extended Mind*, ed. David Menary. Cambridge, MA: MIT Press, 2010: 27–42.

Clark, Kenneth. *Animals and Man: Their Relationship as Reflected in Western Art from Prehistory to the Present Day.* New York: William Morrow and Co., 1977.

Classen, Constance, David Howes, and Anthony Synnott. *Aroma: The Cultural History of Smell.* New York: Routledge, 1994.

Cohen, Elizabeth Starr, and Thomas Vance Cohen. *Daily Life in Renaissance Italy.* Westport, CT: Greenwood Press, 2001.

Coiter, Volcher. *Lectiones Gabrielis Falloppii de Partitus Simularibus Humani.* Nuremberg, 1575.

Coke, Edward. *Upon Littleton.* London, 1628.

Cole, F. J. *A History of Comparative Anatomy from Aristotle to the Eighteenth Century.* New York: Dover Publishing, 1945, 1975.

Corbin, Alain. *The Foul and Fragrant: Odor and the French Social Imagination.* Cambridge, MA: Harvard University Press, 1986.

Cowley, Abraham. *The Poems of Abraham Cowley.* Ed. A. R. Waller. London, 1668.

Crawshey, John. *The Countryman's Instructor.* London, 1636.

Crooke, Helkiah. *Microcosmographia.* London, 1615.

Crowley, Robert. *One and Thyrtye Epigrammes.* London, 1550.

Csordas, Thomas J. "Somatic Modes of Attention." *Cultural Anthropology* 8:2 (May 1993): 135–56.

Culpeper, Nicholas. *Culpeper's Schoole of Physic.* London, 1678.

Cuneo, Pia. "(Un)Stable Identities: Hippology and the Professionalization of Scholarship and Horsemanship in Early Modern Germany." In *Early Modern Zoology: The Construction of Animals in Science, Literature, and the Visual Arts,* ed. Karl A. E. Enenkel and Paul J. Smith. Boston and Leiden: Brill, 2007: 2: 339–59.

Cunningham, Andrew. *The Anatomical Renaissance: The Resurrection of the Anatomical Projects of the Ancients.* New York: Ashgate, 1997.

Dante. *The Divine Comedy.* Vol. I, *Inferno.* Trans. Mark Musa. London: Penguin Classics, 1984.

Dante. *Dante's Inferno: The Indiana Critical Edition.* Trans. Mark Musa. Bloomington: Indiana University Press, 1994.

Darnton, Robert. *The Great Cat Massacre and Other Episodes in French Cultural History.* New York: Basic Books, 1999.

De Grazia, Margreta. *Hamlet without Hamlet.* New York: Cambridge University Press, 2007.

Deleuze, Gilles, and Felix Guattari. *A Thousand Plateaus: Capitalism and Schizophrenia.* Trans. Brian Massumi. Minneapolis: University of Minnesota Press, 1987.

Derrida, Jacques. *The Animal That Therefore I Am.* Ed. Marie-Louise Mallet. Trans. David Willis. New York: Fordham University Press, 2008.

———. "The Animal That Therefore I Am (More to Follow)." Trans. David Willis. *Critical Inquiry* 28 (Winter 2002): 369–418.

Descartes, René. *"Discourse on Method" and "Meditations."* Trans. John Veitch. New York: Prometheus Books, 1989.

Despret, Vinciane. "The Body We Care For: Figures of Anthropo-zoo-genesis." *Body and Society* 10:2–3 (2004): 111–34.

Diamond, Jared. *Guns, Germs, and Steel: The Fates of Human Societies.* New York: W. W. Norton, 1999.

Dillard-Wright, David B. *The Ark of the Possible: The Animal World in Merleau-Ponty.* New York: Lexington Books, 2009.

Donne, John. *The Complete English Poems.* Ed. A. J. Smith. New York: Penguin Books, 1986.

Dunlop, Robert. *Medicine, an Illustrated History.* New York: Mosby, 1996.

Edwards, Karen. "A Milton Bestiary: Mole." *Milton Quarterly* 42:2 (May 2008): 117–19.

Erasmus, Desiderius. *The Praise of Folly.* Trans. Clarence Miller. New Haven, CT: Yale University Press, 1979.

Estok, Simon C. *Ecocriticism and Shakespeare: Reading Ecophobia.* New York: Palgrave Macmillan, 2011.

———. "Theory from the Fringes: Animals, Ecocriticism, Shakespeare." *Mosaic* 40:1 (March 2007): 61–78.

Eustachi, Bartolomeo. *Tabulae Anatomicae*. Rome, 1714.

Evans, E. P. *The Criminal Prosecution and Capital Punishment of Animals*. London: William Heinemann, 1906.

Fanshawe, Richard. *Shorter Poems and Translations*. Ed. N. W. Bawcutt. Liverpool: Liverpool University Press, 1964.

Febvre, Lucien. *The Problem of Unbelief in the Sixteenth Century: The Religion of Rabelais*. Trans. Beatrice Gottlieb. Cambridge, MA: Harvard University Press, 1982.

Fissell, Mary E. "Imaging Vermin in Early Modern England." In *The Animal-Human Boundary: Historical Perspectives*, ed. Angela Creager and William Chester Jordan. Rochester, NY: University of Rochester Press, 2002: 77–114.

Fitter, Chris. "'The Quarrel Is between Our Masters and Us Their Men': *Romeo and Juliet*, Dearth and the London Riots." *English Literary Renaissance* 30:2 (Spring 2000): 154–83.

Fornaciari, G., V. Giuffra, S. Marinozzi, M. S. Picchi, and M. Masetti. "'Royal' Pediculosis in Renaissance Italy: Lice in the Mummy of the King of Naples Ferdinand II of Aragon (1467–1496)." *Memorias do Instituto. Oswaldo Cruz* (Rio de Janeiro) 104:4 (July 2009): 671–72.

Foucault, Michel. *The Archaeology of Knowledge*. New York: Harper and Row, 1972.

———. *Madness and Civilization: A History of Insanity in the Age of Reason*. New York: Vintage Books, 1988.

———. *The Order of Things: An Archaeology of the Human Sciences*. New York: Pantheon, 1971.

Freccero, Carla. *Queer/Early/Modern*. Durham, NC: Duke University Press, 2006.

Fudge, Erica. *Animal*. London: Reaktion Books, 2002.

———. *Brutal Reasoning: Animals, Rationality and Humanity in Early Modern England*. Ithaca, NY: Cornell University Press, 2006.

———. "The Dog Is Himself: Humans, Animals, and Self-Control in *The Two Gentlemen of Verona*." In *How to Do Things with Shakespeare: New Approaches, New Essays*, ed. Laurie Maguire. Malden, MA: Blackwell, 2008: 185–209.

———. "Monstrous Acts: Bestiality in Early Modern England." *History Today* 50 (2000): 20–25.

———. *Perceiving Animals: Humans and Beasts in Early Modern English Culture*. New York: St. Martin's Press, 2000.

———. "Saying Nothing but Concerning the Same: On Dominion, Purity, and Meat in Early Modern England." In *Renaissance Beasts: Of Animals, Humans and Other Wonderful Creatures*, ed. Erica Fudge. Urbana: University of Illinois Press, 2004: 70–86.

Gelli, Giovanni Battista. *Circes of John Baptista Gello, Florentine*. Trans. Henry Iden. London, 1557.

Gibbs, Raymond, Jr. *Embodiment and Cognitive Science*. Cambridge: Cambridge University Press, 2005, 2007.

Gibson, James. *Ecological Approaches to Visual Perception*. Boston: Houghton Mifflin, 1979.

Graaf, Regnier de. *Opera Omnia.* Lyons, 1678.

Grandin, Temple, and Catherine Johnson. *Animals in Translation: Using the Mysteries of Autism to Decode Animal Behavior.* New York: Scribner, 2005.

Greenblatt, Stephen. *Renaissance Self-Fashioning: From More to Shakespeare.* Chicago: University of Chicago Press, 1980.

Grisone, Federigo. *Gli Ordine di Cavalcare.* Naples, 1550.

Guo, K., K. Meints, C. Hall, S. Hall, and D. Mills. "Left Gaze Bias in Humans, Rhesus Monkeys, and Domestic Dogs." *Animal Cognition* 12 (2009): 409–18.

Halpern, Richard. *The Poetics of Primitive Accumulation: English Renaissance Culture and the Genealogy of Capital.* Ithaca, NY: Cornell University Press, 1991.

Hamill, Thomas A. "Cockfighting as Cultural Allegory in Early Modern England." *Journal of Medieval and Early Modern Studies* 39:2 (Spring 2009): 375–406.

Haraway, Donna. *The Companion Species Manifesto.* Chicago: Prickly Paradigm Press, 2003.

———. *When Species Meet (Posthumanities).* Minneapolis: University of Minnesota Press, 2007.

Harcourt, Glenn. "Vesalius and the Anatomy of Antique Sculpture." *Representations* 17 (Winter 1987): 28–61.

Harris, Jonathan Gil. *Foreign Bodies and the Body Politic: Discourses of Social Pathology in Early Modern England.* Cambridge: Cambridge University Press, 1998.

———. *Sick Economies: Drama, Mercantilism and Disease in Shakespeare's England.* Philadelphia: University of Pennsylvania Press, 2004.

Hartlib, Samuel. *The Reformed Commonwealth of Bees, Presented in Several Letters.* London, 1655.

Healy, Margaret. *Fictions of Disease in Early Modern England: Bodies, Plagues and Politics.* Basingstoke: Palgrave, 2001.

Hegel, G. W. F. *Lectures on the Philosophy of History.* Trans. Hugh Barr Nesbit. Cambridge: Cambridge University Press, 1975.

Henderson, Paula. *The Tudor House and Garden: Architecture and Landscape in the Sixteenth and Early Seventeenth Centuries.* New Haven, CT: Yale University Press, 2005.

Hentschell, Roze. *The Culture of Cloth in Early Modern England: Textual Constructions of a National Identity.* New York: Ashgate, 2008.

Heresbach, Conrad. *Four Books of Husbandrie.* London, 1596.

———. *Whole Art of Husbandry Contained in Four Books.* London, 1631.

Heselar, Baldesar. *Andreas Vesalius' First Public Anatomy at Bologna 1540: An Eyewitness Report.* Trans. Ruben Eriksson. Uppsala, Stockholm: Almqvist and Witsells, 1959.

Hillman, David. *Shakespeare's Entrails: Belief, Skepticism and the Interior of the Body.* New York: Palgrave Macmillan, 2007.

———. "Visceral Knowledge: Shakespeare, Skepticism, and the Interior of the Early Modern Body." In *The Body in Parts: Fantasies of Corporeality in Early Modern Europe*, ed. David Hillman and Carla Mazzio. New York: Routledge, 1997: 81–105.

Hillman, David, and Carla Mazzio, eds. *The Body in Parts: Fantasies of Corporeality in Early Modern Europe.* New York: Routledge, 1997.

Hollander, John, ed. *Sonnets*. New York: Alfred A. Knopf, 2001.

Hughes, Merritt Y. "Spenser's Acrasia and the Renaissance Circe." *Journal of the History of Ideas* 4:4 (October 1943): 381–99.

Humphrey, Ozias. *A Memoir of George Stubbs and Joseph Mayer*. London: Pallas Athene Press, 2005.

Hutchins, Edwin. *Cognition in the Wild*. Cambridge, MA: MIT Press, 1995.

Ingold, Tim. "The Animal in the Study of Humanity." In *What Is an Animal?*, ed. Tim Ingold. London: Unwin Hyman, 1988, 1994: 84–99.

———. Introduction to *What Is an Animal?*, ed. Tim Ingold. London: Routledge, 1988, 1994.

Ingraham, Catherine. *Architecture and the Burdens of Linearity*. New Haven, CT: Yale University Press, 1998.

———. *Architecture, Animal, Human: The Asymmetrical Condition*. New York: Routledge, 2006.

Jay, Martin. *Downcast Eyes: The Denigration of Vision in Twentieth-Century French Thought*. Berkeley: University of California Press, 1994.

Jenner, Mark. S. "The Great Dog Massacre." In *Fear in Early Modern Society*, ed. William G. Naphy and Penny Roberts. Manchester: Manchester University Press, 1997: 44–61.

Jonson, Ben. *The Complete Poems*. Ed. George Parfitt. New Haven, CT: Yale University Press, 1975.

Kamps, Ivo, and Melissa Smith. "Utopian Ecocriticism: Naturalizing Nature in Thomas More's *Utopia*." In *Early Modern Ecostudies: From the Florentine Codex to Shakespeare*, ed. Thomas Hallock, Ivo Kamps, and Karen Raber. New York: Palgrave Press, 2008: 115–30.

Keene, Derek. "The Medieval Urban Landscape, AD 900–1540." In *The English Urban Landscape*, ed. Philip Waller. Oxford: Oxford University Press, 2000: 74–98.

Kemp, Martin. *The Science of Art: Optical Themes in Western Art from Brunelleschi to Seurat*. New Haven, CT: Yale University Press, 1990.

———. "Temples of the Body and Temples of the Cosmos: Vision and Visualization in the Vesalian and Copernican Revolutions." In *Picturing Knowledge: Historical and Philosophical Problems Concerning the Use of Art in Science*, ed. Brian S. Baigrie. Toronto: University of Toronto Press, 1996: 40–85.

Kemp, Martin, and Marina Wallace. *Spectacular Bodies: The Art and Science of the Human Body from Leonardo to Now*. Berkeley: University of California Press, 2000

Kete, Kathleen. *The Beast in the Boudoir: Petkeeping in Nineteenth-Century Paris*. Berkeley: University of California Press, 1994, 1995.

Knoeff, Rina. "Animals Inside: Anatomy, Interiority and Virtue in the Early Modern Dutch Republic." *Medizinhistoriches Journal* 43 (2008): 1–19.

Landry, Donna, Cary Wolfe, Bruce Boehrer, et al. "Speciesism, Identity Politics, and Ecocriticism: A Conversation with Humanists and Post-Humanists." *The Eighteenth Century* 52:1 (2011): 87–106.

Laporte, Dominique. *The History of Shit*. Trans. Nadia Benabid and Rodophe El-Khoury. Cambridge, MA: MIT Press, 2000.

Lefebvre, Henri. *The Production of Space*. Trans. Donald Nicholson-Smith. Malden, MA: Blackwell, 1974, 1984.

LeGuin, Elisabeth. "Man and Horse in Harmony." In *The Culture of the Horse: Status, Discipline and Identity in the Early Modern World*, ed. Karen Raber and Treva J. Tucker. New York: Palgrave Macmillan, 2005: 175–96.

Lehane, Brendan. *The Compleat Flea*. New York: Viking Press, 1969.

Lindeman, Mary. *Medicine and Society in Early Modern Europe*. Cambridge: Cambridge University Press, 1991.

Lingis, Alphonso. "Animal Body, Inhuman Face." In *Zoontologies: The Question of the Animal*, ed. Cary Wolfe. Minneapolis: University of Minnesota Press, 2003.

Locke, John. *Two Treatises of Government*. Ed. Mark Goldie. London: J. M. Dent, 1993.

Machiavelli, Niccolo. *The Prince*. Trans. Daniel Donno. New York: Bantam Books, 1966, 1981.

MacInnes, Ian. "Mastiffs and Spaniels: Gender and Nation in the English Dog." *Textual Practice* 17 (2003): 21–40.

Macpherson, C. B. *The Political Theory of Possessive Individualism*. Oxford: Clarendon Press, 1962.

Macrae, Andrew. "'On the Famous Voyage': Ben Jonson and Civic Space." *Early Modern Literary Studies*, special issue, 3 (September 1998). http://extra.shu.ac.uk/emls/04–2/mcraonth.htm.

Mandeville, Bernard. *The Fable of the Bees*. London, 1705.

Marino, Lori. "Dolphin Cognition." *Current Biology* 14 (2004): R910–11.

Markham, Gervase. *A Discource [sic] of Horsemanshippe*. London, 1593.

———. *The English Housewife Containing the Inward and Outward Virtues That Ought to Be in a Complete Woman*. London, 1615.

———. *Second Book of the English Husbandman*. London, 1614.

Marx, Karl. *Capital*. Trans. Samuel Moore and Edward Aveling. Ed. Fredrick Engels. New York: Modern Library, 1906.

———. *Selected Writings*. Ed. David McLellan. New York: Oxford University Press, 1977.

Mascall, Leonard. *A Book of Fishing With Hook and Line.*. London, 1590.

———. *The Government of Cattel*. London, 1662.

McComb, K., A. M. Taylor, C. Wilson, and B. Charlton. "Manipulation by Domestic Cats: The Cry Embedded within the Purr." *Current Biology* 19 (2009): R507–8.

Melville, Elinor G. L. *A Plague of Sheep: Environmental Consequences of the Conquest of Mexico*. Cambridge: Cambridge University Press, 1994.

Merleau-Ponty, Maurice. *The Visible and the Invisible*. Trans. Alphonso Lingis. Evanston, IL: Northwestern University Press, 1968.

Milton, John. *A Critical Edition of the Major Works*. Ed. Stephen Orgel and Jonathan Goldberg. New York: Oxford University Press, 1991.

Moe, Harald. *The Art of Anatomical Illustration in the Renaissance and Baroque Periods*. Copenhagen, Denmark: Rhodos, 1995.

Montaigne, Michel de. *The Complete Essays*. Trans. M. A. Screech. London and New York: Penguin Books, 1987, 1991, 2003.

Moore, John. *A Mappe of Mans Mortalitie*. London, 1617.

More, Thomas. Utopia. In *Three Early Modern Utopias*, ed. Susan Bruce. Oxford: Oxford University Press, 1999, 2008. 3–129.

Morgan, Nicholas. *The Horseman's Honour*. London,1620.

Moryson, Fynes. *The Itinerary of Fynes Moryson*. Glasgow: James Maclehose and Sons, 1908.

Mullaney, Stephen. *The Place of the Stage: License, Play and Power in Renaissance England*. Chicago: University of Chicago Press, 1988.

Mumford, Lewis. *The City in History: Its Origins, Its Transformation, and Its Prospects*. New York: MJF Books, 1967, 1968.

Munro, Ian. *The Figure of the Crowd in Early Modern London: The City and Its Double*. New York: Palgrave, 2005.

Oberle, Martha Ann. "Hamlet's Mousetrap and Trapping Mice in Shakespeare's England." *Discoveries* (Fall 1998): 5–6.

Parrish, Julia K., and William M. Hamner. *Animal Groups in Three Dimensions*. Cambridge: Cambridge University Press, 1977.

Paster, Gail Kern. *The Body Embarrassed: Drama and the Disciplines of Shame in Early Modern England*. Ithaca, NY: Cornell University Press, 1993.

———. *The Idea of the City in the Age of Shakespeare*. Athens: University of Georgia Press, 1985.

———. "Melancholy Cats, Lugged Bears, and Early Modern Cosmology: Reading Shakespeare's Psychological Materialism across the Species Barrier." In *Reading the Early Modern Passions: Essays in the Cultural History of Emotions*, ed. Gail Kern Paster, Katherine Rowe, and Mary Floyd-Wilson. Philadelphia: University of Pennsylvania Press, 2004: 113–29.

Patton, Paul. "Language, Power and the Training of Horses." In *Zoontologies: The Question of the Animal*, ed. Cary Wolfe. Minneapolis: University of Minnesota Press, 2003: 83–99.

Pecquet, Jean. *Experimenta Nova Anatomica*. Paris, 1651.

Pepperberg, Irene. *The Alex Studies: Cognitive and Communicative Abilities of Grey Parrots*. Cambridge, MA: Harvard University Press, 2000.

Philo, Chris. "Animals, Geography, and the City: Notes on Inclusions and Exclusions." In *Animal Geographies: Place, Politics, and Identity in the Nature-Culture Borderlands*, ed. Jennifer Wolch and Jody Emel. New York: Verso, 1998: 51–71.

Pike, David L. "Sewage Treatments: Vertical Space and Waste in Nineteenth-Century Paris and London." In *Filth: Dirt, Disgust and Modern Life*, ed. William A. Cohen and Ryan Jonson. Minneapolis: University of Minnesota Press, 2005: 51–77.

Plat, Hugh. *The Jewel House of Art and Nature*. London, 1653.

Plater, Felix. *De Corporis Humani Structura et Usu*. Basle: Abrosius Froben, 1583.

Pluvinel, Antoine. *Le Maneige Royal*. Trans. Hilda Nelson. London: J. A. Allen, 1989.

Porter, Roy. *The Greatest Benefit to All Mankind: A Medical History of Humanity*. New York: W. W. Norton and Company, 1997.

Potts, Wayne K. "The Chorus-Line Hypothesis of Coordination in Avian Flocks." *Nature* 24 (1984): 344–45.

Proops, L., M. Walton, and K. McComb. "The Use of Human-Given Cues by Domestic Horses (*Equus caballus*) during an Object Choice Task." *Animal Behaviour* 79 (2010): 1205–9.

Prothero, Rowland E. *English Farming Past and Present.* New York: Longmans Green, 1912.

R. W. Gent[leman]. *A Necessary Family Book.* London, 1688.

R. C. *Vermiculars Destroyed.* London, 1690.

Raber, Karen. "From Sheep to Meat, from Pets to People: Animal Domestication 1600–1800." In *A Cultural History of Animals*, vol. 4, *1600–1800*, ed. Matthew Senior. London: Berg, 2007: 73–99.

Ramesey, William. *Helminthologia.* London, 1668.

Ray, Sid. "'Those Whom God Hath Joined Together': Bondage Metaphors and Marital Advice in Early Modern England." In *Domestic Arrangements in Early Modern England*, ed. Kari Boyd McBride. Pittsburgh: Duquesne University Press, 2002: 15–47.

Reiss, D., and L. Marino. "Mirror Self-recognition in the Bottlenose Dolphin: A Case of Cognitive Convergence." *Proceedings of the National Academy of Sciences* 98 (2001): 5937–42.

Roberts, Jeanne Addison. "Horses and Hermaphrodites: Metamorphoses in *Taming of the Shrew*." *Shakespeare Quarterly* 43:2 (Summer 1983): 159–71.

Rowe, Katherine. "'God's Handy Worke': Divine Complicity and the Anatomist's Touch." In *The Body in Parts: Fantasies of Corporeality in Early Modern Europe*, ed. David Hillman and Carla Mazzio. New York: Routledge, 1997: 285–309.

Ruini, Carlo. *Anatomia del Cavallo, Infermità e Suoi Rimedii.* Venezia, 1598, 1618.

Ryder, Michael L. *Sheep and Man.* London: Duckworth, 1983.

Saunders, J. B., and C. D. O'Malley. *The Illustrations from the Works of Andreas Vesalius of Brussels.* Cleveland: World Publishing Co., 1950.

Sawday, Jonathan. *The Body Emblazoned: Dissection and the Human Body in Renaissance Culture.* New York: Routledge, 1995.

Schiesari, Juliana. *Beasts and Beauties: Animals, Gender and Domestication in the Italian Renaissance.* Toronto: University of Toronto Press, 2010.

Schmitt, C. B., and C. Webster. "Harvey and M. A. Severino, a Neglected Medical Relationship." *Bulletin of the History of Medicine* 45 (1971): 49–75.

Schoenfeldt, Michael. *Bodies and Selves in Early Modern England.* Cambridge and New York: Cambridge University Press, 1999.

Scholz, Bernard F. "Ownerless Legs or Arms Stretching from the Sky: Notes on an Emblematic Motif." In *Andrea Alciato and the Emblem Tradition: Essays in Honor of Virginia Woods Callahan*, ed. Peter M. Daly. New York: AMS Press, 1989: 249–83.

Serpell, James. *In the Company of Animals: A Study of Human-Animal Relationships.* New York: Cambridge University Press, 1996, 2008.

Serres, Michel. *The Five Senses: A Philosophy of Mingled Bodies.* Trans. Margaret Cowley and Peter Sankey. London: Continuum, 2009.

———. *Parasite*. Minneapolis: University of Minnesota Press, 2007.

Shakespeare, William. *The Complete Works*. Ed. David Bevington. 5th ed. New York: Longman, 2006.

Shannon, Laurie. *The Accommodated Animal: Cosmopolity in Shakespearean Locales*. Chicago: University of Chicago Press, 2012.

———. "The Eight Animals in Shakespeare, or Before the Human." *PMLA* 124:2 (2009): 472–79.

———. "Invisible Parts: Animals and the Renaissance Anatomies of Human Exceptionalism." In *Animal Encounters*, ed. Tom Tyler and Manuela Rossini. Leiden: Brill Publishing, 2009: 137–58.

Shapiro, Kenneth. "Understanding Dogs through Kinesthetic Empathy, Social Construction, and History." *Anthrozoös* 3 (1990): 184–95.

Shell, Marc. "The Family Pet." *Representations* 15 (Summer 1986): 121–53.

Sidney, Philip. *The Countess of Pembroke's Arcadia*. Ed. Maurice Evans. London: Penguin Books, 1977.

———. *Sir Philip Sidney: "An Apology for Poetry" and "Astrophil and Stella": Texts and Contexts*. Ed. Peter C. Herman. Glen Allen, VA: College Publishing, 2001: 56–210.

Siebert, Charles. "An Elephant Crackup?" *New York Times*, October 8, 2006, http://www.nytimes.com/2006/10/08/magazine/08elephant.html?pagewanted=all.

Singer, Charles. *A Short History of Anatomy and Physiology from the Greeks to Harvey*. New York: Dover Publications, 1957.

Snape, Andrew. *The Anatomy of an Horse*. New York: Howell Book House, 1997.

Spenser, Edmund. *The Faerie Queene*. Ed. Thomas P. Roche Jr. London and New York: Penguin Books, 1987.

Spinage, C. A. *Cattle Plague, a History*. New York: Plenum Publishers, 2003.

Stallybrass, Peter. "'Well Grubbed, Old Mole': Marx, Hamlet, and the (Un)Fixing of Representation." In *Marxist Shakespeares*, ed. Jean Howard and Scott Cutler Shershow. New York: Routledge, 2001: 16–30.

States, Bert O. *Hamlet and the Concept of Character*. Baltimore: Johns Hopkins University Press, 1992,

Stewart, Douglas J. "Falstaff the Centaur." *Shakespeare Quarterly* 28:1 (Winter 1977): 5–21.

Stow, John. *A Survey of London*. London, 1603.

Strachan, David. "Hay Fever, Hygiene and Household Size." *British Medical Journal* 299:6710 (November 1989): 1259–60.

Summers, R. W., D. E. Elliott, K. Qadir, J. F. Urban, R. Thompson, and J. V. Weinstock. "Trichuris Suis Seems to Be Safe and Possibly Effective in the Treatment of Inflammatory Bowel Disease." *American Journal of Gastroenterology* 98:9 (2003): 2034–41.

Tague, Ingrid H. "Dead Pets: Satire and Sentiment in British Elegies and Epitaphs for Animals." *Eighteenth-Century Studies* 41:3 (2008): 289–306.

Tanner, John. *The Hidden Treasures of the Art of Physick*. London, 1659.

Tapper, Richard L. "Animality, Humanity, Morality, Society." In *What Is an Animal?*, ed. Tim Ingold, London: Routledge, 1988, 1994: 47–58.

Taylor, John, attributed "The Coaches Overthrow." London, 1643.

Thomas, Keith. *Man and the Natural World: Changing Attitudes in England 1500–1800*. London: Penguin, 1983.

Topsell, Edward. *The History of Four-Footed Beasts*. London, 1607.

Totaro, Rebecca. "English Plague and New World Promise." *Utopian Studies* 10:1 (1999): 1–12.

Tryon, Thomas. *The Way to Health, Long Life, and Happiness*. London, 1683.

Tuan, Yi-Fu. *Dominance and Affection: The Making of Pets*. New Haven, CT: Yale University Press, 2004.

Tusser, Thomas. *Five Hundred Points of Good Husbandry*. London, 1580.

Ventura, Iolanda. "On the Representation of the Animal World in the Collections of Natural Questions between Late Middle Ages and Early Modern Times." *Reinardus* 21 (2008): 182–200.

Vesalius, Andreas. *On the Fabric of the Human Body, a Translation of "De Humani Corporis Fabrica Libri Septem" by Andreas Vesalius*. 2 vols. Trans. William Frank Richardson and John Burd Carman. San Francisco: Norman Publishing, 1999.

Vitruvius. *Ten Books on Architecture*. Trans. Morris Hicky Morgan. New York: Dover Publications, 1960.

Vyner, Blaise. "Mole Trapping in South Wales." *Folk Life* 17 (1979): 14–19.

Walker, Suzanne J. "Making and Breaking the Stag: The Construction of the Animal in the Early Modern Hunting Treatise." In *Early Modern Zoology: The Construction of Animals in Science, Literature, and the Visual Arts*, ed. Karl A. E. Enenkel and Paul J. Smith. Boston and Leiden: Brill, 2007: 2: 317–37.

Wall, Wendy. "Renaissance National Husbandry: Gervase Markham and the Publication of England." *Sixteenth Century Journal* 27:30 (Fall 1996): 767–85.

Watson, Elizabeth Porges. "(Un)Bridled Passion: Chivalric Metaphor and Practice in Sidney's *Astrophil and Stella*." *Reinardus* 15:1 (2002): 117–29.

Watson, Robert N. "The Ecology of Self in *Midsummer Night's Dream*." In *Ecocritical Shakespeare*, ed. Lynne Bruckner and Dan Brayton. Burlington, VT: Ashgate, 2011: 33–56.

Wayne, Don E. *Penshurst: The Semiotics of Place and the Poetics of History*. London: Methuen, 1984.

Wear, Andrew. *Knowledge and Practice in English Medicine, 1550–1680*. Cambridge: Cambridge University Press, 2000.

Williams, Raymond. *Marxism and Literature*. Oxford and New York: Oxford University Press, 1977.

Wilson, Luke. "William Harvey's *Prelectiones*: The Performance of the Body in the Renaissance Theater of Anatomy." *Representations* 17 (Winter 1987): 62–95.

Winkler, Isabella. "Love, Death and Parasites." In *Mapping Michel Serres*, ed. Niran Abbas. Ann Arbor: University of Michigan Press, 2005: 226–42.

Wolfe, Cary. *Animal Rites: American Culture, the Discourse of Species, and Posthumanist Theory*. Chicago: University of Chicago Press, 2003.

———. *What Is Posthumanism?* Minneapolis: University of Minnesota Press, 2010.

Wolfgang, Franz. *The History of Brutes; Or a Description of Living Creatures*. London, 1672.

Woodbridge, Linda. *Vagrancy, Homelessness and English Renaissance Literature*. Urbana: University of Illinois Press, 2001.

Woolfson, Jonathan. "The Renaissance of Bees." *Renaissance Studies* 24:2 (2009): 281–300.

Woolley, Hannah. *The Accomplisht Ladys Delight*. London, 1677.

Worsley, Giles. *The British Stable*. New Haven, CT: Yale University Press, 2004.

Worsley, Lucy, and Tom Addyman. "Riding Houses and Horses: William Cavendish's Architecture for the Art of Horsemanship." *Architectural History* 45 (2002): 194–229.

Wotton, Henry. *The Elements of Architecture: A Facsimile Reprint of the 1624 Edition*. Charlottesville: University of Virginia Press for the Folger Shakespeare Library, 1968.

Yachnin, Paul A. "Sheepishness in *The Winter's Tale*." In *How to Do Things with Shakespeare*, ed. Laurie Maguire. Oxford, UK and Malden, MA: Blackwell Publishing, 2008: 210–29.

Yates, Julian. "Counting Sheep: Dolly Does Utopia (Again)." *Rhizomes* 8 (Spring 2004), http://www.rhizomes.net/issue8/yates2.htm.

———. "Humanist Habitats, or 'Eating Well' with Thomas More's *Utopia*." In *Environment and Embodiment in Early Modern England*, ed. Mary Floyd Wilson and Garrett A. Sullivan Jr. New York: Palgrave, 2007: 187–209.

Zinsser, Hans. *Rats, Lice, and History*. Boston: Little, Brown and Co., 1934, 1935.

Zuffi, Stefano. *The Cat in Art*. Trans. Simon Jones. New York: Abrams, 2005.

Index

Acknowledgments

My thanks to Ivo Kamps, who read and commented on an early version of this manuscript, and to the three readers for the University of Pennsylvania Press, who gave invaluable advice for revision. For help with translation of Ruini's text from Italian, I thank Isabella Watt, and for providing a variety of Latin translations of Melchior Lorck's engraving couplet, I thank Gregory Heyworth and the many respondents to my query on the Ficino listserv (especially David Lupher and Roger Kuin). While many libraries and collections helped provide the array of images for this volume, Alasdair McCartney at the Wellcome Collection deserves special credit for creating so many new images for me to use. The University of Mississippi generously allowed me a sabbatical year to write this book, for which I am grateful, and has also provided ongoing institutional support for such things as conference travel, giving me opportunities to air ideas and receive valuable criticism from peers. I am constantly aware of how much my graduate students contribute to the freshening of my thoughts on old texts and old subjects; Sallie Anglin deserves special mention, however, for her enthusiasm regarding theories of the body, and her willingness to indulge with me in flights of theoretical fancy. And as always, Doug McPherson has been the best possible partner anyone could ask for, which has helped make this work, and all my work and play, possible.

Unlike many academic books, this one was written quickly during a sabbatical year, and so did not grow so much out of collaboration with other scholars as is usual in our profession. It was shaped, rather, by my daily interactions—some present and actual, some historical and in memory only—with the many creatures who have shared my life, and who demanded to be accounted for somehow in my academic work. Thanks to them all: Sweet Pea and Puff, Sammy and Flute, Willie, BC, Hector, Midget, Tom, Falstaff, Spike, Demetrius, Ellie, Pascoe, Tamara, Melville, Mouse, Baby Daddy, Titus, Cassandra, Boris, Abby, Benny, Wilma, Silvester, Shark, Lily, and Loki. I'm dedicating this book to the memory of my two very best friends, Emerson and Ali: thank you, boys, and sleep well.

CPSIA information can be obtained
at www.ICGtesting.com
Printed in the USA
LVHW112324181222
735494LV00007B/24/J